THE ROYAL
ARMY SERVICE CORPS

Field Marshal The Duke of Connaught, K.G.
Colonel in Chief
Royal Army Service Corps

THE ROYAL
ARMY SERVICE CORPS

A HISTORY OF
TRANSPORT AND SUPPLY
IN THE BRITISH ARMY

BY

JOHN FORTESCUE
LL.D., D.Litt.

Vol. I

PRINTED AND BOUND BY ANTHONY ROWE LTD, EASTBOURNE

PREFACE

THE business of Transport and Supply is so highly technical that it is presumptuous, to say the least, in a mere layman to touch it. The subject, however, is one which has long interested me and which I had the privilege of discussing at length many years ago with such masters as the late Sir Redvers Buller and that most amiable and accomplished officer the late Colonel Charles Bridge. Heartened by their encouragement, I endeavoured to trace the course of Transport and Supply through all of our innumerable campaigns in my *History of the British Army*. It is from that history that most of the information in this present volume is gathered, and, as the sources are there fully given, I have refrained from encumbering the present pages with them.

For the campaigns subsequent to 1870 there are official histories, full of valuable matter, of the campaigns of Abyssinia in 1867-8, of Egypt in 1882 and of the Sudan in 1884. For the final campaigns in the Sudan I have found Churchill's *River War* useful, and for the Ashanti Campaign of 1900 Sir James Willcocks's *From Kabul to Kumassi* of sterling value. But the best material for these later campaigns has been supplied to me by private and public records of the Royal Army Service Corps; and for these I have to thank in particular Lieut.-General Sir Frederick Clayton, Major-General Selden Long, Colonel William Elliott, Colonel Reid, the officer lately in charge of the R.A.S.C. Record Department, and Lieut.-Colonel Badcock of the R.A.S.C. Training College at Aldershot. The two gentlemen last named in particular have met my troublesome questions and requirements with a readiness of help and courtesy which demands my warmest gratitude. Not less thankful am I to all the officers above named and to others, to whom the manuscript was submitted, for their encouragement.

The book has not been an easy one to write, and I am not sure now that I have treated it in the right way. But the life of the Royal Army Service Corps, under its various denominations, was until 1855 intermittent, and for long after that date uncertain and indeterminate. And to write the history of such a Corps is a very different task from that of writing the history of a regiment whose existence has been continuous, though, by the way, even that demands a far greater measure of literary skill than the amateur would suppose. However, the work, for better or worse, is done; and, if it have grave faults, they are at least not due to want of admiration and enthusiasm on my part for the achievements of the Royal Army Service Corps.

J. W. F.

August 1930

CONTENTS

CONTENTS

ILLUSTRATIONS

ERRATA

Chap. II. *title, for* SEVENTEENTH *read* EIGHTEENTH

p. 191, l. 29, *for* a railway ran as far as Pieter-maritzburg, *read* a railway ran as far as Botha's Hill, half-way to Pietermaritzburg, and, as the war proceeded, was extended to the latter place.

CHAPTER I

INTRODUCTORY

A SURVEY of the history of transport and supply from the earliest times through many centuries would furnish full occupation for a man's whole life. I have no profound knowledge of the subject, and I must, therefore, pass over it very rapidly and imperfectly.

The activities of man may be said to be bounded by fresh water. He is himself largely composed of water. He cannot himself live without it; neither can the vegetables nor animals which are necessary to his subsistence.

Man's abode, therefore, everywhere depends upon water, and water is the most masterful and ruthless of all the elements. It attracts large populations to the banks of great rivers, and sweeps them away by tens of thousands in a single careless flood. But for our purpose the points to note are that water is incompressible and heavy. Man may go to the water and, in obedience to water's laws, may lead it to follow him. He may by mechanical appliances force it to ascend from beneath the earth to the surface. In modern times he, by condensation, transmutes salt water into fresh. But, speaking generally, it was quite impossible in former days, and it is a most arduous task in these days, to carry water for any great number of men over any great distance. It may be laid down, then, that all wanderings of man, whether military or other, are governed by the supply of fresh water. And where water is, there is food.

It is likely that every movement of primitive man was in the nature of a military movement, that is to say that he risked encounter with hostile man or with beast. But, however that may be, he can hardly have ventured to any great distance from his own haunts without taking food with him. The fighting men would carry it themselves, and, if an action were imminent, would unload it, leave a few of their number to guard it and proceed to the fight unencumbered. Thus would grow up the habit, already prompted by the collection of the harvest—grain, dates, what not—in the primitive village, of forming what are called magazines. An invading tribe, however, if successful, would count upon living upon the enemy's country; and would have no scruple about allowing their foes to die of hunger or thirst, so they themselves were full. And this heedless instinct of savagery has maintained its strength to quite modern times. In one of Tipu Sahib's invasions of the Carnatic late in the eighteenth century, it was reckoned that a million wretched villagers died of starvation. A raid of Marathas was compared to the descent of a swarm of locusts, which swept the land bare and left the inhabitants to die of famine.

The waste caused by this indiscriminate plunder and destruction of course defeated its own object; and the next step seems to have been the organisation of plunder and the gathering of the produce of the invaded country into magazines. This of course demanded a certain measure of discipline for the just distribution* as well as for the faithful collection of the supplies. But, more to our present purpose, it demanded also transport—carriers, human or animal—to bring the scattered food into one place. The enemy and their women might be impressed for this purpose, and be fed or allowed to

---

* The phrase δαὶς ἐΐση (the equal feast) which so constantly recurs in Homer, suggests what may be called a convention of rationing from very ancient times.

starve as might be convenient. Beasts would of course require forage, and would probably be too precious to be squandered. Man and beast alike can draw thrice the weight that they can carry, and so traction of some kind must have come in very early. The primitive vehicle on land would have been the sledge; but we have no record of the man of genius who first mounted the sledge upon sections of tree trunks rolling freely upon an axle. In any case wheeled vehicles go back to the Pharaohs—I know not to what remoter antiquity—and are of course familiar in Homer.

So far we have been concerned only with the carriage of food. But for the purposes of war other things must be carried, and first of all weapons. These may be classified as shock weapons—those used for delivering cut, thrust or blow at close quarters—and missile weapons for effecting the same purpose at a distance. A man might himself carry his sword, spear or bludgeon for hand-to-hand fighting, and also perhaps a certain number of darts to be thrown by the hand. Or he might carry his sling or his bow, with its ammunition, and a single shock weapon—he could hardly be encumbered with more—for personal encounter. But he could not stand the weight of more than a certain number of arrows or a certain number of stones. It is true that stones are to be found in most places, though not in all, and that no army would be at the pains to carry great loads of them; though slingers naturally preferred "smooth stones from the brook"—water-worn stones. But arrows do not grow on trees; and a reserve supply of them, being imperatively necessary, must be carried somehow, or, in other words, required transport. Spare armour and spare weapons also can hardly have been omitted from an expedition prepared with any foresight.

Lastly, men required—or grew very early to require—some additional clothing to protect them against the cold at night and even, in some cases, shelter against bad

1-2

weather at large. This likewise needed to be carried, and laid additional burden on the transport.

Thus in very remote times we find armies carrying with them food—howsoever obtained—ammunition and what we group together under the term baggage. Let us glance at King Saul's army when David first made his appearance. On his first visit to the camp David brought with him two or more pack-asses laden with a present of bread for his brothers and of cheese for their officers. This points to the quite credible circumstance that good food was not too abundant in the army. He must also have brought with him what we should call his own kit, for before he went out to encounter Goliath he came to "the place of the waggons... and left his baggage in the hand of the keeper of the baggage".* In another passage we are told that Saul once "lay in the place of the waggons", confirming the inference that, even then, the transport was parked in some place apart; and it is evident further that there was an official who did duty as baggage master.

The drivers and other folks connected with the transport and the baggage must necessarily have been non-combatants, and it is very curious that at this same period we catch a glimpse of jealousy between the combatant and the non-combatant branches of the army. In one of his raids David marched a small force almost to a standstill and left a third of it behind to protect the baggage. The remainder that went with him gathered great spoil, and at first refused to share it with the baggage guard. David thereupon laid down a rule which became a standing regulation with the Jews in war: "As his share is that goeth down to the battle, so shall his share be that tarrieth by the stuff; they shall share alike". David, in other words, appreciated the value of

---

* In the Vulgate David's baggage is expressed by the classical term *vasa*, while the keeper of the baggage is *custos ad sarcinas*, *sarcina* being the classical word for a pack or knapsack.

his auxiliary services and honoured them accordingly. Not till late in the nineteenth century was his principle accepted in the British Army.

The next step seems to have been the entry of finance into the domain of transport and supply, though it is impossible to divine the first manner of that entry. The mercenary, hired or professional soldier is an extremely ancient institution, with certain characteristics which tend to cling to him throughout all ages. He was engaged at a fixed rate of pay, but his service was of the nature of a gamble. His employer rarely, if ever, had the money to pay him for long, hoping to gain it by the plunder of his enemy. But the soldier equally looked upon the plunder as his natural right, and was not disposed to allow his employer to get hold of more of it than he could help. Hence the soldier's habit of breaking loose after the storming of a town or after a battle and, to give but one recent instance, the dispersal of the French military chest by the British troops after Vitoria before Wellington could get hold of it for the general service of the army. But a campaign could not go on at all unless the soldiers were fed; and it became the practice to deduct from the soldier's pay a fixed daily sum for the cost of his subsistence. Such business fell necessarily into the hands of the non-combatant service; and the combatants always—very often with reason—suspected the non-combatants of cheating.

Next came in the practice of making over to contractors the duty of providing food for an army in the field, and transport to carry it and all other necessaries. How old this system may be I have no knowledge, but in India I suspect it to be of immense antiquity. Of course such a contractor may have been originally a mere speculator who obtained certain concessions in return for the promise of certain services, neither party having really any intention of abiding by his agreement.

Probably the first contractors differed little from the sutlers of much later times; and I shall now make one great bound into the Europe of the fifteenth and sixteenth centuries and glance at the practice of the mercenary bands of that period.

These bands were the models upon which all the armies of Europe were built, our own army being based principally upon the Germans. They were in practice little communities of men, women and children, which were only kept in order by extremely stringent measures. Their victualling and their transport (except the private carriages of officers) were conducted by sutlers who followed them in the hope of profit, and were not exactly under contract nor exactly independent traders. The soldier received no rations, but bought his food from the sutlers in their open market; the prices, however, being fixed by the Provost Marshal, who was also responsible for the general enforcement of discipline. His duties were sufficiently difficult, for, if he fixed the prices too high, the men grumbled, and, if too low, the sutlers simply forsook the camp and left the soldiers to provide for themselves. It is not difficult to understand the permanent ill-feeling which must have existed between the troops, who always imagined themselves to be cheated, and the sutlers, who always ran the risk of a military riot which might be their ruin.

It would not, I think, be very profitable to follow the course of our mediaeval wars, when discipline was very imperfect, organisation was extremely crude and the practice of living on the country, wickedly and wastefully, was probably the only means of living at all. Contracts in abundance were made—they have been printed in many folio volumes—crown jewels were pledged, and every shift was resorted to in order to raise money; but the interest of these documents, in spite of the human nature that peeps through them, is more academic than practical. In Edward III's time

6

the so-called contract often amounted only to an order to the Mayor and Bailiffs of a town that they should incite merchants to go to the King's camp with certain provisions and other goods, for the sale of which there was promised to them prompt payment (*solutio prompta*). The only real training that Englishmen in time of peace could gather towards providing for the wants of an army was gained by the officers, styled harbingers and purveyors, who preceded the Sovereign during a royal progress and purchased provisions for the court, its train and the rabble that hung upon it. It is probable that there was little less disorder and rascality amongst this rabble than among the followers on a campaign.

Meanwhile a new complication had been introduced into war by the invention of gunpowder and of firearms. Ammunition thereupon at once became heavier; and, further, some of the new weapons—cannon—were so ponderous that they could only be moved upon wheels by animal traction. Every form of wheeled vehicle, including guns, went into one category in those days. A draught-horse was a draught-horse, and might be required to haul guns on one day, and flour or forage on another. Hence it came about naturally that the business of loads lay with one department, and the business of waggons and horses with another. The horses of cavalry were of course an inseparable part of the regimental establishment; but teams and drivers, kept and trained for the peculiar service of the artillery, are comparatively a modern institution, not yet a century and a half old. In fact it may be said that, excepting the horses of the cavalry, every animal required for the service of a campaign was impressed, purchased or hired for the occasion.

In the sixteenth century there were no government victualling yards in England, not even for the Navy, and consequently the provisions for all naval and military expeditions were supplied by contract, often with disastrous results. The English were then far behind other nations in knowledge of war; and such few of them as had any acquaintance with it had learned it by service in foreign armies, particularly the Swedish and the Dutch. In both of these matters had advanced so far that in the seventeenth century there was a regular table of rations for all ranks, and there was also an officer responsible for the feeding of the troops, with a waggon master under him. This points to the comprehension of transport and supply under a single head; and, so long as money lasted, there may have been some method and order about the organisation. But few commanders in the field were adequately supplied with cash; and, when cash failed, they had no alternative but to turn their troops loose upon the inhabitants, friendly or hostile, to live, both men and horses, upon "free quarter". When this was done, the rations for all ranks were duly laid down on paper; but, even if the regulations were carefully observed, they were still oppressive and must inevitably have led to incessant friction and outrage. The truth is that military discipline depends upon regular feeding, and that the regular feeding of an army equally depends upon military discipline. The two things are mutually interdependent. Without discipline there can be no just distribution; without just distribution there must be waste of victuals; and the inevitable consequence of waste of victuals is waste of men.

Our own army grew out of the civil dissensions between Sovereign and Parliament which came to a head in 1642. There was a certain number of officers upon both sides who had seen active service with the Swedish, Dutch and other armies; but, if they had any experience in the victualling of troops in the field, it was not utilised. The Parliamentary army had a Commissary for the Provisions and a Carriage-Master-General; but neither of them seems to have been of the slightest use.

8

Both armies lived, practically, upon the country, that of the Parliament paying its way by means of tickets issued by the Commissary. The redemption of these being very uncertain, there was naturally loud outcry. In fact both armies were generally on the verge of starvation, when not actually famished, and were cursed as plagues by the countryfolk. The quarrel might have sputtered out into an indecisive and ignoble end, but for two circumstances. The Parliament had the City of London at its back, which signified the principal financial resources of the country; and it had also a man, Oliver Cromwell, who understood the value of strict military discipline.

In 1645 the Parliament remodelled its army, putting it on a regular footing and providing that it should be regularly paid; and therewith the issue of the struggle was decided. On what may be called the General Staff of the New Model Army we find a Commissary-General of Victuals, a Commissary-General of Horse Provisions and a Waggon-Master-General; on the Staff of the Horse (we may call it the Cavalry Division, for it was nearly seven thousand strong) there was a Commissary-General; and on the Staff of the Train (engineers, artillery, and its escort of two battalions) there was a Commissary of Ammunition and a Commissary of the Draught-Horses. A Commissary, it should be explained, was simply an officer to whom certain duties were committed; and the term was not yet applied exclusively to those concerned with transport and supply. The organisation seems sufficiently crude. Food and forage are under distinct heads and transport under a third. The Commissary of Horse was Ireton and, as he commanded the left wing of cavalry at Naseby, his duties may have been purely combatant. Then the Train has its own Commissary of the Draught-Horse and also a Commissary for Ammunition, suggesting once again a division of responsibility for the waggon and for its load. Lastly, all finance was placed in the hands of three Treasurers-

9

at-War. However, even so, the New Model was a far more efficient fighting machine than any army that had come before it. The soldier was more or less regularly paid, and one result was that private speculators—vintners and sutlers—followed the army, subject to military regulation, and opened a market, after the manner of the German mercenary bands, where the soldiers could buy their food. "Free quarter", now under much stricter regulation, still continued intermittently at times of stress until in 1649 it disappeared altogether, and so the army grew fit for the work which it was to do under Cromwell in Scotland and Ireland.

In Scotland there was small sufficiency of provisions and the people hid away what they had, so Cromwell's army depended upon victuals shipped from England. For this reason the English could not move far from the coast, and the Scots manœuvred continually to cut them off from it. Transport was evidently very scarce, for the men carried seven days' rations of biscuit and cheese on their backs. During Monk's campaign in the Highlands, where he marched, roughly speaking, from south to north, he set up a chain of magazines along the eastern border, which formed so many bases of supply. Starting with a train of pack-horses, he carried provisions to last him to the next line of supply and there replenished. Thus he was able to press the Highland tribes continually until, worn out by constant chasing and by the destruction of their provision grounds, they submitted.

In Ireland, which later became the victualling yard of the world, the Parliamentary armies were starving and stationary till Cromwell took command. Even he was obliged to depend upon provisions shipped from England and was therefore tied to the sea, while the inclemency of the climate forced him to carry tents, which must have been a sad encumbrance to his transport. But after a month or two the inhabitants, tempted by ready money, brought in victuals freely for sale, and the Parliamentary army was much better supplied by its nominal enemies than the Royalist army by its nominal friends. Still, it was a very rough campaign attended by a great deal of sickness, and the troops even under Cromwell's immediate command got out of hand. He had deliberately sacked Drogheda to inspire terror; and Wexford was consequently inclined to surrender without resistance. Cromwell, as he hoped, had actually arranged the terms and secured something which would help to pay the cost of the war. But no sooner did the men get wind of this than they stormed and plundered the place out of hand. Cromwell was evidently much annoyed, but was fain to excuse the undisciplined pillage and massacre by the plea that "God would have it so". The final reduction of Ireland was accomplished, as usual, by small mobile columns with, it can hardly be doubted, pack-animals for transport.

It remains only to glance at Cromwell's one colonial expedition—that to St Domingo—which was undertaken without any provocation because England was bankrupt at the close of the Civil War and Cromwell thought to relieve her by the plunder of Spain. For this campaign he sent out six thousand men—not regular troops but a hastily enlisted rabble. The rendezvous, as was the rule in those days and for a century and a half later, was at Barbados, the most windwardly of the Antilles, and the expedition, by extraordinary good fortune, reached it in three weeks. The provisions, shipped by the victuallers of the Navy, were very defective, and no more, of course, could be obtained in Barbados, where no grain is grown. The troops were weak and sickly owing to bad food; and they were further discouraged by an order prohibiting all plunder. Three Commissioners accompanied the expedition with instructions to take charge of the spoil, and, as at Wexford, the soldiers had no idea of forfeiting what they considered to be their rights for the benefit of the State. The expedition ended in disgraceful failure, though it captured Jamaica, where the force was practically annihilated through sickness.

With the year 1661 we enter upon the history of the Regular Army; and a few words must be devoted to its nature. It was not an army but a collection of regiments, horse and foot. The officers of all ranks purchased their commissions and the colonels and captains were proprietors of their regiments and companies. The agent who conducted the finance of the regiment, the surgeon who looked to the welfare of the men's bodies, and the chaplain who ministered to their souls were all of them the colonel's servants. The regimental paysheet was the beginning and end of its finance, any allowances for contingent expenses being disguised as the pay of fictitious men. General officers, unless by particular provision for special service, received no pay as such, and had to content themselves with their regimental salary unless they obtained the colonelcy of a regiment or the governorship of a fortress. To the latter was attached a regular salary. A colonelcy brought with it the privilege of clothing the men of a regiment by the stoppage of twopence a day from the pay of every one of them. This might be a profitable business, but could be turned to heavy loss. For the rest, the greater part of the balance of the men's pay was stopped for their subsistence. They were quartered in alehouses and fed by the colonel's contract with the landlord until the passing of the Mutiny Act in 1689, after which the daily tariff for feeding the soldier was laid down by Act of Parliament. The men were thus much on a level with their fellows of the labouring class in civil life. Their wages were spent in housing, clothing and feeding them; but the tools of their trade—their weapons—were furnished by the Board of Ordnance at the public expense.

Thus the whole life of a soldier was bound up within

the four corners of his regiment. Practically everything in the Army was regimental. There was a small—a very small—headquarters' staff which looked to points of discipline, and there was a War Office, consisting of a very few clerks for the auditing of the regimental accounts. Until the Union of England and Scotland in 1707 there were an English, a Scottish and an Irish establishment; after that union there were until 1800 a British and an Irish establishment, with different rates of pay; provisions being cheaper in Ireland. In Ireland, too, the soldiers were quartered in barracks instead of in billets, but were fed by contract. The artillery and the engineers, after they came into existence, were quite apart from the rest of the Army. They were subject not to the Commander-in-Chief but to the Master-General of the Ordnance. The officers received their commissions not by purchase but through nomination of the Board of Ordnance. The men were clothed not by the colonel but by the Board of Ordnance, and promotion went not by purchase, which was unknown in the Ordnance Corps, as they were called, but by seniority. Few officers, therefore, rose to general rank, and as late as 1778 there were still doubts whether an officer of artillery, though a General, could command cavalry and infantry in the field.

Transport and supply, being considered wholly matters of finance, were committed to the Treasury, which appointed its deputies or commissaries, to manage the business in all its branches, not excluding the carriage of sick and wounded.

The general duties of the Army in time of peace comprised those of the police and the preventive service within the British Isles, and the maintenance of garrisons in the British possessions abroad. To these were added in time of war the defence of the realm and of the Empire, the conduct of operations in pursuance of these objects, and the manning of the fleet.

The British Empire was already in being when the Regular Army was first established; but the colonies were supposed to look to their own defence. In the few places where a British garrison was to be found, that garrison was inalienably attached to the same quarter and was maintained for that service alone. In the case of Tangier, however, which was the only foreign station held in any strength in Charles II's time, the regiments were retained after the fortress had been abandoned, and were swept into the Regular Army.

It was with the dethronement of James II and the accession of William III that the long struggle with France for the possession of the New World was fairly begun. From that date, therefore, we may begin to examine our subject more closely, for the Army was employed incessantly, and was steadily augmented in order to cope with its increasing duties. It must be premised that the aristocratic revolution of 1688, when scrutinised with attention, reveals itself as a very base and unclean business. The whole country was demoralised. No one knew what might happen, and the majority of men did their utmost to make themselves safe for the present and to remain on good terms, so far as they could, with both of the contending factions. It must be added that administration was then in its infancy, and that the first banks in London had only just come into existence. The system of credit, under which we now live, was not to be fully developed for another century and a half; and one result of this was that salaries in the seventeenth and eighteenth centuries were very irregularly paid. In the seventeenth century holders of salaries petitioned for payment every quarter, and were lucky if they obtained it—very lucky indeed if they obtained it in full. Hence to practically every office there were attached fees, licit or illicit, which formed the only certain income upon which the holders could depend. The Governor of a colony, for instance, upon reaching his government, would issue a new Commission of the Peace and take two guineas from every justice. Even the private soldier long paid a fee, politely called a stoppage, for the privilege of receiving his wages. Naturally those who were entrusted with the expenditure of large sums had the greater opportunity of enriching themselves and took advantage of it. The very form of the accounts showed that dishonesty was expected. Any sum of money entrusted to a public servant for disbursement was debited against him with the ominous word *Charge*, as if he had stolen it. Then, if he accounted for it satisfactorily, he received his *Discharge* and ultimately, probably after the lapse of years and some expenditure in fees, his *Quietus*, which signified that he could make his mind easy.

THE CAMPAIGN IN IRELAND. William's first important campaign was in Ireland, and for this service the money was entrusted to William Harbord, Treasurer of the Army. The finances of the country were in extreme disorder, but Harbord was not the man to make the best of them. The troops sent to Ireland were raw recruits with bad officers; and the only chance of putting some discipline into such a rabble was to pay them and feed them regularly so that they should have no excuse for misconduct. But Harbord would provide no money for anyone except his own troop of horse, which consisted of himself, two clerks whom he called officers, and a standard which he kept in his bedroom. The provision of hospitals was a part of his charge; but there were none and, even if there had been, there were no medicines. Harbord, being a politician and a member of Parliament, could always find an excuse for returning to England and evading unpleasant duties and enquiries, and he actually had the impudence to urge the Commander-in-Chief, the veteran Duke of Schomberg, to march against the enemy.

But the army could not march and, though stationary, was starving. The Commissary-General, by name Shales, had been Purveyor to the camp of ten or twelve thousand men formed by James II at Hounslow in 1685, and should therefore have had some experience both of supply and transport. He duly accumulated victuals—bad victuals it is true—at the base, Belfast, and he purchased a number of horses in Cheshire. But instead of transporting these to Ireland, he let them out to the farmers in Cheshire for the harvest, and pocketed their hire. Unpaid by Harbord, unfed by Shales, officers and men became absolutely demoralised. All ranks from the colonels downward scrambled for such money as was to be had; and by the time that the troops were withdrawn into winter quarters six thousand out of fourteen thousand of them had perished. No one was punished for these miscarriages. Shales was called to account and made some good points in his defence. Probably he and Harbord were no worse than hundreds of others, and, even if they had been honest or competent, would have been baffled by the stupidity and rascality of superiors and subordinates. The root of the whole matter was that no one in authority in England at the moment, King William excepted, had the slightest idea of the meaning of war or of the organisation necessary for conducting it.

One small point may be noticed as typical of the friction that could arise out of the old system of transport. The Board of Ordnance looked to the Commissary-General to provide horses for the artillery. The Commissary-General replied that the artillery was no business of his. The Commissary of the Artillery managed to collect a few horses, and then the Commissary-General tried to borrow them for general purposes of transport; whereupon the Commissary of the Artillery declined to spare them.

After the disastrous experience of 1689 Cromwell's

methods of conducting an Irish campaign were examined by some sensible man, and were followed in 1690 and 1691. There is no need to go further into them.

WILLIAM III's CAMPAIGNS IN THE WEST INDIES. I turn now to two expeditions, unknown except to a few people, which were undertaken by William III against the French in the West Indies. They are instructive chiefly as illustrating the friction between Navy, Army and Treasury.

In both of these ventures there were, as usual, a naval officer in supreme command of all ships and naval business, a military officer in charge of the soldiers, and a Commissary-General who was in control of stores and provisions, paymaster, muster-master and Judge-Advocate-General—a combination of functions which was centred in one man for the sake of economy. Since the principal object of these expeditions was plunder and prize money, the interests of these three persons might very well not coincide in respect of any given operation; and practically it was in the power of any one of them to wreck any single plan that might be projected by the other two.

In the first of the two expeditions—in 1693—Commodore and General turned against the Commissary and put him out of action by confining him in a small vessel by himself under the custody of a serjeant's guard.

In the second expedition, which was despatched against St Domingo in 1695, the Commodore and the Commissary were knaves and the military commander, an old soldier of much experience, was an honest man. The Commodore and Commissary, having come early to an agreement to exclude the General from all share in prize money, inveigled him ashore at Madeira on the outward passage and tried to leave him behind. Failing in this, they laid themselves out in every way to thwart him, the Commodore by withholding the co-operation of the ships, the Commissary by refusing to land provisions, guns and ammunition. They succeeded so far that the Commodore beguiled the soldiers into doing most of the hard work, while he carried off the plunder for himself and the Commissary. The end of the whole story was tragic. The Commodore died and his ill-gotten gains were seized by one of his captains. The Commissary died; great numbers of officers and seamen died, and the General alone of the commanders returned home to tell the tale.

CAMPAIGNS IN FLANDERS. Flanders has always been a cockpit, the country being fertile and abounding in sluggish streams convenient for water carriage. In the seventeenth century the French mapped it out somewhat after the manner of a chessboard, whereon certain moves, in the stage then reached in the art of war, led inevitably to certain other moves; so that if an army left one camping-ground pointing in a given direction, its next camping-ground could be predicted with certainty. The Dutch, naturally, were not less familiar with it than the French and understood thoroughly how to carry on war therein. War was a less difficult matter then than now. Armies did not try to meet each other and force a decision. They were too costly and too precious. Actions were fought from time to time; but the great professors of the art of war laid down that the most profitable way of conducting it was to move into an enemy's country, entrench yourself to the teeth and subsist at his expense. A wise commander would almost certainly choose some place with convenient roads—the old Roman roads were the best—or waterways; and then the ousting of him became a difficult matter. As a rule, if one army so entrenched itself, the hostile army moved up to its front and entrenched itself likewise; and so they would remain looking at each other for weeks. The feeding of a stationary force being always easier than that of an army in motion, the skill and energy of the Commissaries were not put to any very severe test; but the difficulty which generally caused one army or the other to move was that of forage. If one commander could control a richer and wider area than his adversary, he could after a short time predict almost to a day when his adversary would be obliged to seek another camping-ground. If an army did not remain positively inactive, it might equally remain stationary for days and weeks by conducting a siege. The French Court loved a siege. The Sovereign would arrive in state to assist at it, with a full company of comedians to amuse him of evenings and a painter or two to immortalise the operations of the siege on canvas. Thus wars were prolonged for years until financial exhaustion brought them to an end.

To this pedantic school of warriors William III belonged, though he was fonder of a fight than most men of his time. Marlborough was the man who broke down the system by swifter and more active movement in search of a decision. His arrangements for supply and transport therefore needed greater elasticity and more perfect organisation. Unfortunately I have been unable to discover much in detail about them; but, if Marlborough's own orders are undiscoverable, those of General Wade and the Duke of Cumberland, when fighting over the same ground in 1744-7, are to hand; and it may be assumed with some certainty that they were based upon Marlborough's. A country which has been a favourite fighting-ground for centuries cannot fail to produce a race of contractors ready to provide for armies; and the methods of all of them must, roads, rivers and country remaining unchanged, have been much the same.

The essence of Marlborough's system of transport and supply for the army in Flanders was a contract with Sir Solomon Medina—presumably a Jew and certainly a very able man—for providing it with bread and bread waggons. In Cromwell's time the soldier's ration had been bread and cheese, but by the opening of the eighteenth century cheese had disappeared, and the Commissary's duties bound him to supply bread, fuel and forage only. Apart from bread the soldier depended for his subsistence upon sutlers; and sutlers were a regimental affair—one grand sutler for every regiment, and one petty sutler for each troop of horse or company of foot. The allowance seems a large one, for a troop of horse rarely exceeded seventy-five men, or a company one hundred. So important were the sutlers, however, that they received an allowance of forage for their horses, which were limited to fifteen for a regiment of horse, twelve for a regiment of dragoons (mounted infantry on inferior horses), or twelve for a battalion of foot. Taking the campaign of Ramillies as a sample, we find that Marlborough in 1706 had of British troops five regiments of horse, two of dragoons and nineteen battalions of foot, so that at this rate the sutlers' horses alone would have numbered two hundred and eighty. The major, who was in those days the regimental staff officer, was responsible for the quality of the sutlers' goods and for their selling them by fair weight and measure. The adjutant was originally the major's assistant, and in France is still called *aide-Major*. It was ordered that the men should mess regularly, and should have bacon "or other flesh meat" twice a week; this regulation being evidently designed to prevent the soldier from spending the whole of his pay upon drink. For vegetables parties were sent out to gather roots. Commanding officers were further required to encourage butchers (who were likewise licensed) to follow the regiments with sheep and cattle on the hoof and to sell the men meat, so that they should have no excuse for falling back upon liquor.

Thus the victualling of the men depended, in the matter of bread, upon one gigantic contract, and in all other matters upon a multitude of petty contractors or speculators—whichever term may be preferred. The bread contract was on so great a scale that by established usage the Commander-in-Chief received from the contractor a percentage which gave him a fund for the purchase of secret intelligence. A part of the soldier's wages was stopped to pay for his bread, and the remainder was supposed to be expended in supplementing this diet at the sutlers' canteens. Marlborough, fighting, as is commonly the case with British commanders, for the most part in a friendly country, was very stern against plunder; but to judge from the life of the celebrated sutleress, Mrs Christian Ross, the sutlers and their followers were the most shameless thieves of all.

With regard to forage, the second of the Commissary's charges, there are many passages in Marlborough's despatches. The bulk of it was taken by foraging parties, often with much waste and much hardship to the peasants, though every effort was made to lessen these risks. Sometimes the folk on the land were allowed to compound for exemption from foraging parties by supplying so many thousand sacks of grain. It appears that a deduction was made from the pay of at least some mounted troops in payment for forage, and that the State supplemented this stoppage when forage was dear. Contracts were invariably made for the supply of forage during winter quarters, which would enable the price of the ration to be fixed.* It does not appear that forage was ever sent over from England. But the whole business of forage was difficult and complicated to the last degree, giving birth to mountains of illegible and almost unintelligible accounts.

In the matter of fuel, the Commissary's third charge, there seems to have been no difficulty in Flanders, though we shall hear of trouble later in Holland.

* See *Marlborough's Desp.* III, 582, 635; IV, 405; V, 186.

To pass now from supply to transport, it would appear (though it would be bold to assert it as a certainty) that the bread contractor's waggons and teams formed the only public source of transport for the army as a whole. A "bread waggon" (the usual term employed) seems to have been, broadly speaking, any horsed or wheeled vehicle provided by the bread contractor, and was by no means consecrated only to the sole conveyance of bread. Thus one bread waggon was allowed to each regiment as an ambulance; and indeed bread waggons and their teams were used for every kind of purpose. Marlborough would employ either the horses or the waggons or both for carrying ammunition or moving guns; and that although the artillery teams were distinct from others, being hired under a different contract. In short, a horse was a horse and a waggon was a waggon, to whatever purpose they might be devoted; and Marlborough's staff had a weary task in adjusting the conflicting claims to them, for there were none too many at any time. For the siege of Lille in 1708 Marlborough required sixteen thousand horses to drag the guns and the ammunition, and managed somehow to get them. He seems to have had a certain number of English draught-horses, for he testifies to their superiority; but the horses of Holland, Flanders and Germany, being cheaper, were preferred.

Roads, except the old Roman roads, being few and bad, pack-animals were largely employed as well as vehicles. The great silver pilgrim bottles (in the possession of Lord Spencer) wherein Marlborough carried his wine, were evidently designed to be slung on either side of a pack-horse. It is probable that most of the officers' baggage was carried by pack-animals and part, at least, of the equipment of the sutlers also.

Since baggage was a regimental matter, the number of different authorities in charge of transport must have been considerable; but on the march all vehicles and baggage animals were subject to the Waggon-Master. If any moved without his orders or strayed from their place without his permission, the penalty was that the load should be plundered there and then, even if it belonged to the Commander-in-Chief. And here it must be noticed that officers of high rank generally and the Commander-in-Chief in particular had a vast quantity of baggage, their retinue apparently compelling them to keep a costly table. Lord Peterborough in 1707 lost his heavy baggage in Spain. It included sixteen waggons, over fifty mules and several valuable horses, the worth of the whole being estimated at £8000, which would be equivalent to quite £40,000 at the present day. The Waggon-Master's task in keeping so many unruly elements in order must have been severe, yet, as he was responsible only for the waggon and not for its load, he need not have found it excessive.

CAMPAIGNS IN GERMANY AND SPAIN. So much for the campaigns in Flanders. But there are other campaigns also to be considered at this period —that of Marlborough himself on the Danube and those of Galway and Peterborough in Spain. It is noteworthy that, when he passed into Germany, Marlborough was obliged to change his bread contractor. Once again he found a Solomon—Solomon Adam—of whom he spoke very highly. Other arrangements for the passage of the troops through an infinity of petty German principalities, and for the renewal of their shoes and the like matters, testify to Marlborough's diplomatic skill and the prevision with which he took thought for every detail. Once in Bavaria after the victory of the Schellenberg he found a fertile country with abundant supplies, and what he did not use he deliberately, though reluctantly, destroyed, so as to bring the Elector of Bavaria to terms. In fact success made easy the problem of supply.

The operations in Spain were not very important,

the force employed being small. It was landed first at Lisbon, but the country between that capital and Madrid had been so much devastated by two years of war that it sailed round to Barcelona. This place was captured, but further operations were suspended for want of transport. "I cannot get carriages to transport the baggage of our troops to their garrisons", wrote Peterborough; "I cannot get ammunition carried to a fortified place; I cannot get provisions put into a place which must expect a siege." Lack of money was chiefly responsible for this state of things, and this trouble continued. It was impossible for either side to move any great number of troops—even so many as twenty thousand—and it must be conjectured that they depended for transport upon hired pack-mules and for supply upon anything that could be purchased for money or credit. Wellington, a century later, failed to discover any contractor who could provide bread and waggons after the fashion of Flanders; and it is hardly to be supposed that Peterborough and Galway were more fortunate.

FOREIGN GARRISONS IN TIME OF PEACE. In the year 1714 the war ended with the Peace of Utrecht and England found herself the richer by two Mediterranean possessions, Gibraltar and Minorca, and by the acquisition of Nova Scotia on the other side of the Atlantic. Foreign garrisons were a novelty to the Regular Army. In Britain that army (it will be remembered) was billeted in alehouses and fed, by stoppage of the men's pay, according to a tariff fixed by Act of Parliament. In Ireland there were barracks, and the men were fed by contract. But the new possessions were strange lands, and the politicians in England had not the slightest idea how to deal with them. The victualling of them was entrusted to contractors, but in the contracts the most simple necessities were overlooked. In the case of Minorca, brandy, oil, bread, salt and tobacco were duly supplied to the soldiers, but the item of meat, even salt meat, was entirely omitted. At Annapolis, a lonely half-savage station, the men were supposed to drink nothing but water. Consequently they mutinied, and their officers were obliged to buy molasses at their own cost and to brew them beer. The officials at the Treasury seem to have thought that, if they provided bread for soldiers, all other necessities would descend upon them from Heaven. Perhaps this was natural, seeing that a single contract with Sir Solomon Medina had sufficed to tide Marlborough's army through nine or ten campaigns; but they had forgotten the existence of sutlers, or possibly imagined that they too were sent from Heaven, even to so remote a spot as Annapolis. The neglect of the civil administrators was indeed incredible. Gibraltar had been in our possession by treaty for six years before it occurred to anyone that the fortress should always contain two months' provisions in advance. Even then it was the King himself who suggested it. When Gibraltar was besieged by the Spaniards in 1727, there was a dearth of salt in the garrison, and for a time the Governor himself had to content himself with biscuit at his table, there being no bread from want of flour. Yet this so-called siege was not a siege at all, for the Spanish fleet could not close the sea to the British, and therefore provision ships could sail in at any time. The Treasury had, in fact, not yet learned its work in the way of providing for the army over sea. In 1711 the garrison at Gibraltar were obliged to burn their huts from want of fuel, and in 1730 they were still without a roof over their heads and suffering much loss from exposure and from dysentery.

Yet other garrisons—small enough—in America and the West Indies were for the most part attached permanently to their stations, though the regiments of the line were beginning to undertake duty in the Antilles.

At New York there were four companies which maintained the frontier guards against the French and Indians. These must have been fed by local contract, but, through the fault of the Board of Ordnance, they were not properly clothed; and, out of two weak companies, forty-nine men died of cold in a single winter. In Bermuda, once again through the neglect of the Board of Ordnance, not one ounce of stores was landed between 1696 and 1739. In the true Antilles, Jamaica, Antigua and other islands, the planters granted a special allowance to the garrison over and above their ordinary pay; but, to judge from the state of things in the nineteenth century, the men were fed chiefly upon salt provisions drawn from the Navy's victualling yards. Their quarters were generally very unhealthy, notably in Jamaica, and the life of a battalion in the West Indies, even in the early years of Queen Victoria, did not exceed two years, owing to the ravages of yellow fever.

The transport and supply service of the Army was still in this primitive state when England entered upon the long contest with France for the New Empire in the West and the sovereignty of India in the East. It would be tedious to go through the whole of the campaigns between 1742 and 1763 individually, so it will be convenient to deal with them by spheres of operations.

THE CAMPAIGNS OF GERMANY AND FLANDERS, 1743–8. These were conducted according to the precedent of Marlborough's wars and need not detain us.

OPERATIONS IN THE WEST INDIES AND ON THE SPANISH MAIN. These consisted practically always in the siege of the enemy's principal fortress guarding the harbour, the reduction of which signified the fall of the island, or (in the case of Porto Bello and Carthagena) of the enemy's local capital. In all such campaigns the Navy took as active a part as the Army. The troops were never far from the ships, and they were fed with ships' victuals, which were carried up to them by bluejackets or by negro carriers, purchased or hired from the British islands. No doubt a few mules and horses could be captured or impressed upon the spot and were probably used as pack-animals, West Indian roads being few and the paved ways so narrow and steep as to be difficult for wheeled traffic.

OPERATIONS IN NORTH AMERICA. The two gates of the North American continent in old days were Quebec, which was in the hands of the French, and New York, which was in the hands of the English. The Power which should hold both would be master of the continent, for from both there was access by water to the Great Lakes, and so to the great rivers which run south to the Gulf of Mexico. Quebec, of course, lying at the mouth of the St Lawrence, was the more important and commanding gate; and the capture of Quebec was as much a naval as a military enterprise, akin to the attacks upon West Indian islands. From New York the favourite way to the Great Lakes was up the River Hudson and then either northward by Lakes George and Champlain, or westward by Lake Oneida. The transport, therefore, consisted entirely of boats, with gangs of men stationed wherever the rapids of the Hudson interrupted the navigation, to carry the boats into practicable water. This required some organisation and some discipline which the Americans were never able to accomplish for themselves; but, speaking generally, the problem of transport and supply was comparatively simple, for provisions could be carried by water from England straight to the Lakes. The provision of boats was a matter for contract, presenting no great difficulty, for there were plenty of expert boat builders in America. The establishment of magazines along the waterways was also a simple matter, for there were fortified posts at the most important points. For crews much use was made of Indians. One great difficulty was eliminated by the fact that boats require no forage and that there was abundance of timber on the way for purposes of repairs.

There were, however, a certain number of expeditions overland, the most important of which were two despatched to uproot the French posts planted on the Upper Ohio in rear of the British settlements in Pennsylvania. The first of these, the ill-fated enterprise entrusted to General Braddock, was mismanaged from the first. The troops sailed from England to Hampton Roads and thence up the Potomac to Alexandria. Thence the way to Fort Duquesne (the modern Pittsburg) was long and circuitous and lay through a poor country where waggons, horses, supplies and forage were scarce. Had they landed at Philadelphia the march would have been shortened and would have passed through a fertile and populous district full of supplies of every kind. The colonists on the spot were unwilling to exert themselves in the least on behalf of Braddock. Contracts were indeed made both for waggons and victuals, but these were broken or disavowed; and it was only by the mediation of Benjamin Franklin that Braddock managed to collect about one hundred and fifty waggons and six hundred pack-horses. His force numbered about two thousand fighting men, and his objective lay about one hundred miles away as the crow flies, through forest-clad mountains along a rough track no more than twelve feet wide. Improving the track as he went, Braddock took eight days to cover thirty miles; but even so his horses, having no forage except such poor stuff as was to be found in the forest, were weak and falling down fast. The men also were failing owing to fever and dysentery. Braddock therefore decided to move on with two-thirds of his force only, leaving the heavy baggage to follow as best it could, and taking with him ten guns, a sufficient number of pack-horses and only thirty waggons. On the 7th of July, the thirty-seventh day after quitting his base, he was still

28

eight miles from his objective when his force was surprised and virtually annihilated. Had he succeeded in
reaching Fort Duquesne and in driving the French from
it, he must have retired again immediately from want of
supplies.

Not until three years later, in 1758, was a second
attempt made to expel the French from the Ohio. This
time the commander, General Forbes, decided to advance from Pennsylvania and to push on by slow stages,
establishing magazines at intervals of forty miles, so that
his final advance might be as little encumbered as
possible. With great difficulty he collected provisions,
horses and waggons at Philadelphia during May and
June, and in July reached his advanced base, the village
of Carlisle, rather over a hundred miles to the west of
Philadelphia. Here he was detained for several weeks
by sickness, while his advanced parties under Colonel
Bouquet of the Sixtieth—a most efficient officer—
formed a fortified magazine at Raystown, sixty miles to
the west of Carlisle, and sent detachments forward to
make a road over the Alleghanies. Forbes described
the country as "an immense uninhabited wilderness,
overgrown everywhere with trees and brushwood, so
that nowhere can one see twenty yards". However,
Bouquet worked on and began to fill another magazine
at Loyalhannon, some fifty miles west and north of
Raystown and within less than fifty miles of Fort
Duquesne.

With the month of October came heavy and continuous rain, which ruined the new road. The horses,
unable to bring their own forage forward, broke down
fast from overwork and starvation. The force, about
four thousand strong, was by this time assembled at
Loyalhannon, but the magazines were emptying faster
than they could be refilled. In desperation Forbes,
though sick unto death and too weak to stand, decided
to move on with twenty-five hundred picked men,

29

carrying their packs and a blanket, but leaving all tents and baggage behind. The rain had now turned to snow, but on the evening of the seventh day's march—24th of November—he came before the ruins of Fort Duquesne which had been evacuated by the French. They likewise had been in difficulties over their supplies, which had forced them to disperse their troops. Forbes left a garrison of two hundred men to hold the post, being unable to collect victuals enough for more, and early in December led his column painfully back to Philadelphia. He had been carried in a litter for every step of the outward and return marches, but it had been his head and his will which had achieved a most difficult enterprise. He died a few weeks later; and the next troublesome little expedition of this kind was entrusted to Bouquet.

In 1763, after the peace which transferred Canada from the French to the English, the remoter parts of the country were held by a chain of weak posts extending in the north from Niagara round the southern shore of Lake Erie to Detroit, with outlying posts about Mackinaw, at the northern extremity of Lake Huron, and also at the southern end of Lake Michigan. The length of this chain was, roughly speaking, a thousand miles; but, though there was communication by water all the way, the garrisons from sheer neglect were miserably fed, subsisting for months together on flour and peas, the salt pork supplied to them being uneatable. There was another chain of posts along the route of Braddock's march from Pennsylvania to Pittsburg, and thence northward to Lake Erie. A sudden well-concerted rebellion of Indians made an end of all the posts on the lakes except Detroit, and dangerously threatened those between Pennsylvania and the Ohio. The re-establishment of order on this latter line was entrusted to Bouquet, who at once moved from his headquarters at Philadelphia to Carlisle, where he arrived at the end of

June. He had given orders for victuals to be accumulated there, but the whole country was in a state of panic, and nothing had been done. He was detained for eighteen days before he could collect waggons, oxen, horses and supplies, his resources being constantly diminished by the entreaties of starving settlers. On the 23rd of July he reached Raystown, and by the 2nd of August, after following the track of Forbes, he had covered one hundred and fifty miles from Carlisle and lay at an intermediate post between Raystown and Pittsburg. Here he left his oxen and waggons and proceeded with three hundred and fifty pack-horses and a few driven cattle only. On the 5th and 6th he fought an action which cost him a fourth of his force and laid open to him the way to Pittsburg, whence, having reinforced the garrison, he returned to Philadelphia.

In the following autumn (October, 1764) he again advanced from Pittsburg through dense forest into an unknown country between Lake Erie and the Ohio, his force mustering about fifteen hundred fighting men. His transport consisted entirely of pack-horses, and he drove with him also oxen and sheep "on the hoof". Progress was necessarily slow, but the bare penetration of these fastnesses for one hundred and fifty miles sufficed to bring the Indians to reason, and Bouquet accomplished his purpose without the firing of a shot. The entire campaign until his return to Pittsburg seems to have lasted about seven weeks, and it was a triumph of organisation over immense difficulties of supply and transport. Bouquet evidently regarded it as such, for he appended to his own modest account of his operations a table, working out the exact amount of transport required for a force of given strength in an expedition against the Indians, and giving the load of each waggon and pack-horse somewhat in the style of our mobilisation tables of to-day.

This, so far as I know, is the very first printed table of the kind in the English language.*

OPERATIONS IN INDIA. The story of our early campaigns in the plains of India is at once familiar and obscure. From all that we can gather, they were conducted with extreme comfort and even luxury, the officers travelling, as a rule, in palanquins with an immense retinue of servants, and the army being accompanied by an indiscriminate rabble which hoped to make something, either by trading or looting, out of the operations. The fighting men were comparatively few, and their subsistence was provided for by contracts with native contractors. The systems varied in the three presidencies; but the description of that which reigned in Bengal given by Lord Napier of Magdala in 1867 probably applies pretty accurately in all. "The Commissariat", he wrote, "have had but a small quantity of their own carriage to manage [in the eighteenth century they probably had none]; the greater portion has been hired carriage managed under a kind of social organisation peculiar to itself, and which goes on somehow, one hardly knows how." The Commissary in those primitive days was appointed for the occasion, and the post was much coveted. The East India Company, most reprehensibly, made it their practice to underpay their employees and leave it to them to fill their pockets by private trading or corrupt dealing. Hence the Commissary was expected to make money out of his appointment, and so he did, very often at the expense of the men's stomachs. Robert Clive himself was once a Commissary and enriched himself accordingly, though he was a sufficiently good soldier to see that the men were properly fed. Before 1763 British armies never moved

* The book is a little thin quarto, printed at Philadelphia in 1766, and now commands a fancy price. I owned a copy at one time and had the pleasure of showing it to Sir Redvers Buller, who knew of its existence and of the peculiar interest of the appended tables, but had never before seen it.

to any great distance, except by sea, in India; and the old arrangements sufficed. When later they were called upon to operate among the more warlike races and in the hills, then difficulties, as shall be seen, presented themselves immediately; and the military training in India, where officers of energy and talent were generally seized upon early for civil employment, was not calculated to encourage men to face them.

CHAPTER II

AMERICA AND INDIA IN THE SEVENTEENTH CENTURY

THE year 1763 saw the establishment of the first British Empire, and within twelve years began the quarrel with the American Colonies which, being taken up successively by France, Spain and Holland, resulted in the loss of those colonies, of one or two West Indian islands, and very nearly of India. It will be convenient to glance at the several spheres of operations in turn.

THE CAMPAIGNS IN AMERICA. This was the most detestable kind of war—that against a civilised enemy in a wild and untamed country—of which the latest example is the South African War of 1899–1902. The difficulties of feeding armies in the field in such a theatre must always be enormous, and they were felt as much by the Americans as by the British. It must not be forgotten that the American rebels—most rightly from their own point of view—took the offensive at the outset. They were already masters of New York, and they made a dash upon Quebec so as to seize both the main gates of the continent. But they had neglected to provide for transport and supplies; and the column of two thousand men which marched upon Quebec lost two hundred men dead from starvation and fatigue, two hundred more sick, and three hundred more deserters from the same cause. The remnant came before Quebec, famished, having been obliged to eat their dogs; and

34

their attack upon the city was easily repelled. They were driven out of Canada with no great difficulty, the British, of course, using the waterways for purposes of transport.

But at Boston, where the British had struck their first blow in the action of Bunker Hill, the British troops were paralysed by want of land transport. They were beleaguered by a greatly superior force, and, though they might have attacked it with temporary success, they could have reaped no profit from their victory, for they could not follow up their enemy. The neighbourhood of Boston being bitterly hostile, it had been impossible to collect animals and vehicles at the last moment; and General Howe begged that transport might be sent him by sea from elsewhere. But this the British Government declared to be impossible, and probably with good reason. Later one regiment of cavalry was sent out from England complete, and half the horses perished on the voyage. The rebel agents, if they could not check the purchase of transport from the loyalists (who were the majority) at other points in America, could certainly have made the embarkation of animals very difficult. Moreover, even if horse transports had been at hand, which they were not, the casualties in any voyage along the American coast during the winter must certainly have been heavy. The end of the matter was that in March, 1776, Howe evacuated Boston by sea and retired to Halifax, which became the base for future operations.

There were, however, at Halifax no natural stores of food even for Howe's small army of nine thousand men; and the General suffered tortures of anxiety owing to the tardy arrival of provision ships from England. Not until August could he begin the operations for the recapture of New York, which was easily effected. Throughout this short campaign Howe could never move far from the waterways, being dependent on water transport and supplies from the ships. By

35   3-2

November he must have collected a little land transport of some kind, for he landed a flying column of two thousand five hundred men which marched for a short distance inland, but was soon brought to a temporary halt by starvation. Howe's movements, apart from water transport, were, in fact, confined to crossing the space between the waterway of the Hudson and the waterway of the Delaware; and when he reached the latter he could advance no further because the Americans had removed all boats. The campaign therefore came to an end.

In the following year, 1777, Howe sailed with fourteen thousand men for the Chesapeake, landed at the head of an inlet only thirteen miles west of the Delaware, advanced twenty miles, beat the Americans at Brandywine, and by the capture of the defences on the Delaware opened that river to the fleet and gave himself a new base at Philadelphia, where the population was loyal and supplies were abundant. He must have picked up most of his land transport on the spot, for the voyage from New York to the Chesapeake occupied twenty-four days, which would have killed many horses, if they had been embarked, and weakened the rest. As a matter of fact he landed on the 25th of August, and did not come into contact with the enemy twenty miles away until nine days later. Probably he was gathering in transport every day.

At about the same time General Burgoyne started from the Canadian side to move by way of Lake Champlain to the Hudson and down that river to New York. His regular force numbered just over seven thousand, to which he hoped to add two thousand Canadians and a number of Indians. The difficulty of his advance lay in the intervening space of about thirty miles between Skenesborough, at the southern end of Lake Champlain, and the navigable waters of the Hudson. To cross this space—hilly ground covered

36

with forest—he required land transport to convey not only his supplies and stores but his boats. This transport he endeavoured to obtain through contractors in Canada; but the contracts were not fulfilled. The number of horses supplied was insufficient, and the Canadians showed great unwillingness to accept employment with the transport. Burgoyne concentrated at Fort Cumberland at the northern extremity of Lake Champlain on the 20th of June. His first stage was to Crown Point— sixty miles—where he halted for three days to establish magazines, and the next to Ticonderoga, five miles farther on, which was in the occupation of the enemy. The operations for driving the Americans out lasted from the 1st to the 7th of July; and on the 10th Burgoyne with his whole force had reached Skenesborough, at the southern extremity of Lake Champlain. From this point the route lay through forest, and the Americans in their retreat had felled trees at every few yards along the track. It took Burgoyne exactly twenty days to cover the next twenty miles southward from Skenesborough to Fort Edward; and here he was brought to a stand. He had a formidable enemy in his front against whom he dared not advance without plenty of artillery, and his horses were too few to carry his supplies and boats across to the River Hudson, far too few to form magazines. His force was greater than he could feed, yet too small to garrison posts and furnish escorts along his line of communication. He ought to have halted at Fort Edward, and indeed was anxious to do so; but he had positive orders to prosecute his march upon New York and conceived that he had no alternative but to obey.

An effort to capture an American magazine, and so to make good his wants, led him about six miles farther south to the Hudson at Saratoga. The effort failed. Enemies closed in upon him from every side, and after hard fighting he was surrounded and forced to surrender, his troops being reduced by their losses to no more than thirty-five hundred men. The disaster was due primarily to the mad orders which had been sent to him from England, and which forced him to persist in a hopeless enterprise. But the hopelessness of the enterprise lay in the insufficiency of the land transport and the consequent impossibility of feeding the troops at any distance from the main waterways.

CAMPAIGN OF 1778. Emboldened by the success of the Americans, France now declared war upon England; and the British Government decided to give up the northern colonies, except New York City and harbour, for lost, and to direct all future endeavours against the southern colonies. From want of sufficient shipping the retreat from Philadelphia to New York was conducted by land, though many of the stores were sent round by sea. The train of baggage, we are told, was immense, so that evidently the Commissaries had been able to collect plenty of horses and waggons in Pennsylvania. The Americans showed little enterprise during the movement, and the Army reached New York without serious loss (September 1st, 1778).

In November a small expedition left New York by sea and, landing two miles from Savannah, the capital of Georgia, captured it with little difficulty (December 29th, 1778). It was joined by a small reinforcement drawn from the garrisons of East Florida, which, being unable to obtain horses, made its way along the creeks and watercourses of East Florida, so as to use boats for transport, and for days together lived chiefly upon oysters.

The next enterprise was the capture of Charleston, for which objective about eight thousand men sailed from New York on the 26th of December, 1779. The convoy was dispersed by a storm. Nearly all of the horses embarked on board ship perished, and it was not possible to invest Charleston until April. Large captures of horses were made during the siege, and, after Charleston fell, there was no difficulty in obtaining plenty of them. This city accordingly became the principal base for operations in South and in North Carolina, though it was necessary to hold also minor marine bases at Beaufort and at Savannah to the south and at Georgetown to north of it. Inland there was an area of about one hundred and fifty miles square to be controlled, chiefly by means of posts situated upon the great rivers; and the officer to whom this duty was entrusted was Lord Cornwallis. I tried, when writing the history of this campaign, to arrive at some idea of the organisation of his transport and supply service, but could find nothing except masses of unenlightening accounts. Cornwallis's force was small. The largest field force that he could assemble rarely amounted to five thousand men. Much of Carolina was rich and fertile, yet we find Cornwallis constantly in difficulty over the filling of his magazines and with his troops in the field half starved. The enemy's armies were, of course, competing with him, and the rebels did their best to intimidate the loyalists who would have helped him. His chief Commissary served in Flanders in 1793 and 1794, and was so nervous there about making contracts for supply as well as for transport that he was evidently without experience of them. The conclusion that I draw is that Cornwallis fed his men chiefly with provisions sent from England by sea; and that the campaigns in the Carolinas really differed little in principle from those conducted in the West Indies.

The American War of Independence was, in fact, essentially a naval war, and was not won by the Americans at all, but by the French fleet. Washington's letters are one long complaint of the starvation of his armies; and it is evident that the Americans were hopeless in the matters of transport and supply. The British held New York, thereby securing Canada and overawing the northern colonies, entirely in virtue of supplies received by sea from England. The country all around was eaten up by the American armies; and the American Generals were consequently helpless. Washington was never more desperate than in April, 1781. By October the French fleet, after three years of failure, had decided the issue in his favour.

I come to the conclusion that only while General Howe had his headquarters at Philadelphia, and could use the resources of the rich and fertile province of Pennsylvania, was any British force in America well equipped as to transport and supply.

INDIA. I now turn to events in India during this same period of the American War. There in 1767–8 we had to encounter a new enemy in Hyder Ali, the soldier adventurer who had made himself a kingdom in Mysore, and who thoroughly understood war. Against him was matched the Council of Madras, feeble, incompetent and corrupt, but none the less served by a good soldier, General Joseph Smith, who did much to make good their shortcomings. Nothing would induce the Council to furnish him with transport, nor even to allow him a free hand in the field; and the reasons for this are worth setting down. One member of the Council held the contract for victualling the European troops and for furnishing the army with transport. The whole of the Council from the Governor downward had a share in this venture. They therefore appointed the contractor above mentioned and another of their members to be Field-Deputies, who should assist the General in his operations. The contractor was further appointed Commissary-General, so that altogether he combined three functions. As a member of Council he was the General's superior, as Field-Deputy his colleague, and as Commissary-General his colleague. Naturally the campaign did not go well, and had not Hyder Ali been terrified of the very name of Smith, it might have ended more dishonourably than it did—in an agreement to revert to the *status quo ante bellum*.

In 1780 Hyder Ali again invaded the territory of Madras, and once more, owing to the corruption of the Council of Government, the army was crippled by the want of transport and supply. In consequence of a disaster to the British arms the veteran Sir Eyre Coote was called in to take command, but he fared little better than his predecessors. The astute Hyder Ali had swept up all transport cattle with his ubiquitous cavalry; and Coote was obliged to confine his operations to the vicinity of the coast, where a small flotilla could follow him by sea with supplies. At one moment the French fleet appeared on the scene, and, had it remained there, Coote's army must have surrendered from famine and India would have been lost. Throughout the following year the spectre of starvation haunted Coote in all of his operations, and until the news of peace with France reached Madras in June 1783 our empire in India was in continuous peril. As a diversion to relieve the pressure on Madras, a small force was in 1782 landed on the western coast to threaten Mysore from that side. The General, Matthews, started without transport, supplies or reserves of ammunition, depending for all these things upon captures from the enemy, but even so met for a time with some measure of success. The history of the presidential administrations at this time is not agreeable reading.

Lord Cornwallis was sent as Governor-General to India in 1786, in order to purify the administration both civil and military, and was emphatic in proclaiming a policy of peace. But in 1790 he found himself compelled by the aggression of Hyder Ali's son, Tipu Sahib, to invade Mysore. According to the rotten principles upon which war was managed in India, the operations were conducted from Madras as a base, though the theatre was three hundred miles distant from it. The campaign did not prosper, and in 1791 Cornwallis made entirely new plans. Tipu had foiled him in great measure by devastating the country over which the British must advance; and Cornwallis devoted all his energies to the collection of supplies and transport from Bengal, employing for the first time elephants in large numbers. Deceiving Tipu as to his intentions, he ascended the ghauts, and stormed Bangalore out of hand. There he found a great store of forage, just in time to save his transport cattle, which were already dying by hundreds of starvation. Having gained this advanced base, he resumed his march after a week's halt; but the captured forage was by that time exhausted; and six weeks later he found himself still one hundred miles from his objective, Seringapatam, and with insufficient cattle to carry his supplies and the material necessary for a siege. He called upon the officers to give up to him their private transport and offered pay to thousands of women and boys to carry each of them an eighteen-pound shot. Even so, however, he realised that he could take with him no more than twenty days' provisions and fifteen out of fifty-two siege cannon.

Thus equipped he moved forward; and a cloud of smoke rose continually before him, showing that Tipu Sahib's light horse were burning every village and every blade of forage above ground to ashes. The ways were very rough; the country was very rugged; rain fell constantly and the exhausted cattle dropped down by hundreds in their yokes. With a great effort Cornwallis reached Seringapatam, and laid his plans to surprise and defeat Tipu's army. He failed, and was obliged to destroy the whole of his siege train and retreat. So many bullocks had perished that the guns and all the public conveyances of the army were dragged by men; while the horses of the cavalry were taken for conveyance of the sick. Hundreds of followers died of famine, and even the sepoys were starving when at the end of the first day's march Cornwallis met unexpectedly a host of Maratha allies with vast quantities of supplies, which, of course, they sold at monopolist's prices. He was thus able to retire with comparative ease to Bangalore. This was the first campaign of the British fought on the hills of India, and its results were not encouraging.

In the following year, 1792, Cornwallis began his operations by opening a new line of communication and capturing a succession of Tipu Sahib's hill fortresses to guard it. Using these as magazines, he was able, having collected fresh transport animals, to move slowly and deliberately; nor could Tipu's devastation of the country in his front avail to stop him. Concentrating at Savandroog, about thirty miles west of Bangalore and about forty miles, as the crow flies, north-west of Seringapatam, he marched on the 25th of January with twenty-two thousand fighting men and fifty thousand followers, came before Seringapatam on the 5th of February and stormed it on the 6th.

It may be convenient here to abandon strict chronological order and to deal at once with the final and decisive campaign of Mysore in 1799. The Commander-in-Chief was General Harris, who seems to have had no idea of conducting military operations in any but the primitive fashion of the Government of Madras. There was, however, an officer present, a young colonel of thirty named Arthur Wellesley, who took great exception to that Government's methods. "In India", he wrote, "armies take the field with arsenals and magazines which they always carry with them." Harris had an advanced base at Vellore, eighty miles west of Madras and about one hundred and eighty miles as the crow flies from Seringapatam; but he might as conveniently have concentrated at Madras itself from the number of encumbrances which accompanied the army. The fighting men numbered thirty-one thousand, and the followers one hundred and fifty thousand. The public transport, according to long custom, consisted mainly of the wild and undersized cattle of the Carnatic, which were attached to guns and waggons without any previous training either of animals or drivers. The private transport of the officers far exceeded that of the army at large; and the force actually moved upon its objective in a hollow square, having three miles of front and seven of depth, wherein were assembled one hundred and twenty thousand bullocks, besides elephants, camels, horses and asses. Tipu Sahib followed his usual practice of devastating the country before the British as they advanced, and Harris was obliged to follow a zigzag course, taking any direction in which forage was to be found. Notwithstanding this the cattle began to fail very early. Large quantities of ammunition were abandoned; and within ten days of the army's entry into Mysore matters were so serious that an enquiry was held. It was then discovered that the bullocks were starving, owing to certain absurd rules laid down by the Madras Commissariat. These rules were summarily abolished; a number of superfluous stores, which Wellesley had begged Harris to leave behind, were destroyed; and the unwieldy mass, floundering forward, at last came before Seringapatam. The traversing of the last eighty or ninety miles took twenty days.

Then came the business of the siege, which had hardly begun before it was discovered that the stores of rice, reckoned on the 5th of April at thirty-three days of full rations, had, through some rascality, dwindled by the 15th to eighteen days of half-rations. Harris was obliged by the prospect of actual starvation to assault prematurely; but his success justified him. Nine days after the fall of Seringapatam came in a gigantic convoy of forty thousand draught and pack bullocks, twenty-one thousand sheep, and also abundance of grain, which banished all further anxiety as to supplies. But the whole story of the campaign, happily elucidated for us in some measure by the biting criticisms of Wellesley, showed how helpless, inefficient and often corrupt were the presidential Governments of India in old days. Its most important result was that it set Wellesley thinking, with consequences which shall presently be seen. But we have now reached the period of the great war against revolutionary and imperial France, and must first follow a number of campaigns in divers parts of the world.

CHAPTER III

WARS OF THE FRENCH REVOLUTION AND EMPIRE.

FIRST PERIOD, 1793-1805.

Pɪᴛᴛ's plan for breaking the power of revolutionary France was to capture all her colonies, destroy her transmarine trade and reduce her by financial exhaustion. He therefore turned the very few troops which composed the Army mainly against the West Indian Islands. Since the operations differed little from those of former campaigns, the troops being practically always on the sea shore and drawing their supplies from the ships, there is no occasion to say more of them. It must suffice that several islands were captured, that tens of thousands of men perished of yellow fever, and that France was not appreciably the worse.

The fact was that revolutionary France, being bankrupt, had sallied forth to plunder her neighbours, coveting particularly the wealth of the Bank of Amsterdam. The Dutch being utterly unprepared and apathetic in respect of their own defence, Pitt sent out to the Low Countries first only three battalions of the Guards to encourage them, adding later three more battalions and cavalry, to the total number of about seven thousand men, under command of the Duke of York. About twenty thousand Hanoverians and Hessians were added to these the British contingent which was to work in concert with the Dutch and a considerable army of Austrians. By April, 1793, the Austrians had driven the French from the Low Countries, and the Allies were strung out in a long line from Ostend to Condé, for the invasion of France. The British base was the Scheldt.

With characteristic carelessness Pitt sent over the first contingent of British troops without any Commissary at all; and it was not until they had been in Holland for a fortnight that Commissary Watson sailed from England. He was a man who had seen service in America, and his first action was to represent that a field bakery for the use of the army was absolutely necessary. In England, of course, no such thing was ready, and it would have taken months to prepare it; but the Hanoverians, better understanding war, had a bakery more or less in order at Hanover; and the Duke of York, at Watson's request, arranged to take it over and expand it for the requirements of twenty thousand men, paying all expenses in ready money. It seems that Watson at the outset was charged with the duty of providing for the Hanoverians as well as the British, which was a very difficult matter. The Dutch, insanely jealous and incredibly inefficient, manifested their self-importance by keeping the movements of their troops strictly secret. No sooner had the route of the Hanoverians for joining the army been fixed, than they moved some of their own troops in that direction and laid violent hands upon all the forage. Then it was found that the approaching Hanoverians could not afford, with their low wages, to purchase food on the line of their march. The natural result was a mutiny. They were reassured by a promise of increased pay, and therewith returned to their duty; but it was not a pleasant opening to the campaign.

Then, as was the rule in the Low Countries, came up the question of contracts for the whole business of transport and supply, and here Watson's experience failed him. In America, as has been told, the armies were fed almost entirely with victuals from England, provided by English contractors in agreement with the higher officials of the Treasury. Watson was so slow and cautious in concluding his contracts that the army could not move; and, even after he had been at the front more than two months, his arrangements were still so incomplete that the whole of the Duke of York's troops, both British and Hanoverian, were "put to the greatest distress" both for food and forage. The fact seems to indicate that, in former campaigns in the Low Countries, contractors had practically dictated their own terms and made it worth some one's while that their offer should be accepted.

The campaign finally opened in June, and after some very feeble operations, for the Austrians, who were in supreme command, were incredibly slow, the Duke of York's contingent moved off to the siege of Dunkirk. The Government had promised that a siege train and a flotilla should meet them by sea; but the siege train was late in arriving and the flotilla never arrived at all. The Duke was obliged to destroy his siege artillery and retreat; and the campaign came to an end, without disaster indeed but without credit. The Hanoverians seem to have been neglected by their own people to an extent which ruined their efficiency both physical and moral. They were not properly fed, being very irregularly supplied with meat, and such of them as were not in hospital were constantly on the verge of mutiny.

For the campaign of 1794 Pitt increased the Duke of York's cavalry to twenty-eight squadrons but would still spare no more infantry. The artillery had been found most defective, drivers being scarce and both guns and ammunition waggons being drawn by horses harnessed tandem, after the fashion of Marlborough's time, instead of two abreast. So great had been the trouble in 1793 with transport both of guns and supplies that in this year two important new departures were taken by the formation of a corps of gunner drivers, and of a transport corps denominated the Royal Waggoners. Incidentally the institution of gunner drivers relieved the Commissariat of a burdensome duty; for it had frequently fallen to its lot to provide drivers and teams for guns on foreign service. The Royal Waggoners were an entirely new departure, but unfortunately came into being at a most unfavourable time. Pitt had taken the disastrous step of offering commissions broadcast to any who would bring in a certain number of recruits. Hence there arose terrific gambling in the recruiting market with the result that the crimps filled the ranks with children, half-witted or decrepit men, and that schoolboys rose over the heads of old officers to the command of battalions. The mischief thus done to the army in a few months was not entirely eradicated for many years; and naturally such a time was the very worst for raising a wholly new corps, which had yet to make its reputation and establish its traditions.

The Royal Waggoners consisted of five companies each of one hundred and twenty men, one tenth of whom were, or were supposed to be, artificers. Since the order for their formation had been issued in March they naturally were not ready for the opening of the campaign in April. It began brilliantly; but the Austrians, having important business in Poland, first did their best to get the British destroyed in action in May, and finally in July marched away and left the British to their own devices. Pitt thereupon reinforced the British to a strength of twenty-five thousand men, and among these reinforcements came the Royal Waggoners. They had been recruited from the scum of London, and did not make a good impression. "A greater set of scoundrels", wrote Sir James Craig, the Chief of the Staff and an excellent officer, "never disgraced an army. I believe it to be true that half of them if not taken from the hulks* have at times visited them...they have committed every species of villainy and treat their horses badly." It is fair to say that the rest of the army, officers and men, was not much better; but being dressed in blue the Royal Waggoners attained an evil pre-eminence as the Newgate Blues. The task set to the Duke of York of defending Holland against overwhelming superiority of numbers was, with such material, utterly impossible. His retreat to the west coast being cut off, he was obliged to retire through the depth of an arctic winter to the Ems. All discipline disappeared. Drivers, waggons, soldiers and robbers floundered on in one huge disorderly mob. Yet there must have been some supplies, for, though thousands perished from cold and exhaustion, we do not hear that food was lacking, and it is certain that on one day of the retreat forty soldiers were found frozen stark and stiff round a rum cask. We know also that a large train of officers' baggage came safely to the Ems. But the whole affair was so disastrous and disgraceful that it was hushed up. The losses of men and horses were terrible. On arrival at the Ems, thirty-three battalions, though they had not suffered severely in action, could produce only six thousand men. As to the Royal Waggoners, we hear no more of them, and they seem to have vanished past resurrection.

The old army having by this time been destroyed and the first effort to make a new one having failed with ignominy, there were no more operations upon any scale until 1799, though the West Indies continued to devour men by thousands. There are, however, one or two little enterprises worth a few remarks because they exemplify the utter indifference of the Cabinet towards the questions of transport and supply, and the constant peril to which they exposed the troops in consequence.

* Hulks of ships on the lower Thames in which convicts were confined. See Charles Dickens's *Great Expectations*.

THE OCCUPATION OF THE ISLE D'YEU, 1795. It being a part of British policy to give countenance to the counter-revolutionary or Royalist movement in Brittany, General Doyle was sent in September, 1795, with about five thousand men, including two thousand cavalry, to occupy the Isle D'Yeu, about twenty-five miles north of the mouth of the Loire. The island which is about six miles by four, was easily taken, but was found to contain no forage, no pasture, insufficient corn to feed the eighteen hundred inhabitants (all Royalists), not more than forty oxen and only a few miserable sheep. In this place, which contained but one dangerous roadstead, Doyle found himself set down at the approach of the autumnal equinox with seven days' provisions and three weeks' fuel at short allowance. He had two thousand hungry horses and not a scrap of food for them, and he could find no shelter for his men except by dispersing them dangerously among several small villages. His force was too weak to repel a regular attack, which the French could easily deliver in overwhelming numbers, and he could not re-embark, because his transports had been taken away from him.

The next six weeks were a time of torment to Doyle. Foul weather prevented provision ships from coming regularly to the island, and only at great risk were supplies from time to time landed and fifteen hundred of the cavalry re-embarked and sent back to England. His men were sickening fast from exposure; five hundred horses were dying of hunger; there was not (a curious detail) a single candle in the whole of the force; and there seemed to be every probability that not only the troops but the inhabitants must perish from starvation. At last, six weeks after Doyle's landing on the island, three months' provisions were painfully accumulated; and then Doyle received orders to re-embark his men on a squadron of the Royal Navy. But re-embarking was a difficult matter, since the first gale would force the ships to go to sea. Moreover, the squadron was itself so short of victuals that the Admiral could not run the risk of taking men on board and being driven to sea with more mouths than he could feed. Nor dared he embark the supplies on the island before the men, lest he should be driven to sea before the men were on board, in which case they would be left on the island to starve. The Admiral, therefore, was fain to send to England for transports; but by taking skilful advantage of favourable weather he managed to get both the men and sufficient supplies on board his squadron, and brought them safely back to England by the end of December. The casualties, though not a shot had been fired, amounted to forty-five men dead of sickness through exposure, and from four to five hundred horses. It was no fault of the Ministers that every man and horse was not starved to death.

THE EXPEDITION TO THE CAPE OF GOOD HOPE, 1795. For the security of the voyage to India an expedition of three thousand men under Major-General Sir Alured Clarke was sent to occupy the Cape of Good Hope, then a Dutch possession. The commander carried a letter from the Prince of Orange—titular ruler of the Netherlands—to the Government at Cape Town ordering them to deliver up the place to the British; and for this reason—or for no reason—the British Government declined to provide Clarke with any artillery or with any Commissary or military chest, or even with any supplies apart from those carried by the escorting squadron of the Royal Navy. The Dutch Governor at Capetown declined to surrender and drove all cattle near the coast inland, so that the invaders should get no fresh meat. This was a serious matter, for there was much scurvy among the crews of the men-of-war. Even if any of the inhabitants had been friendly and inclined to sell provisions, the military commander had no money with which to pay him; so that the situation imperatively demanded the use of force. Ships were sent to St Helena to borrow guns and gunners, and meanwhile the troops landed at Simonstown, succeeded in driving the Dutch from the point—Muizenberg—where the road left the coast to turn inland upon Capetown, and there began the formation of a small magazine.

Every ounce of supplies was necessarily carried up on the backs of sailors and soldiers. As the Government had not provided food for the soldiers, they had to live on the squadron's victuals, with the result that blue-jackets and redcoats alike were perforce placed upon short allowance. The soldiers also were weak after being for weeks cooped up on board ship; and altogether nine days were taken up in the making of this dépôt. Then on the 14th of September the force advanced without a draught-animal or pack-animal of any description whatever. Every man carried four days' rations; the guns—nine of them—received from St Helena were dragged by volunteer seamen from the transports, and all supplies and stores were brought along somehow by soldiers and sailors. The enemy had a thousand regular troops with nine field guns, and could call out the entire Boer population; and Clarke, with so many men employed as beasts of burden, can have had no superfluity of fighting soldiers; but on the 14th of September— three months after his first landing—he advanced upon Capetown. The Dutch hovered round the column, firing at long range, but Clarke's losses were trifling until after a march of six miles he found the enemy in position at Wynberg. He drove them out and pursued them for two miles, when his overburdened troops could go no farther. However, on the following day the Governor of Cape Colony surrendered, and the possession of Capetown and of Table Bay put an end to all difficulties.

THE CAPTURE OF MINORCA, 1798. An enterprise nearly akin to that at the Cape was undertaken in 1798 by General Charles Stuart, who was probably the ablest officer in the Army. He was commanding a mixed force of British and foreigners in Portugal at the time, but he concentrated his four battalions at Gibraltar before proceeding upon his venture. He had with him no transport nor even teams for his few field guns; and his information concerning the enemy was extremely vague. Landing on the north coast, he repelled a strong Spanish force which opposed him on the shore, and so made good his footing. But he was at a loss to know what to do next. The island was rugged and mountainous, and the roads were so bad as to make any movement very difficult. He ascertained, however, that the enemy's force was divided between Port Mahon on the east coast and Ciudadella on the west, fifty miles apart, and that there was a strategic post—Mercadal—in the mountains, eight or ten miles inland, which severed connection between the two. He sent a flying column of six hundred men to seize Mercadal, captured the small Spanish garrison which held it and took also some small magazines attached to it. This gave him some modicum of supplies, and next day he moved up there with his main body, bluejackets from the men-of-war helping to drag the guns.

There he learned that the Spaniards had withdrawn nearly all of their men from Port Mahon and were concentrating at Ciudadella. He at once sent a detachment to Port Mahon, received the surrender of the handful of Spanish soldiers in the place, and thus gained a safe port for his ships, and a good number of transport animals, probably pack-mules. Then leaving one hundred men only at Port Mahon, he advanced upon Ciudadella. There the Spaniards were entrenched about five thousand strong. Stuart had fewer than four thousand, probably not more than three thousand. He had no more than six light guns, the carriages of six more having fallen to pieces. But he solemnly threw up batteries, made a great display of force and fairly "bluffed" the Spanish commander into immediate surrender. The whole of the operations lasted just eight days, and are interesting as an example of what may be done by a leader of resolution and resource. The Spanish commander, having no information as to Stuart's strength, was presumably right to concentrate his whole force at one point. Had he kept it divided, retaining half of it in its original station at Port Mahon, Stuart would not have been able to secure that harbour nor to collect transport. Stuart, it may be added, so thoroughly understood transport and supply, that the Duke of York had written to him from the Horse Guards, asking him to give a full explanation of his system. Unfortunately he died before he had any chance of showing what he could do in military operations upon a grand scale.

THE NORTH HOLLAND EXPEDITION OF 1799. By the year 1799 the star of the French was beginning to wane, and Napoleon had not yet restored it, as he was to do at Marengo, to its former brightness. There seemed to be a chance for England to strike a telling blow; and, always justly anxious while an enemy commanded the mouth of the Scheldt, the British Government decided that the blow should fall on Holland, where the Russians had promised to give help, and where it was hoped that the Dutch would rise in insurrection to shake off the French yoke. A new method of augmenting the army was found by bribing militiamen to become regulars; and in August ten thousand men under Sir Ralph Abercromby were shipped to North Holland with orders to effect a landing. What precisely Abercromby was to do when landed the Ministers did not explain, because they had no very clear ideas themselves. They provided him with a siege train, because they had a vague notion that it might be wanted, but they refused to furnish horses enough to draw it. Above all they declined to make any provision for transport. Abercromby protested again and again. "The British troops want the means of conveyance for artillery, sick, baggage and provisions", he wrote, "and you know we have not a foot of ground until we acquire it. I hope it is not a crime to state these facts." A little later, after receiving a return of the Russian troops that were expected, showing an enormous train of waggons, he discoursed anew upon the same text. "The Emperor of Russia may make a General into a private by his *fiat*, but he cannot make his army march without their baggage. It is self-evident that an army is not a machine that can move of itself; it must have the means of moving... As our numbers increase, so must our arrangements, and rest assured that an army cannot move without horses or waggons." It is rather singular that a General should have been obliged to repeat these obvious facts after six years of war.

Abercromby spoke to deaf ears. The armament sailed on the 13th of August and met with gales which made any landing impossible until the 27th. By that time water and provisions were already so short that the Admiral was on the point of sailing for the Ems. However, on the 27th Abercromby, after rather sharp fighting, effected his disembarkation upon an open beach, a short distance to the south of Helder, the Portsmouth of the Netherlands. By good luck Helder was evacuated by the enemy immediately afterwards, and thus Abercromby was assured of a safe harbour for his ships. But for this, the fleet and the transports might have been blown off the coast, and he would have been left stranded without any reserve of food or ammunition. Still, though he had gained a base, he had no means of moving; and he was obliged to take up a defensive position outside Helder where, from want of transport, he had the greatest difficulty in feeding his troops. After a few days he found a few horses and waggons, which made things easier; but meanwhile reinforcements of five thousand additional men had joined him, and the Government had sent with them no more than thirty-five bread waggons. The Government had hoped that, in a country seamed by canals, much could be done by water carriage, but this had proved to be a delusion. The canals were of varying gauges. A few large barges, captured at Helder, could not enter the smaller canals about Abercromby's position, and the enemy had carried off all smaller craft. However, Abercromby managed to maintain himself until further reinforcements raised the army to fifty thousand men, three-fourths of them British, when the command was taken over by the Duke of York.

The full allowance of land transport supplied by Government for about thirty-seven thousand British soldiers was one hundred bread waggons, as many forage carts, twenty hospital waggons and ten forge carts. Of these fewer than half were on the spot, the remainder being in England and quite possibly in course of construction. Fuel was wanting, and was only made good by breaking up Dutch ships captured at Helder. The Treasury had made such a muddle of the bread supply that, even when Abercromby had only fifteen thousand men, it was suddenly discovered that there was less than one week's bread in store. As a climax to the general confusion not a single sutler presented himself, and consequently there was not a drop of spirits to be obtained by the army.

Soon afterwards the campaign opened. So long as the operations were confined to the well-canalised districts, it was possible with great difficulty to feed the troops from hand to mouth. When they passed beyond it—as the necessities of the case demanded that they must—they broke down completely from want of wheeled transport. The Duke was obliged to retreat to some fortified lines which he had thrown up round Helder, and his few waggons took two days to traverse nine miles. When he arrived within them he found only nine days' victuals in store. Until the Duke of York arrived it had not apparently occurred to the Commissary-General that it would be prudent to have a month's supplies in hand. Later, it was discovered that, in making his calculations, he had omitted to provide for the retention of a month's provisions upon all of the transports in case of re-embarkation; and that the taking of this very necessary precaution had upset all his arrangements. Happily the French were not aware of this complication; and, being very anxious to be quit of the Duke of York, they allowed him to withdraw under a capitulation of very easy terms.

The whole story is curious and instructive, but its chief interest for us is that this grossly mismanaged expedition witnessed the new birth of the Royal Waggon Train. Not much time was allowed for its formation, for its creation was only ordered on the 12th of August, and it went on active service within a month. It was, however, composed of cavalry soldiers who were of superior class to the infantry, received higher pay and had been taught to look after their horses. Its organisation was likewise based upon that of cavalry. It consisted of five troops, each comprising four officers who bore combatant rank, and seventy-one of other ranks, whereof sixty were drivers. All ranks received the pay of cavalry, and the whole were under command of a Waggon-Master-General. Within five weeks of its raising it was augmented by three more troops of the like composition; but these cannot have been completed until after the expedition returned from Holland, for its strength on the eve of re-embarkation did not exceed twenty-five officers, two hundred and seventy-five other ranks and five hundred and fourteen horses. Probably the original five troops were never at full strength during the campaign; and indeed the Duke of York reported at the close of the campaign that the Waggon

Train had been inadequate to the wants of the army. This is hardly surprising, for the mobilisation tables of a century later require, for an army corps little exceeding the Duke's force in numbers, five hundred and fourteen four-horse vehicles, besides pair-horse and six-horse carriages and pack-animals. However, adequate or inadequate, the Waggon Train had been reborn and was destined to last for a generation.

THE EGYPTIAN CAMPAIGN OF 1801. The next important campaign was that in Egypt, in which it was impossible for the Waggon Train to take part, or indeed for the Government to provide land transport of any kind. In those days of small ships and voyages of uncertain length it was physically impossible to send horses for great distances over sea. The bulk of forage and of water forbade it, to say nothing of the injury caused to the animals in a gale. But the Government was quite as casual over this expedition as over the last. They took it for granted that an army sent to Egypt could get no fresh water until it had won access to the Nile by the capture of Alexandria; but, until such access had been gained, they hesitated not to allow sixteen thousand soldiers to depend for water upon supplies carried by the ships and landed on the backs of bluejackets. It did not occur to them that if the fleet were driven off the coast by a gale the army might die of thirst. "There are risks", wrote the indignant Abercromby, "in a British warfare unknown in any other service."

Abercromby, as is well known, forced his landing at Aboukir on the 8th of March, 1801, and to his great relief found water by digging near the roots of palm trees. Even so, the uncertainty of the sea made his situation very perilous. On the 9th and 10th the wind blew so hard that it was impossible to land supplies and stores. These were, however, got ashore on the 11th, and on the 12th Abercromby began his advance upon

59

Alexandria, twelve miles from his landing-place, using the salt lake Maadieh, on his inland flank, as a means of water transport. His sixteen guns were dragged through the heavy sand by men, which put him at serious disadvantage in the two actions that he was compelled to fight on the way, for the French, having full teams of horses for their guns, could manœuvre their artillery as Abercromby could not. Thirteen days elapsed between the debarkation and the decisive action which gave the British possession of Alexandria, and in that time thirty-five hundred men out of fifteen thousand five hundred went on the sick list, worn out by the work of beasts of burden. Abercromby was mortally wounded in the final battle before Alexandria, but his successor, having with difficulty collected animals to draw his guns and ammunition waggons, finished the campaign by an advance up the Nile, using the river for water transport.

The army was then reinforced by five thousand men from India who had landed at Kosseir, in the Red Sea, and marched across the desert to the Nile at Keneh. A staff officer arriving in advance managed to secure a certain number of camels, and went forward to Keneh to send supplies of water and provisions to different stations on the route. From the side of Kosseir parties of sepoys were employed in searching for springs and digging wells at different points. The journey was divided into seven stages, at the first, third and fifth of which water was to be obtained, the seventh stage ending at the Nile itself. Baird's plan was to pass his force across the whole distance in small parties, of which the first was, on reaching Keneh, to send back its camels and water-bags to the fifth stage; the second party, on arriving at the fifth stage, was to send back its camels to the third stage; and the third party, on reaching the third stage, was to return its camels to the first stage; and so on until the whole should have crossed the desert.

The first party accordingly marched from Kosseir on the 19th of June; but the water-skins almost emptied themselves from leakage on the way, so that, when the first division reached the third stage, it was necessary to forward to them the water and camels of the second party. It seemed likely that the entire project must be abandoned as impracticable had not water fortunately been found by digging midway between the third and fourth stages. Thus by the 8th of July—that is to say within nineteen days after the start—two British battalions and a few companies of sepoys, or about two thousand men, had reached Keneh safely. Since the French army had capitulated on the 27th of June there was no occasion to hurry the troops from India into Lower Egypt. The remainder of them, reinforced to a strength of four thousand, therefore marched to Keneh at their leisure with the loss of only three men.

One battalion which had been landed at Suez started from thence to cross the desert to El Hanka with an allowance of three pints of water per man, carried by camels. The thermometer rose to 116° in the course of the march, and the water had become thick owing to the cracking of the water-skins under the intense heat. The officers, however, had a little stock of wine which they shared with their men, and they cut their baggage from the backs of the camels and set exhausted men upon them in its place. The battalion started at 6 p.m. on the 6th of June, halted from 4 p.m. to 7 p.m. on the 7th, and again from 11 p.m. until 4 a.m. on the 8th, and reached the springs of El Hanka between 4 p.m. and 5 p.m., having traversed seventy miles in forty-eight hours. Not a man had tasted food since leaving Suez from fear of intensifying thirst. However, all came in except nine men who died of exhaustion.

In 1801 the Treaty of Amiens gave a short breathing space to the contending parties; but in 1803 war again broke out against France in Europe and against the

Marathas in India; and, it will be convenient to take the Indian operations first.

THE MARATHA WAR OF 1803. If Europeans had not come to India during the dissolution of the Mogul Empire in the seventeenth and eighteenth centuries the Marathas would have become masters of India. Of the three European nations which had at first disputed for predominance in the great peninsula—British, French and Dutch—the first-named had gained supremacy. But the Marathas, though quarrelling among themselves, had not forgotten their former ambition. The French were constantly intriguing with them against the British, and in 1803 matters came to such a point that the issue had to be decided by arms. Circumstances dictated that there should be two distinct fields of operations, and accordingly two armies were set in motion, one in Hindustan under General Gerard Lake, subject to the general direction of Calcutta, and the other in the Dekhan under General Arthur Wellesley, subject to the direction of Bombay.

Since the capture of Seringapatam in 1799 Wellesley had been ruler of Mysore; and petty operations in hunting down banditti and the like had taught him much as to the feeding of an army in the field. He had taken particular note of Tipu Sahib's draught-bullocks which could walk four miles and trot six miles an hour, and which, after Tipu's death had been taken into the Company's service. But nothing could induce the East India Company to maintain a body of trained drivers, a point upon which Wellesley laid great stress. His words upon the subject are still worth quoting.

Money will purchase cattle at any time; but unless men are provided to take care of them and to drive them, the money is thrown away and the service must come to a stand.

A bullock that goes one day without his regular food loses a part of his strength; if he does not get it on the second day he may not lose the appearance of being fit for service, but he is entirely unable to work; and after these animals have once lost their strength and condition, so much time elapses before they recover that they become a burden upon the army, and the whole expense of their original purchase and subsequent food is lost.

The drivers hired for the service of Bombay are in particular the worst that I have seen (1) because they are entirely unaccustomed to the care of cattle, (2) because of ten of this description of persons hired at Bombay nine of them desert.

There remains but one mode of having bullock-drivers and therefore bullocks when they are required and that is to have in the service at all times a corps of bullock-drivers, regularly trained and managed.*

This letter was actually written after the decisive battle of Assaye had been fought, but it was only a recapitulation of former recommendations many times repeated. Wellesley was in fact the first (and very nearly the last) man to give any attention to the care of animals in an Indian campaign. He actually issued one general order forbidding bullock drivers to let their animals trot.† No detail was too small for him to notice in the business of transport and supply; for he recognised that it was of supreme importance. Moreover, against so formidable and elusive an enemy as the Marathas, he wished to depart from the evil, slovenly and corrupt traditions of India. There was to be no more trailing over the country in a hollow square, three miles by seven, with a moving city in the midst of it. "The only mode," he wrote, "by which we can inspire either our allies or our enemies with respect for our operations will be to show them that our armies can move with ease and celerity at all times and in all situations."

His difficulties were great, for the Bombay Government was supine and inefficient. Wellesley had arranged for the formation of a dépôt on the Malabar coast, within easy reach of Bombay by sea and of Poona by

* Letter to Government of Bombay—4th of November, 1803.
† 9th of February, 1803.

land, and the Bombay Government had promised to provide transport to move supplies from thence overland. Not a bullock arrived. They promised to furnish him with pontoons, but not one was forthcoming. Wellesley had to make good these deficiencies as best he could, but he was determined to beat the Marathas in his own way. He knew they would always avoid a general action if they could, except in some very strong defensive position, which they had a perfect genius for selecting, and which would cost many lives to assault. He knew also that they lived on the country and consequently could not stay in such a position for more than a limited period. With a good transport and supply service he could feed his own troops for an indefinite time; and if the Marathas slipped away, he could overtake them and fight them on the march. His *impedimenta* must, therefore, be reduced as far as possible. No useless hordes of followers must be permitted to accompany the army. Officers must be content with pack-animals for their baggage, for he would not permit them to have wheeled vehicles. But, above all, the beasts of burden must be well fed and carefully tended, for upon this hung, not only the mobility of the army, but the good nourishment, physical strength and moral force of the men.

There were a few preliminary movements before the serious work of the campaign began, wherein Wellesley was able to compare his system with the helpless confusion of other Generals. "I make long marches with the greatest facility, and all my cattle are fresh", he wrote (22nd of February, 1803). "I wish I could say as much of General Stuart. He has lost a number of cattle and the remainder are in a very bad state. I see no remedy but that which I have already recommended to him—to diminish his monstrous equipment and to leave behind him everything not absolutely necessary." "Your cattle", he wrote to Stuart a few days later

(3rd of March), "were very fine and complete in drivers when they left Seringapatam"; from which it is pretty evident that they had deteriorated in condition entirely owing to Stuart's neglect.

It would be easy to fill a volume with extracts from Wellesley's letters respecting transport and supply, yet it is impossible to say exactly how his transport was organised. There were purchased cattle and hired cattle; there are allusions to Government's supplies and to "brinjarries" (*banjaras* or native grain dealers) whose numbers are given in one place as twenty-six thousand—a figure which compels us to construe the word as meaning bullocks and not dealers. But, whatever the organisation may have been, the cattle were always in good condition, and the campaign was brilliantly begun and ended in five months.

In the north, General Lake, having no Mysore bullocks and being tied to the Bengal system of transport and supply ("which goes on somehow, one hardly knows how"), went to work in the old fashion. He moved off from his concentration ground in a huge hollow square, his army numbering about fifteen thousand men, and the followers about ten times that number, with at least as many bullocks. Lake was a fine fighting man, and, so long as he had to do only with pitched battles in the plains, was successful enough. But when he had later to deal with an enemy who avoided action, he made bad mistakes. At last he had to chase an elusive adversary from the Jumna almost to the Indus at Attock, and then for once he was obliged to take strong measures. He reduced the proportion of tents by one half, forbade the use of wheeled vehicles by officers, and made every fighting man carry six pounds of flour, which were to last him six days. Thus lightly equipped he made some extraordinary marches and achieved some notable successes; but, immediately that the more ordinary work of a campaign had begun once again, the system of Bengal reasserted itself. We hear during his siege of Bhurtpore (January, 1805) of a convoy of twelve thousand bullocks laden with grain which, having an escort of no more than fourteen hundred men, were mostly carried off by the enemy. A few days later we hear of a second convoy of fifty thousand bullocks and eight hundred laden carts; and, since the safe arrival of this was a matter of life or death, Lake went out in person with reinforcements for the escort and, not a little through the sheer terror of his name, brought the convoy in without the loss of a waggon or a bullock. But this was the way in Bengal. The authorities seem to have had no idea of keeping a force in the field regularly supplied. They would allow an army's victuals to sink almost to starvation point, and then with an immense effort hurl square miles of provender in its direction and trust to luck to bring it to its destination. Lake took two years over his campaign, which, even when closed, left his work undone.

Whether Wellesley himself could have wrought any solid improvement in the Commissariat of Bengal may be doubted. After the conclusion of his operation against the Marathas he settled down to the administration of Mysore, and, being very much his own master, could make some headway against the stupidity, supineness and corruption which he found all round him. But he could stamp no lasting impression upon it. His campaign, as compared with those of previous wars in India, was a startling novelty. Never before had an army been so orderly, so well supplied, so well disciplined and so rapid in movement. But India is a country of low standards with a climate that forbids to the majority of white men the effort to raise them permanently. We shall see all the shortcomings of the Indian Commissariat still unblushingly uncorrected more than sixty years after the battle of Assaye.

CHAPTER IV

WARS OF THE FRENCH EMPIRE.
SECOND PERIOD, 1805-1809.

LEAVING India now, it is necessary to glance at the various expeditions undertaken between 1805 and the opening of the Peninsular War in 1808. Since they were mostly, so to speak, roving expeditions, in which troops were not disembarked for any long time, they present no special features of great interest and may be dismissed with comparative brevity.

THE CAMPAIGN IN SOUTH ITALY, 1806. This was undertaken by a small body of British troops, quartered in Sicily and held ready, with their transport ships, to embark and land at any point in the Mediterranean where they might strike a telling blow. A chance offered itself in the presence of a small French force of five to seven thousand men under General Reynier in Calabria. The transports were kept ready victualled, so that the men had only to step aboard; and thus it was that a force of about five thousand men sailed from Messina for the bay of St Euphemia in the hope of destroying Reynier and upsetting the whole of the French operations in southern Italy. There were no facilities for transporting animals, and but few horses were embarked, namely those of the staff and of regimental commanders, sixteen dragoon horses, and teams for three out of six light field guns. In addition to these there were mules enough to carry ten mountain guns and the camp kettles of the men.

67   5-2

The troops forced their landing against slight resistance on the 30th of June, and spent three days in landing animals, supplies and stores through a heavy surf. On the 4th of July they advanced four or five miles inland, and beat Reynier handsomely at the action of Maida. They then retired to the beach for supplies, advanced again after two or three days, captured some French magazines containing provisions and forage, and returned to Messina, having been absent for just a fortnight. An energetic commander might have accomplished much more; nor, the population being friendly, could there have been much difficulty in improvising some kind of transport for so small a force.

THE EXPEDITION TO BUENOS AYRES, 1807. Our one campaign in South America was caused by a filibustering Commodore who, after the second capture of the Cape of Good Hope, sailed away with a single battalion to Rio de la Plata and occupied Buenos Ayres. The population quickly rose and overpowered this battalion; but early in January, 1807, reinforcements arrived which captured Monte Video. In June further reinforcements came, which raised the strength of the force to rather more than seven thousand men; the General, Whitelocke, having orders to capture Buenos Ayres.

From Monte Video on the east bank of the Rio de la Plata to Buenos Ayres on the western bank the passage by water is about one hundred and sixty miles. It was decided for sufficient reasons to land at Enseñada de Barragon, about one hundred and thirty miles from Monte Video by sea and twenty-nine miles from Buenos Ayres by land. Little was known about the country to be traversed except that it contained few farmhouses and not a single tree, though it swarmed with cattle. There was, therefore, no prospect of finding fuel or breadstuffs, though fresh meat would be abundant. As regards transport, horses were difficult to procure, and such as were obtainable were unbroken and soon gave way under the burden of unwonted work and insufficient food. For June is midwinter south of the line, when the native grass—the only discoverable forage—contains little nourishment. Whitelocke thereupon decided that his men must carry three days' rations upon their backs and replenish at Reduction, a point on the shore about twenty miles from Enseñada and ten from Buenos Ayres. He therefore gave his commissariat officers no orders to procure animals for purposes of transport; and his only means of carriage were half a dozen small mule carts to bear supplies from the water's edge to any chosen dépôt. According to his own account, the Commissary, until the ships actually anchored before Enseñada, was under the impression that the troops would land, not thirty miles, but only five miles from Buenos Ayres.

The disembarkation began on the 28th of June, and three days' rations of biscuits and spirits were landed on the same day. Sixty pack-saddles had been brought forward for the transport of these supplies, and sixty horses, taken from the light dragoons, were appointed to carry them; but no information was given to the Commissary of this fact. The army began its march on the 29th through two miles of swamp, knee-deep in water, with the result that a great deal of the food carried by the men was soaked with mud and rendered uneatable. On the 30th the pack-saddles and horses were landed and the work of loading began. The unbroken horses naturally rebelled at once. Several galloped away and were never seen again; others dashed off with their saddles but without their loads; and altogether, of eight tons of biscuit landed, about one ton was sent to the army, a small quantity was re-embarked but the greater portion was lost or ruined in the swamp. The rum-casks, which had been placed in the mule carts, fared as badly. The wheels stuck fast, and the Commissary had no choice but to stave in the casks and leave them where they lay. The guns, which had also stuck in the swamp, were hauled out by the efforts of some hundreds of men. Altogether the first day's march was not a success; and the General and the Commissaries were at daggers drawn.

There was already difficulty about the feeding of the men. Some had never received orders to carry their three days' rations; many others, as has been told, had lost theirs in the swamp. The next place where supplies could be obtained from the fleet was Reduction, two days' march distant, so that there was every prospect of the troops lacking food for at least one day and possibly, if any mishap occurred, being starved altogether. Whitelocke cursed his Commissaries and poured his complaints into the ear of his second in command, Sir Samuel Auchmuty. "Sir," answered Auchmuty, "if a General does not himself attend to the supply of his troops they will often lack provisions."

On that day, the 30th of June, the men received but half a ration of biscuit. They had been much harassed on the march by mismanagement, and when they staggered into Reduction next day (1st of July) they were greatly exhausted. Two miles of swamp lay between them and the shore, over which every ounce of provisions from the fleet must be carried; but Whitelocke would not grant them a halt. Some oxen had been procured and slaughtered on the morning of the 2nd, but, before the meat could be cut up and distributed, the General ordered the troops to march and would not allow them to carry the meat in their haversacks. The men lagged terribly and many dropped on the way; but at the close of the march sheep and fuel were found, and on the morning of the 3rd of July the troops entered the suburbs of Buenos Ayres. There bread and liquor were obtained from the houses, and all ranks enjoyed the first real meal that they had eaten since their landing.

On the 5th of July Whitelocke delivered the unsuccessful attack which brought him to a court-martial and to dismissal from the service. He fully deserved his fate if only for the mishandling of the troops on the march. The minutes of the court-martial reveal many details which appear in no narrative of any other campaign, and among them the friction between Whitelocke and his Commissaries is conspicuous. They complained that the General never gave them warning of his movements and that consequently they could make no arrangements; and, since Whitelocke never knew himself what he intended to do, it is probable that their complaint was just. Whether the Commissaries really understood their business or not, it is not easy to say; but since John Bissett, the future author and already a man of wide knowledge and experience, was one of them, I am disposed to think that they did. The whole story is curious as an example of the problems which Generals and Commissaries, owing to the ignorance and thoughtlessness of Ministers, were obliged to solve as best they could at the shortest notice. It will hardly be believed that one party of four thousand men in this very expedition was originally designed to land on the west coast of South America and march over the Andes and across the continent to Buenos Ayres, leaving a chain of posts on the way to preserve communication along the trifling distance, as the crow flies, of nine hundred miles.

THE PENINSULAR WAR. It is hardly necessary to dwell on the Expedition to Copenhagen in 1807, when the force was set down to a siege, within reach of its ships, and where the operations did not last a month. We come now, therefore, to a period of real moment in the history of transport and supply, namely the Peninsular War.

The Iberian peninsula had been succinctly described, not without truth, as a country where large armies starved and small armies were beaten. The Spanish proverb runs, "War with all the world, peace with England", but the British were not wholly without experience of operations in Spain. Setting aside the Black Prince's campaign in the fourteenth century, we have already followed the fortunes of the small force sent there during the War of the Spanish Succession while Marlborough was fighting in Flanders. A body of seven thousand men was also despatched to Portugal in 1762, and a still weaker detachment was sent to Lisbon under Sir Charles Stuart in 1797. Nevertheless the fact remained that the British had never put forth their full strength hitherto in any quarter except the Low Countries. Marlborough's march to the Danube was an extraordinary event, and the British contingent, which took part in it, was but a small fraction of Marlborough's army. The campaign of Dettingen was a Hanoverian rather than a British affair, after which, as after Blenheim, the scene of action reverted immediately to Flanders. Broadly speaking, it may be said that the British after the sixteenth century had no experience of war on a large scale except in the Low Countries, where hostilities were so familiar that everyone was ready and able to carry every detail of them (except actual fighting) for anyone who was prepared to pay sufficient money.

The French invasion of Spain and Portugal in 1807 was undertaken to coerce both countries into accepting Napoleon's decrees which prohibited all commercial intercourse with England. It was very unscrupulously, not to say treacherously, pushed forward, and was deeply resented by the Spaniards who, in shame and fury, rose in insurrection on the 2nd of May, 1808. One of the smaller northern provinces—for the insurrection, though universal, was organised (so far as it had any organisation) by provinces—invoked the help of England; and the British Government resolved to send a force thither under Sir Arthur Wellesley to seize, if possible, a naval base at Lisbon. The Portuguese had followed the Spaniards in insurrection, and could therefore be counted upon as friendly. The only force near the spot, apart from the garrison of Gibraltar, was a little body of five thousand men under General Spencer who were kept afloat in copper-bottomed transports ready for action in any part of the world. These conditions in themselves forbade the carrying of any great number of animals. Spencer followed the movements of the insurgents along the southern coast of Spain, threatening but not actually disembarking, until he heard of Wellesley's departure from England, when he made haste to join him.

Wellesley brought with him nine thousand troops, including one regiment of cavalry, and eighteen guns. Teams for his artillery were at first denied to him, but it chanced that the Commander-in-Chief (as distinct from the Treasury) had organised a small waggon train of two troops for the service of Ireland, evidently with the object of enabling a small column to move at any moment to repress disturbances. Wellesley begged first for the horses (cast horses from the cavalry) and, having obtained them, asked next for the officers and drivers also. There was some difficulty about this, which was surmounted by adding these two troops to the Royal Waggon Train and sending them out as a part of it. The horses embarked were thirty-four for the staff, three hundred and six for the artillery and two hundred and twenty-four for the cavalry, or five hundred and six in all. The vehicles of all descriptions consisted of eighteen gun carriages, as many ammunition waggons, four camp-equipment waggons and three forge carts. It would not have been prudent to send out more, for no one could tell how long the troops and animals might be detained on board ship, nor when they would land, nor where, nor what weather they might encounter in the interval.

The armament sailed from Cork on the 13th of July, Wellesley going ahead of it in a frigate. The Admiral on the station reported that the Portuguese insurgents had made over to him the only fort which guarded Mondego Bay about one hundred miles north of Lisbon; and there, though it was but an open beach, Wellesley decided to land. The disembarkation began on the 1st of August; and, owing to the surf, it was five days before the nine thousand men landed with their horses, artillery, supplies and stores. Then Spencer arrived, and the landing of his men, about six thousand, took three days more. The time was spent by Wellesley in collecting transport, and in drawing up two memoranda for his Commissaries in which he set forth the quantity of supplies that he would take with him, and the number of carts and of pack-mules (for which latter he expressed a decided preference) that would be needed to carry them, the spare ammunition and so forth. One would have thought that the Commissaries might have worked out these details for themselves, but apparently they could not.

In ten days Wellesley had collected sufficient carriage of one kind or another to convey thirteen days' supplies, mules enough for his reserve ammunition and horses enough to mount sixty dragoons. He was also able to arrange for stores of forage to be prepared for him as he moved south. But the French had been in the country before him and had already taken toll of the animals, so that he was unable to obtain teams for Spencer's guns. Wellesley marched on the 10th of August, taking the coast road so that he might retain touch with the ships (for the country could furnish no supplies) and relieving the men of their packs so that they might the more easily carry four days' bread. The owners of the country bullock carts refused to allow them to go farther from their homes than the nearest village at which they could be replaced by others; so that the composition of these was daily changing. On the 16th Wellesley fought a rearguard action with a French detachment at Roliça, and on the 18th he halted at Vimeiro near the mouth of the river Maceira, where he had decided to disembark reinforcements which had come out from England. Here he was attacked on the 21st by the French, whom he beat off easily; but not expecting such foolhardiness on the part of the enemy, he had parked his transport too far in advance, with the result that many of the drivers vanished, together with a large proportion of the four hundred bullock carts and five hundred pack mules which he had with him. For this reason among others Sir Harry Burrard, who succeeded Wellesley in command on the day of the fight, declined to pursue. The campaign ended in the evacuation of Portugal by the French army under the Convention of Cintra.

It was at Maceira in August, 1808, that there landed a young German of the Commissariat, named Augustus Schaumann, whose diary, printed in 1924, gives us curious details of his department. He was introduced at once to the Portuguese bullock carts, which he describes as follows:

They consisted of rough planks nailed on to a massive pole or shaft. At right angles to the shaft and under the planks two blocks of semi-rounded wood were fixed, having a hole in the centre, and through these holes the axle was fixed. It was a live axle fixed firmly to the wheels. As these axles are never greased they make a terrible squeaking and creaking, and when a number of these carts are moving together it is enough to drive one quite mad.

I saw these vehicles still in use in Portugal not many years ago, and when one thinks of but one of their defects—the difficulty of turning them round—it is easy to understand that Wellesley from the first held them in detestation. Wellesley, however, was for the moment in disgrace owing to the Convention of Cintra, and the winter campaign of 1808-9 was conducted by Sir John Moore.

Of the troops that were to be placed under his command about twenty-five thousand were already in

Portugal and fifteen thousand more under Sir David Baird were under orders to sail from England, land at Coruña, and join Moore in Spain. The plan of campaign was vague. The French had been driven by the insurgents behind the Ebro; and a number of Spanish mobs, called armies, without any organisation or cohesion, were assembled to drive them out of Spain. They left—or said that they had left—a gap in their line, which was to be filled by Moore's army. This signified that Moore would have to march some three hundred miles to the scene of operations, with the prospect of hard fighting to follow. Careful provision for transport and supply was, therefore, of the first importance; and unfortunately waggons and mules alike were hardly procurable in Portugal. The Commissaries, albeit zealous, were, by Schaumann's own confession, absolutely without experience except in the concluding of contracts. The chief of them Moore described as an honourable man, well fitted for an office in London but useless in the field. His assistants were in every respect inferior persons. Moore warned the Secretary for War that for the higher duties of the Commissariat he must seek out capable men of business from London at large, since he would never find them in the Treasury. This severe judgment was belied by the subsequent success of Commissary General Kennedy, who had been with Wellesley in his short march from the Mondego to Lisbon; but at the time it was probably not far from correct.

Moore's difficulties were heightened by his want of money. The British Government, itself terribly embarrassed by dearth of specie, had hoped that the General might obtain cash on the spot by drawing bills on the Treasury; but these proved to be not negotiable at Lisbon. Matters were complicated by the bankruptcy of a Portuguese contractor upon whom Moore had depended for transport. Meanwhile a Spanish Commissary appeared at Lisbon with rather doubtful promises that the Spanish Government would look to the subsistence of Moore's army. Moore was not satisfied by these assurances, but time was pressing, and he thought it his duty to take all risks. But he did not blind himself to the consequences. "I am advancing", he wrote, "without the knowledge of a single magazine being made, or that we may not starve when we arrive." On the 18th of October he set his troops in motion, though he was barely able to do so by cutting down their light baggage to a point which caused discontent, and by taking with him only ammunition enough for immediate use and a very scanty supply of medicines.

Meanwhile on the 14th of October Baird arrived at Coruña with thirteen thousand men, including eight hundred artillery with guns and teams. Three regiments of cavalry, two troops of horse artillery, and three hundred men of the Waggon Train, all with their horses, were under orders to follow him. It was supposed that he would be able to canton his troops in Galicia until they were mobilised, and that the junta, or governing committee, of the province would welcome him with open arms. Much to Baird's surprise, the junta refused him permission to land anything except his artillery horses. They had their own armies plaguing them for transport and victuals, and found them more than enough. For the rest, reports as to the supply of horses and mules in Galicia were discouraging; nothing had been heard of a Commissary who had been sent to purchase transport animals in Asturias; and money was almost unprocurable. With great difficulty Baird's Commissaries obtained £4800, paying 17 per cent. premium or 5s. 2d. for the dollar. This rate seemed appalling in 1808; but it was cheap as compared with that of the years immediately to come.

After much parleying Baird was allowed to begin the debarkation of his men on the 26th of October; but meanwhile he could not get an ounce of bread for them nor a scrap of forage for his horses, while all efforts to obtain more than four or five mules for transport were in vain. However, things slowly improved. The junta of Galicia agreed to advance £25,000; the British Ambassador at Madrid furnished £50,000 more. The troops were pushed slowly inland in small divisions; a contractor was found to supply them regularly with victuals; and the Commissary sent word from Asturias that mules were obtainable there for hire. Then on the 8th of November arrived three troops of the Waggon Train (three hundred of all ranks), two troops of horse artillery, and two regiments of cavalry, with a promise that a third regiment of cavalry would embark shortly, and that with it would come three months' supply of oats and hay and half a million dollars in specie. Baird's troubles, therefore, seemed likely to come to an end.

How Moore fared, it is not altogether easy to say. It seems from Schaumann's account that along the route of the army's march in Portugal dépôts of supplies had been prepared at sundry points, also that there was certainly one ammunition column which consisted of two hundred Portuguese bullock carts. These were exchanged for Spanish carts when the Spanish frontier was reached, and the hire of these last was a dollar a day, paid daily. At Zamora there was great baking of biscuits by Spanish women in requisitioned ovens, to the amount of twenty-five thousand pounds a day. Here on the 17th of December appeared, to use Schaumann's words, "fat General Hamilton of the waggon-train with his useless waggon-corps". On the 20th, after many vicissitudes, Moore was able to concentrate his army, about twenty-six thousand effective men, at Mayorga, about fifty miles north and east of Zamora, and to begin his bold dash upon the French communications with France. He knew that he must inevitably retire very soon; and on the 24th the retreat began by way of Benavente upon

Coruña. On the 28th the Commissaries at Zamora received orders to send all the biscuit that they could to Benavente. They left two hundred thousand pounds behind them, which were later destroyed. The leading divisions of the British army had already reached Benavente on the 26th; and the troops got out of hand, refusing to wait for the regular distribution of food and fuel, and helping themselves. Many of the oxen and waggons had already broken down, and the drivers in many cases deserted with their teams. The weather was frightful, the rain poured down incessantly, and the roads were knee-deep in clay. There was much confusion; but the retreat continued, by divisions, and on the 30th the entire army united at Astorga, about forty miles north-west of Benavente.

Here the disorder was increased by the arrival of some thousands of a defeated Spanish army, whose commander, Count Romana, had broken his promise to Moore not to cross the track of his retreat. The next dépôt of supplies was at Villafranca, thirty-six miles to the north-west as the crow flies and not less than fifty miles as the road ran. Moore had barely two days' bread to carry him over this distance, but he would not listen to Romana's proposals to stand and fight. In such a retreat the only way is to hustle the troops ruthlessly on, and he gave his orders accordingly. From Astorga the way lay through the mountains of Galicia, where rain had turned to snow; and, though the foundation of the road was good and solid, it was covered with melted snow and mud, through which men and beasts waded knee-deep. Discipline in many battalions seems to have ceased altogether, though there were still steady troops enough to form a formidable rearguard. At Villafranca the men stormed the supply dépôts at the bayonet's point and helped themselves; but Moore, after destroying such victuals as were unconsumed, continued to hound his men towards Coruña. At Lugo, fifty miles as the crow flies from Villafranca, Moore halted and offered battle, whereupon discipline to some extent reasserted itself and the empty ranks became mysteriously full again. But the French, who had also suffered greatly, declined an action; and Moore, slipping away on the night of the 8th, obtained a good start of his pursuers. The weather was so terrible that Moore was obliged to grant his men another halt on the 10th; but on the 11th they came down into the low ground and the sunshine, and the retreat was over.

A successful action enabled the British to re-embark for England, and prepare for another campaign. The cost of the retreat in men was heavy, though not so great as was supposed, for thousands of stragglers made their way to Portugal and rejoined the troops there. The cost in animals is quite impossible to calculate. Many circumstances combined to bring about this result. In the first place Moore had been sent out to Spain by the Government under a total misconception of the true state of affairs; and his raid into Spain was simply an effort to fulfil, at great risk, the British Government's intentions. He started from Portugal, as we have seen, very imperfectly equipped with transport, and his Commissariat was, from want of experience, very inefficient. He brought upon himself almost the whole might of Napoleon's strength in Spain, and dared not retreat to Portugal by the way of his advance lest he should be (as he certainly would have been) cut off and destroyed. He, therefore, took the line of Baird's advance from Coruña; having previously ordered Baird to form dépôts upon the route. This Baird had done at Benavente, Astorga and Villafranca, where considerable quantities of supplies had been accumulated. But the evacuation of the superfluity of these towards the rear— that is to say towards the various halting-places on the road to Coruña—had been found impossible owing to lack of transport. There was not much carriage left in

Galicia and to such as there was the provincial junta claimed, with justice, priority of right. It is likely enough that the Commissaries, from want of experience, began the work of evacuation too late; but, without a proper transport service of their own, it is difficult to see how they could have accomplished much. That was one principal reason for the losses and confusion of the retreat—the want of a properly organised transport service under military direction and subject to military discipline. The Waggon Train seems to have deserved Schaumann's epithet of useless; but in any case it was too small. A second and more important cause was the bad discipline of the troops themselves. They behaved well enough during the forward march, but they were so much disappointed and disgusted at the order to retire that they abandoned themselves to grumbling and misconduct. The officers, who thought that they knew much better than the General, made no attempt, for the most part, to quell this bad spirit in the men, and were among the worst and noisiest of the grumblers. The failings of the Commissariat were bad, but the failings of the regimental officers were worse. There is no better example than Moore's retreat of the truth put forward in an early page of this book, that, if military discipline depends upon regular feeding, equally regular feeding depends upon military discipline.

THE CAMPAIGNS OF 1809 IN THE PENINSULA. Moore's army embarked for England in January, 1809, and by April it was back again under the command of Sir Arthur Wellesley. It was only after much hesitation that the Cabinet had decided to carry on the contest in the Peninsula, and only with great reluctance that it sanctioned the appointment of Wellesley. The struggle indeed seemed hopeless, for the French had over two hundred thousand men in the Peninsula and against such a force a handful of thirty thousand British troops was as naught. But, though the Spanish armies were worthless, the Spanish population was eternally active in mischief. Every isolated French soldier and even every small French party were waylaid and murdered. It was not safe to send a despatch with a smaller escort than five and twenty men. The French armies, therefore, were fully occupied in holding Spain down, and could ill spare troops to drive the British from Portugal. It was upon this calculation that Wellesley had recommended the continuance of the fight in the Peninsula. He reckoned that if the Portuguese were properly trained and disciplined he could put into line seventy thousand men. He did not believe that the French could overcome these seventy thousand with a smaller force than one hundred thousand; and he was confident that this was a greater number than the French could spare.

Other matters also came into account. In the first place the British had the command of the sea. They had an excellent marine base at Lisbon, and, if they could hold it, they could pour into it men, supplies and stores indefinitely by the cheapest and (in those days) the speediest mode of transit—the sailing ship. The French, on the other hand, must move every man and every ounce of supplies and stores by land, mostly by bad roads, which signified fatiguing marches of hundreds of miles, with endless wear and tear of men, of their clothing, of their boots, of their arms, of animals and of vehicles. Moreover every straggler who fell out in Spain could be accounted a dead man; and small convoys, unless accompanied by strong escorts, were certain of being trapped or intercepted by banditti or armed peasants.

Next, and this was most important, it was the practice of the French armies to live on the country. France, rendered bankrupt by the follies of the Revolution, had sallied forth to plunder her neighbours, and to maintain her armies upon their territory at their expense.

Napoleon had continued the system. Perhaps he had no choice; but, though it was economical in respect of money, it was wasteful in respect of men. In order that his troops might live, he had to advance always on a broad front, and to concentrate hastily by forced marches for action. How many men he thus marched to death is past calculation. They do not appear in the casualty lists of his victories. Moreover, since troops will always live by marauding rather than starve, the discipline of Napoleon's armies was never good. It is certain that no great commander was more prodigal of men's lives than Napoleon.

Now the English system had always been exactly the reverse of Napoleon's. The English had no great store of men to draw upon, and though, like Napoleon, they kept war so far as possible remote from their own territory, they could only transfer it to a friendly country, because no other would admit them. To live at "free quarter" upon a friendly country would have been to render it hostile, so they had always paid their way, and their commanders had been particularly severe against plunder and marauding. In brief, whereas Napoleon's system was to squander men in order to save money, the British system was always to squander money in order to save men.

Thus it appears that a contest of the British with the French in the Peninsula—or indeed in any other European country—was much the same in principle as that between the British and the Marathas in India, and that the key to success for the British was an efficient system of transport and supply.

Of course, if the French had concentrated every man that they had in the Peninsula and had marched against the British, they could have driven them into the sea in one campaign, no matter how efficient the British Commissariat. Napoleon had proved that in his dealing with Sir John Moore. But such concentration signified the

loss of Spain, or at any rate the necessity for recon-
quering it; and Napoleon had no wish either to evacuate
Spain or to reconquer it. What Wellesley saw, with
astonishing insight, was that Napoleon was not strong
enough, even with three hundred thousand men, both to
hold the Peninsula and to drive the British from it.
Moore's campaign, disastrous though it seemed at the
time, was really a great success. He forced Napoleon to
scatter his forces over a far greater area than the French
could possibly keep in subjection, and thus weakened
their hold upon every part.

During the interval between the re-embarkation of
Moore's force and the new debarkation of Wellesley's,
Sir John Cradock, who commanded the few British
troops in Portugal, had been unable to make any preparations, not knowing for most of the time whether he
might be ordered to re-embark. In March, however, he
made enquiries as to mules and horses for his artillery,
cavalry and transport and found that they were unobtainable. Forage also was scarcely to be found, and the
British cavalry horses were already half starved. He
sent to the coast of Barbary to see if mules could be
purchased there, but in vain. Then in April Wellesley
arrived, but even he could not create pack-mules when
they did not exist. So precious were they that he
actually sent ships round to Cadiz to fetch one hundred
mules which had been collected by a British regiment
for its own use. He was fain to fall back upon ox
waggons; and in May he concentrated at Coimbra in
readiness for the coming campaign.

The enemy immediately within reach was one French
army under Marshal Soult to the north at Oporto, and
another under Marshal Victor to the east at Merida on
the Tagus, the two being two hundred miles apart and
out of communication with each other. Leaving twelve
thousand British and Portuguese to watch Victor,
Wellesley marched with forty thousand against Soult.

Starting on the 6th of May, he surprised Soult at Oporto on the 12th, and drove him northward, pursuing him into the bleak and mountainous province of Tras os Montes until on the 17th he abandoned the chase. His transport could not keep up with him; the men were on short allowance of bread; their boots were worn out; and sickness was increasing owing to fatigue and exposure. The Commissariat had not distinguished itself. Moore's Commissary-General, Robert Kennedy, of whom we shall see more, had been replaced by one Murray, and the change had not been for the better. "Our Commissariat is very bad indeed," wrote Wellesley at this time, "but it is new and will improve, I hope." As to the waggon train, its waggons were too broad for the Portuguese roads, so the horses were made over to the cavalry and artillery, and the vehicles, when employed at all, were used as ambulances.

Then came the turn of Marshal Victor, who had retired up the Tagus. Wellesley's preparations were much retarded by want of cash. He had been obliged to borrow £10,000, which was very reluctantly spared by the city of Oporto, before he could march against Soult, and he was obliged to beg for a further £100,000 from Cadiz before he could move in search of Victor. He started from Abrantes on the 27th of June, still very short of transport, but relying on the assurance of the Spaniards, who were working with him, that everything needful for his twenty-three thousand men would be supplied. On the 10th of June the British army joined the Spanish at Plasencia; and then it appeared that no animals were forthcoming. The Spanish authorities had indeed sent commissioners to collect mules, but the people had foiled them by driving the beasts away. The army struggled forward as best it could till the 27th, on which day and the 28th was fought the battle of Talavera. The men had little to eat on these two days, and on the 3rd of August Wellesley retreated. His casualties had been heavy and he was obliged to sacrifice a quantity of baggage in order to procure carriage for two thousand wounded soldiers. On the 4th the army met with some herds of swine upon which they fell like men possessed; on the 5th they had nothing to eat but a little boiled wheat and parched peas. The heat was terrific, and had not the French, equally with the English, been practically condemned to inaction by want of food, the army might have fared badly. On the 19th of August, Wellesley wrote:

> We are starving, our men falling sick, and nothing to give them in the way of comforts; and our horses are dying by hundreds in the week. We have not had a full ration of provisions since the 22nd of July; and I am convinced that in that time the men have not received ten days' bread and the horses not three regular deliveries of barley. We have no means of transport, and I shall be obliged to leave my ammunition on the ground on quitting this place. We now want eighteen hundred horses to complete the cavalry, and two or three hundred for the artillery.

Not until the retreat ended at the Portuguese frontier ten days later did the army return to its normal amount of food. Such was the result of trusting to the Spaniards for transport and supply; and Wellesley—Lord Wellington since Talavera—did not forget the lesson.

CHAPTER V

WARS OF THE FRENCH EMPIRE.
THIRD PERIOD, 1809-1815.

AFTER 1809 the Peninsular War assumed something of a new complexion, as shall presently be explained; and it will be well before pursuing it further to glance at another expedition, generally known as the Walcheren Expedition, which was undertaken in 1809. The object of the enterprise was the destruction of Napoleon's naval establishments on the Scheldt, which were a perpetual menace to England; and the time was not ill-chosen, since Napoleon was already engaged not only with the British and Spaniards in the Peninsula but with Austria in Central Europe.

The preparations were made on an unprecedented large scale. The troops numbered forty thousand; the King's ships of all sorts and sizes were over one hundred and eighty pennants, and the transports brought up the total number of vessels to six hundred. The armament left England at the end of July; by the 31st the fleet had anchored off the mouth of the East Scheldt; and by the 3rd of August the siege of Flushing, which was the first operation, had been taken in hand. Flushing fell on the 16th of August, but the entire enterprise, as is well known, was wrecked by malarial fever, which killed four thousand men and laid over eleven thousand of the survivors on the sick list. Two details, however, are of interest to our present subject, and may be briefly touched upon.

87

First, the troops were fed upon ships' provisions—
exceedingly salt meat and hard and indigestible biscuit.
To allay the thirst and discomfort thus brought about,
the men resorted to spirits, and to relieve the thirst thus
increased they filled themselves with fruit, which was
abundant, and with tank water. They thus succumbed
to typhus and typhoid fever.

Next, the military Commander-in-Chief was much
hampered by the instructions given by the Treasury to
the Commissary-General, who, of course, was expected
to provide a certain amount of land transport as well as
fresh meat. The Treasury's instructions were that the
inhabitants should receive for any articles supplied
no more than the market price as it stood before the
disembarkation of the army. Further, the Treasury
expected all expenses to be paid and specie to be
obtained on the spot by bills drawn upon London.
Now, even if it had been possible (which it was not) to
negotiate these bills at Hamburg, Rotterdam or Amsterdam, it could only have been at a discount of 15 to 20
per cent.; while, as circumstances actually stood, they
were mere valueless paper, which might be realised
some day. The Commissaries, therefore, pressed that
allowance might be made for these drawbacks in the
price paid to the inhabitants. They wrote:

> We have not only drained them of cattle, but have often taken
> their cows, which were of greater value to them for the support
> of their families than can be made good by the highest price paid
> for beef. We have also taken all their horses, waggons and
> drivers without further remuneration than their rations, and
> that at time of harvest.

The Commander-in-Chief, Lord Chatham, heartily
supported the Commissaries and begged for more
specie. The Treasury declined to furnish any more
specie, saying that, if requisitions were not satisfied
upon the terms laid down, then they must be collected
by force. The Secretary for War also wrote privately

that there was no foreign coin at disposal, and that the Government dared not risk the disturbance that would be created if it were known that guineas were being sent abroad. Chatham stuck to his point, and declared that either allowance must be made for discount in favour of the inhabitants, or guineas must be sent. The Treasury answered by reasserting its contention, adding (a characteristic piece of pedantry) a legal opinion in favour thereof, but sending none the less £40,000 in dollars. As a matter of fact, no great harm came of the wrangle, for typhoid fever meanwhile disposed of the whole matter. But the operations were hindered and the Commander-in-Chief was painfully embarrassed, for it was his duty, if he could, to advance and capture Antwerp; and this he could not possibly do if he turned the peasants against him by harsh requisitions. They would have driven away all their transport before he could reach them, and might have risen in his rear (for the soldiers were perishing so fast that it was difficult to secure his communications) and cut off his retreat.

Thus the old problem of transport and supply played its part in wrecking the Walcheren Expedition. It delayed the General's movements and thus set the naval Commander-in-Chief quarrelling with him.

THE PENINSULAR CAMPAIGN OF 1810. Let us now return to the Peninsula where the most critical of all the campaigns was close at hand. Napoleon, having got the better of Austria and seen the failure of the British at Walcheren, was now free to turn all his strength against Spain; and he lost no time in doing so. Between October, 1809, and September, 1810, he poured into the Peninsula nearly one hundred and forty thousand men; and actually by the beginning of February, 1810, his armies in Spain and Portugal numbered close on three hundred thousand. Could Portugal, or at any rate Lisbon, be held against such a force? Wellington thought that it could, though, in case of accidents, he begged the

Government to send transports for the re-embarkation of the army. He had to deal with an enemy which, like the Marathas, lived upon the country, and he thought that he might beat them with the old weapon of an efficient service for transport and supply.

It was by this time plain to him that the old system of the Treasury, to do everything by contract, was impracticable in the Peninsula and that he must build up a new one for himself, teaching his Commissaries their new and difficult business.

One great initial difficulty, it must be repeated, was the dearth of specie, which was due principally to the quarrel between Spain and her precious-metal-producing Colonies. The exchange against England all over the Mediterranean varied, during the war, roughly from 20 to 50 per cent. There was traffic in specie at Lisbon, Oporto, Cadiz, Gibraltar and Malta; and at all of these stations there were different rates and different British officers competing for a small supply. Once, for instance, Lord William Bentinck on the east coast of Spain, outbid Wellington by paying 6s. 3d. for the 4s. 2d. dollar. At last in 1812 Wellington sent a Commissary to Gibraltar to settle an uniform rate of exchange for all British demands, and thereby the situation was greatly eased. But note that Wellington had to do this for himself, and that the Treasury, whose duty it was to look to these things, took no thought of them. We shall find this difficulty of specie constantly recurring to the end. Among the thousand inconveniences caused by it, one raised by the unfriendly action of the United States deserves, perhaps, particular mention. A great deal of the flour, on which the British army in the Peninsula lived, was exported to Lisbon from America. In normal times this would have been paid for by the products of British factories; but the United States had passed in 1806 an Act prohibiting the importation of British goods, and therefore the flour could only be purchased with specie.

In the Commissariat at large, matters, though not yet quite satisfactory, were improving as the Commissaries gradually gained experience. The Commissary-General, Murray, went home broken down after the campaign of 1809, with a handsome tribute from Wellington to his good service. He was succeeded by Robert Kennedy, and meanwhile one of the junior Commissaries, Mr Ogilvie, had revealed a perfect genius for his business. Others of the commissariat staff besides Murray had, however, also given way through overwork. The fact was that the Treasury could not be brought to understand that these campaigns in the Peninsula were something quite new. They had no idea that a Commissary's duties could extend beyond the supervising of contracts and the accountancy attaching thereto. As late as at the beginning of 1812 the Commissary-General found himself forced to explain to the Treasury, in a pathetic letter, that his business was to manage the whole business of transport and supply for the army in detail, and not merely to draw cheques and pay contractors to do these things for him. He was careful to point out that under the new system he saved the profits which had hitherto accrued to contractors; but he urged that he simply must have more men. The Treasury was still puzzled. It had contracts on the brain; and it expected the Commissary-General, in addition to the duty of feeding the army in the field, to grapple with the whole business of accountancy. At last in despair the Commissary sent home a map, showing the position of his thirty-seven principal dépôts, and finally he travelled home himself to explain the situation in detail. The officials imagined that an army remained always as a single compact body, and they recognised that such a body required a magazine. But why should a magazine need more than a single commissariat officer to take charge of it? He could as easily issue supplies to five thousand men as to five hundred. Such were the arguments which the

Commissariat at the front had to combat for the best part of two years. Meanwhile, overworked and under-manned, the Commissariat had to press into the service anyone that they could find—Portuguese as well as British—with the inevitable results of fraud, malversation and an evil name for the department. In 1812, when much progress had been made in breaking down the obstruction of the Treasury, the whole staff of the Commissariat in the Peninsula for a force of forty thousand men little exceeded seven hundred of all ranks.*

I pass next to transport. Wellington resolved very early to abjure wheeled transport as far as possible and to depend chiefly upon pack-animals. One cart only was allowed to each regiment to carry men who fell sick on the march. All others were strictly forbidden. Officers who had engaged ox carts for their private baggage were ordered to discard them and to procure pack-mules or pack-horses instead. Upon this point Wellington was adamant. General Cotton, who commanded the cavalry division, begged, before the advance on Talavera, that the three days' forage with which his troop-horses were burdened might be carried on carts. He was peremptorily refused. Wellington was a good horse master, but nothing would induce him to allow his army to be encumbered with the native bullock

* Commissaries of all ranks	...	...	87
Clerks	...	...	255
Interpreters	...	...	13
Storekeepers ...	...	...	78
Receivers and Issuers ...	...	...	57
Conductors of Stores ...	...	...	154
Bakers	...	...	41
Coopers	...	...	23
Carpenters	...	...	3
Bricklayers	...	...	3
Wheelwrights	...	...	2
Farrier	...	...	1
Office keepers ...	...	...	2
			719

carts. He himself had one single private carriage which he very rarely used for his own purposes but frequently lent to sick or wounded officers.

But the question was how to obtain mules; and it was answered first by transporting them from Tangier, though mainly by hiring them, with their muleteers, from Spain. The Tangier mules were imported principally for what I may call by the later name of regimental transport. One mule or pack-horse was allowed to every troop of cavalry and to every company of infantry to carry the camp kettles, with five additional mules to each battalion and six to each regiment of cavalry to carry the paymaster's books, the regimental surgeon's chest, the armourer's tools, entrenching tools, and, in the case of the cavalry, the equipment of the saddler, veterinary surgeon and farriers. There was, however, a curious division of property in respect of these animals. Those that carried the entrenching tools and the equipment of armourer, saddler and veterinary surgeon alone were the property of the public—that is to say, were supplied and owned by the Commissariat—the remainder being purchased by the officers out of a fund called "bat, baggage and forage allowance" which was issued to all officers to fit themselves out for work in the field. The arrangement did not work smoothly. Before Sir John Moore's campaign the Treasury deducted income tax from the aforesaid allowance under the impression that it was part of the officers' emoluments, instead of a meagre fund to enable them to bear heavy expense. This piece of folly was, however, easily corrected; not so other disadvantages. Wellington made it a strict rule to allow no regiment to join the army until it was fully equipped with regimental transport, and the Commandant at Lisbon used to warn the officers that they must not depend on the Commissariat for mules, and to stimulate them by the promise that the regiment first equipped with transport should be the first to be sent up to the front. But mules and pack-horses were often scarce, and the local dealers were greedy; and matters generally ended in the officers throwing themselves upon the mercy of the Commissariat. Peremptory Generals, such as Robert Craufurd, would sometimes take the commissariat mules for their officers without further parley. Again, if a regimental mule died or became useless, the officers, having no funds to replace it, would try to lay hands on a public, a captured or a stolen mule, upon all of which the Commissary-General, in virtue of a general order, rightly possessed priority of claim. Then again, the prohibition of carts for baggage of course brought all kinds of forbidden burdens on the backs of the public mules of the regimental transport, and this abuse, despite of strict regulations and sharp rebukes, was exceedingly difficult to check. The whole arrangement was in fact new, and the army made as much difficulty about accepting it as the Treasury.

The regimental transport carried no food nor forage. The soldier's daily ration at this time was one and a half pounds of bread or one pound of biscuit, one pound of meat and a ration of wine or spirits. There was a standing order that, whenever the Commissariat could issue the quantity, the infantry must carry three days' bread and the cavalry three days' forage. The remainder of the supplies was borne upon mules hired (as has been already mentioned) in Spain, and driven by their own muleteers. These mules, as Schaumann tells us, were exceedingly fine animals, strong, hardy, patient and capable of constant heavy work on a very short allowance of food and water. The muleteers were as hardy as their beasts. They could run alongside them at a trot for ten miles on end, and seldom changed their clothes or slept under shelter from year's end to year's end. They were always cheerful and they seem to have been, taken altogether, remarkably honest. They had their own organisation under chiefs who bore the title of *capataz*, or overseer, and who were for the most part in every way, except literary education, superior men. The rate of hire was one dollar a day for each mule, with rations for the men though not for the animals, each muleteer having charge of his own mules. Sometimes, from want of ready money, the hire was weeks and months in arrear, and then the mules were supplied by the Commissariat with forage. The final arrangement made was to allow two-thirds of a dollar and a ration of eight pounds of corn daily for each mule. The total number of mules, at the disposal of the Commissariat, over and above those of the regimental transport before referred to, was close upon nine thousand for an army of fifty-three thousand men.

THE CAMPAIGN OF 1810. This organisation for transport, if not actually perfected, was certainly well advanced during the winter of 1809–10. In the spring and summer of 1810 Napoleon designed to sweep the British out of the Peninsula, and had set apart sixty thousand men under his best General, Massena, for the task. It was practically certain that Massena must enter Portugal by Almeida, reducing that fortress as a first necessary step to his further advance. Wellington, there-fore, took up his position in that quarter, taking care that no supplies for man or beast should be left in the vicinity. Massena's preliminary operations were pro-tracted, although he was lucky in taking Almeida early owing to an accidental explosion; and, looking to the denudation of the country, he dared not advance upon Lisbon without accumulating a fortnight's supplies. This took time and, even when the victuals had been collected, he had no transport to carry them, and was obliged to turn over one-third of his artillery horses to his Commissariat for the purpose. In one of his corps it seems that the infantry carried, every man, ten days' biscuits and four days' bread, there being no transport for provisions excepting eighty mules for the head-quarters staff. Finally, abandoning all his communications, Massena began his advance southward on the 15th of September with sixty-five thousand men.

Wellington had thrown up fortified lines at three different points to arrest Massena, but the Marshal avoided the two more northerly of these, and Wellington steadily retreated before him, turning on the 27th to fight a delaying action at Bussaco. On the 10th of October he entered his last defensive position—the famous lines of Torres Vedras—with the Atlantic on his left flank and the Tagus, with a flotilla of gunboats, on his right. Massena dared not attack, and Wellington, with his own transport and supply service in good order, knew that he had only to sit still until starvation compelled Massena to retreat. The Marshal, hoping that a change of Government in England might bring about the voluntary withdrawal of the British army, clung to his position, first actually before the lines and later thirty miles back, at Santarem, until the 2nd of March, 1811, when he was forced to retreat, after losing thousands of men and animals through sheer starvation. By that time, even after sacrificing hundreds of ammunition waggons and transport waggons, he had not horses enough to draw even the whole of his guns. His transport train simply vanished. With enormous difficulty he collected fifteen days' bread to nourish his army during the retreat, but the men were obliged to carry it—if it were carried at all—themselves. Harassed at every step by Wellington and in constant danger of total destruction, Massena recrossed the frontier where he had crossed it, with an army in rags, shoeless, ammunitionless, divided, discouraged and demoralised. He had lost twenty-five thousand men—two thousand fallen in action, eight thousand prisoners, fifteen thousand dead of sickness and starvation. The mortality among his horses was even greater than among his men. The track of his retreat was hideous beyond description, being marked by corpses at almost every step.

THE CAMPAIGN OF 1811. The result of the campaign was the final clearance of the French out of Portugal; and Wellington was able to make at least a show of taking the offensive. He blockaded Almeida in the north-east and invested Badajoz in the east. Massena advanced from Salamanca to try to save Almeida but was driven back at Fuentes de Oñoro (May 5th). Soult moved forward from Seville and compelled Wellington to raise the siege of Badajoz, but was defeated at Albuera and fell back in his turn. Wellington again invested Badajoz; but was once more obliged to abandon the siege by an advance of the joint armies of Soult and of Marmont, who had succeeded Massena in command of the Army of Portugal. But, though greatly superior in numbers, the French accomplished nothing, and Portugal was safely held.

At the end of 1811, looking to Napoleon's designs for invasion of Russia and the consequent withdrawal of many French troops from the Peninsula, it was evident to Wellington that he could take the offensive in earnest, and that he would need some efficient wheeled transport. He therefore set his acting Commissary-General, Mr Bisset, to design suitable carts. These vehicles had iron axle-trees and brass boxes, most of which had been captured from the French, and, the model having been chosen, the construction was begun at Oporto and Almeida during the winter of 1811. Each cart was drawn by a pair of oxen, the animals being purchased and the drivers specially hired. Experience had taught Wellington to be as careful of drivers as of beasts. The full number of these waggons, some of which were to be constructed in England, was eight hundred, and the organisation was as follows:

32 brigades, each of 25 waggons and 54 bullocks.
16 divisions, each of 50 waggons and 108 bullocks.
2 grand divisions, each of 400 waggons and 864 bullocks.

Each division was under charge of a clerk or other junior officer of the Commissariat, the subordinate conductors being all of them, apparently, Portuguese or Spanish.

It is somewhat remarkable that Wellington entered upon this, the most brilliant of his campaigns, under most serious disadvantages. In the first place, his efficient and experienced Commissary-General, Kennedy, had been persuaded by his wife, who had been persuaded in turn by her sister, to resign in order that he might return to England. Wellington did not readily forgive these two ladies, but he accepted the inevitable and asked for Bissett to be sent out in Kennedy's place. His Quartermaster-General, George Murray, also asked for leave in December, 1811, and actually left in May, 1812, being replaced by an officer from home, Colonel Willoughby Gordon, who was not only useless in the field but disloyal. Lastly specie was terribly scarce. The pay of the Spanish muleteers was already, in July, 1811, six months in arrear. They were very patient, but there was one thing which, if they knew it, they would not do—they would not help to feed the despised Portuguese. As the Portuguese formed an important part of the army and their Commissariat was deplorable, the matter was sufficiently serious.

However, Wellington decided to take the offensive early, and first to secure the two eastward gates into Spain, Ciudad Rodrigo and Badajoz. Marmont's army, living on the country, was widely scattered for purposes of subsistence, and, long before he could concentrate it at Salamanca, Wellington had snatched away Ciudad Rodrigo (January 19th, 1812) after twelve days of open trenches. At the end of February Wellington marched south upon Badajoz—knowing perfectly well that Marmont, though his army might be concentrating, had neither magazines nor transport—and captured that fortress likewise (6th April). Thus he could push his advanced base forward to the Portuguese frontier; and he further lightened the burden upon his land transport by improving the navigation both of the Douro and of the Tagus, so as to save one hundred miles of dreary hauling over bad roads through Portugal to Spain. His last petty stroke before he invaded Spain was the destruction of the bridge over the Tagus at Almaraz, which thrust the communications between the French armies north and south of the river one hundred miles back to the bridge of Toledo. And here again the French were paralysed by want of victuals. "I know", wrote General Foy, an excellent officer, "that the place for my division is at Almaraz, but how can I move my troops through a desert, when for several days they have not received even a half ration of bread, and when the prospect of seeing bread come to us grows more remote?" Marmont to north and Soult to south were in the like difficulty. They could only feed their troops by dispersing them over a wide area until harvest should come.

At last in June Wellington invaded Spain in force, though with fear and trembling, for the pay of the troops was three months and of the staff five months in arrear, the Spanish muleteers had not been paid for twelve months and the outstanding bills for meat alone amounted to £200,000. Success carried him forward. On the 22nd of July he defeated Marmont at Salamanca; on the 12th of August he entered Madrid; and on the 19th of September he invested Burgos. Therewith all the French armies in Spain (except that on the east coast) united against him; and he was obliged to retreat. Up to the time of the battle of Salamanca, all had gone well, and Wellington had paid the Commissariat a high compliment. "Notwithstanding the increased distance of our operations from our magazines and that the country is completely exhausted, we have hitherto wanted nothing, thanks to the diligence and attention of the Commissary-General, Mr Bissett, and the officers of the department under his charge." But in the retrograde movement from Burgos, matters did not go so smoothly. Whether through inexperience or, as is more probable, through the neglect of the Quarter-master-General, who was chief of the staff, Commissary Bissett had omitted to empty the magazines on the line of advance from Lisbon to Madrid and thence to Burgos, and to transfer the contents to the line of retreat from Burgos to Salamanca and thence to Ciudad Rodrigo. Kennedy, who had returned just before the siege of Burgos was raised, thus found himself suddenly saddled with this difficult duty, while Wellington at the same time required of him the evacuation of all sick, wounded and other encumbrances from the principal advanced dépôt at Salamanca. Kennedy's troubles were aggravated by the misconduct of the officers and men in charge of the convoys, who drove the Spanish muleteers and waggoners by hundreds to desertion. There was, therefore, failure of supplies at some points of the retreat, with considerable disorder and indiscipline. Wellington damned this misbehaviour in a sweeping general order, not being aware, apparently, that on two days at least the whole army, and on other additional days, certain divisions, had received no rations. On the whole it seems that the staff was far more to blame than the Commissariat for the confusion.

However, in spite of all mishaps, Wellington had liberated two-thirds of Spain from French domination; and the disastrous destruction of the French army in Russia, leading as it did to the withdrawal of great numbers of French troops from Spain, opened a bright prospect for the campaign of 1813. The army rested during the winter. Its discipline was greatly improved and promised to become still better owing to the establishment of a corps of military police. Cash was coming in more regularly, the Government having found a new source of gold in India. But the supply of specie was still insufficient; and it may be worth while to state briefly how Wellington tried to overcome the difficulty on his own account.

Payment for goods purchased by the Commissariat for the army was made by bills drawn by the subordinate Commissaries upon the Commissary-General. These were known as commissariat bills. The "sharks" (to use Wellington's phrase) in Lisbon soon began to buy these securities at depreciated rates, thereby greatly injuring British credit. Wellington thereupon forbade the liquidation of such purchased commissariat bills by bills drawn upon the Treasury. The "sharks" thereupon raised a howl, which was echoed by their correspondents in London; and Wellington withdrew the obnoxious prohibition. The result was that cash in return for Treasury bills became unobtainable. Wellington, thereupon, solved the problem by enacting that no purchased commissariat bill should be discharged by a Treasury bill unless the holder deposited a quantity of coin, equivalent to the amount of his commissariat bill, in the military chest in return for a second Treasury bill. The system worked well and brought in monthly three quarters of a million to a million dollars, without friction and without complaint. But when in due course the transaction came before the Treasury, it was too much for the official mind. It was vigorously criticised; Wellington was furious; and the Treasury was somewhat taken aback to find that the General and not Kennedy, the Commissary-General, was responsible for it. Probably the whole idea emanated from Kennedy; but he, being very jealous of the political Commissary-General, Mr Herries, in London, steadily declined to give Herries any information about anything. In the first shock caused by Wellington's vigorous protests the Treasury for a time yielded to him, and allowed him to continue his policy concerning commissariat bills. But a few months later they put a final end to it, whether rightly or wrongly, I cannot presume to say. It is certain only that the "sharks" got their own way, and that Wellington believed that the monied interest had gained its point by threatening to turn out the Government.

A second method employed by Wellington to raise ready money was to order large quantities of corn, and to sell such quantity of it as was not needed for his own army, to the Portuguese Government at a profit. Thereby incidentally he helped to save the Portuguese from starvation, besides raking a useful little sum into his military chest. The Board of Trade, however, condemned the whole proceeding, and Wellington was fain to admit that his time might more profitably be employed than in speculating in grain. But, he added, a Commander-in-Chief, who had to carry on a war with only one-sixth of the necessary amount of specie, must necessarily be driven to strange shifts and should be encouraged, rather than the contrary, to seek out resources of his own.

THE CAMPAIGNS OF 1813–14. There is no need to pursue further the history of the Peninsular War. In June, 1813, Wellington advanced and by the second week of July he had driven the French armies opposed to him across the frontier. He shifted his marine base first to Santander and later to Passarges; and in the first week in October he crossed the French frontier itself. The French commanders found it a very different thing to live on their own country from subsisting on an invaded country, and they were constantly in want of supplies. The English, on the other hand, paying good money, could obtain both provisions and transport with ease. Moreover, the British troops had learned discipline at last, and their behaviour in France was exemplary, whereas the French soldiers, through sheer starvation, were always plundering, marauding and fighting with their compatriot peasants. In fact Wellington's army had reached the stage when he could say that with it he could go anywhere and do anything; and the essence of its perfection was the organisation, slowly and painfully evolved, for transport and supply. When that was established, discipline was established; for the two, let it be again repeated, must ever go hand in hand.

THE WATERLOO CAMPAIGN, 1815. The Peninsular War ended in a suspension of arms on the 18th of April, 1814. Napoleon was relegated to Elba whence he escaped to France on the 1st of March, 1815. Within that short interval the army, perfect in all its auxiliary departments, which Wellington had so carefully built up, had been already destroyed. Some part of it, as shall presently be told, had been sent to America, but the bulk of it had disappeared. Thus, for instance, Wellington asked for one hundred and fifty guns, but the Ordnance could only provide forty-two, not because the actual weapons were wanting, but because there were not gunners nor horses for more, and not drivers enough even for so many. He was obliged to call upon the Commissariat to find horses for the small-arm ammunition carts, entrenching-tool carts, engineers' waggons and pontoon waggons. The waggon train he asked for at once, but the bread waggons sent from England were condemned by Commissary-General Dunmore, an officer who had learned his business by long service in the Peninsula. In fact all the work that Wellington had done between 1809 and 1814 required to be done again; and, if the campaign had not been begun, continued and ended within four days, the shortcomings might have proved very serious.

For the rest, the Commissariat, in spite of its good work, seems to have received but little consideration in Wellington's campaigns. They were non-combatants and, by force of old tradition, were expected always to give way to the combatant. Especially was this the case when quarters were in question. The most insignificant combatant claimed the right to turn a Commissary out of his quarters and occupy them himself. Schaumann tells us that he had seen Kennedy himself, the Commissary-General, huddled with the whole of his twenty-four clerks into a windowless broken-down hovel, and writing hard by candle-light, while Wellington's youngest volunteer aide-de-camp occupied the best dwelling. Kennedy was indeed knighted for his services but, when the Peninsular medal was issued in 1843, the officers of the Commissariat, who had enabled the combatants to win their victories, did not receive it. Such unreasonable contempt was a great misfortune, for it almost justified Parliament in its steady discouragement of the auxiliary departments of the Army in time of peace.

THE AMERICAN WAR OF 1812–14. For the sake of convenience I have deferred the consideration of the war with America, which was going forward during the three last years of the Peninsular War. The original cause of quarrel arose out of the irreconcilable interests of belligerents and neutrals; yet these differences might have been adjusted but for incidental circumstances. The first was that the President of the United States, for purposes of faction, desired to flout England, and the second was that many Americans were eager for the conquest of Canada. A little judicious pressure from Napoleon upon the ignorant and short-sighted Government at Washington sufficed to make them take the plunge, and on the 17th of June, 1812, the United States declared war upon England.

To all outward appearance Canada lay at their mercy. The British frontier from Quebec to Mackinaw—roughly eight hundred miles—was practically defenceless. There were few troops on the spot and little hope of reinforcing them. Moreover the campaign was found to be in essence a naval campaign on the Great Lakes, where the Americans had far greater resources than the

British for the building and manning of ships, while the British Navy could not reach the fighting area owing to the rapids of the St Lawrence and the falls of Niagara. Nevertheless the British held their own, in spite of heavy reverses on the water, and more than one slight reverse on shore. But the forces employed everywhere were very small, and their operations never strayed far from some waterway, because practically no transport was possible except water transport. It should be mentioned that the New England States, which had been the bitterest of our enemies in the rebellion of 1775, were strongly adverse to the War of 1812, and did not hesitate to make a good profit by selling food-stuffs to the detested English.

Apart from the frontier, there were raids upon different points of the American coast, which were practically naval operations, and there was the attack upon New Orleans, into which the Army was dragged by the cupidity of an Admiral. The conditions thus thoughtlessly imposed upon the troops before New Orleans were incredibly unfavourable. To all intent six thousand men were cooped up on an isthmus fourteen hundred yards broad, between the Mississippi and a deep swamp. In front was the enemy in a strongly fortified position; on the river were American armed vessels, flanking the only line of advance; in rear was a shallow lake and beyond it lay the sea. The only base of supply—the fleet—was eighty miles distant and accessible only by open boats; and this waterway for the last four miles of its course was so narrow that it would barely admit two boats abreast. When water carriage ceased, the track from the landing-place to the camp— a distance of four miles—was so bad after a high tide or after rain that provisions and stores could only be brought forward upon men's backs. Victuals, beyond a few cattle, were unobtainable upon the spot. Again, this line of communication was insecure, for it was open to hostile attack on one flank, where the fleet could not spare boats enough to guard it, while at any time foul weather might interrupt the delivery of supplies. Further, the boats of the fleet were not numerous enough to carry away more than half of the troops at one time; so that, in case of a retreat, there was always the chance that one moiety of the force might be intercepted afloat, and the other moiety might be stranded and overwhelmed without possibility of retreat ashore. Lastly, the total quantity of provisions on the fleet, when the military Commander-in-Chief landed, did not exceed one month's store, which, considering the prospect of the return voyage, was none too great. In fact the naval officers who planned this abortive enterprise ought to have been tried by court-martial.

It need only be added that the attack upon New Orleans was a costly failure, and that the troops were only with the greatest difficulty withdrawn. Too late came the news that the whole of the work done had been to no purpose, for peace between England and the United States had been signed a week before the first British troops had landed by the Mississippi, and more than four weeks before the delivery of the attack.

It now remains to summarise the progress and changes that were accomplished within the Commissariat Department at headquarters, that is to say within the Treasury itself, during the long struggle with France between 1793 and 1815.

SKETCH OF THE COMMISSARIAT DEPARTMENT, 1793–1815. In 1793 there was a nominal Commissary-General, whose office appears to have been a sinecure, for no money (excepting, of course, his salary) was issued to him, and all contracts for food and carriage were made by the Treasury. In 1797 a measure of decentralisation was taken by the appointment of District Commissaries to make local contracts for the troops at home. At first some of these corresponded directly with the Treasury, and others with the Commissary-General; but after twelve months' trial the whole were placed under the Commissary-General. That functionary's duty and authority were, however, strictly limited; and the general distribution of duty and authority was as follows:

Contracts for the feeding of troops in camp (large camps were formed of the regulars, fencibles and militia for home defence) lay with the Commissary-General.

Contracts for the feeding of troops in barracks (this was the period when barrack-building in Great Britain was begun in earnest) lay with the Barrack-Master-General.

Contracts for the troops in charge of beacons and field-works were the business of the General Commanding the District.

Contracts for the subsistence of troops abroad were entrusted to the Victualling Board of the Navy.

Stores for troops at home were the business of the Barrack-Master-General; stores for troops abroad of the Commissaries of (marine) transport. Thus we find three principal departments concerned with the supply duties of the Army—the Treasury, the War Office and the Admiralty. But the confusion did not end there. Every commissariat officer received a commission from the War Office, and a "constitution" from the Treasury. He drew part of his pay from one office and part from the other; and thus he was irrevocably bound to serve two masters. Such absurdities could not continue without death to efficiency, and they were swept away by the intervention of Sir Brook Watson, the Commissary whom we have already seen in Flanders with the Duke of York. By 1806 the whole of these multifarious contracts had been subjected to the sole authority of the Commissary-General.

The change, however, was attended with much unnecessary expense. In 1805 the Commissariat establishment at home counted, inclusive of the Commissary-General but exclusive of his central office in London, just one hundred District Commissaries, assistants of various grades and Central Commissaries, with one hundred and fifteen subordinates of all descriptions.*

The Central Commissaries numbered forty-three, one to each English county, and had apparently been appointed in apprehension of a French invasion. But as the Duke of York had already, in preparation for such an event, parcelled out the country into thirteen military districts, and as there were nineteen District Commissaries, it should seem that the Treasury, while taking the War Office into partnership, would have nothing to say to the Horse Guards. But the military forces of the Crown were at that time subject to so many different authorities that some redundancy may have been inevitable at the outset. Thus the regular infantry and cavalry were under the War Office for administration and under the Horse Guards for training and discipline. The artillery and engineers acknowledged no master but the Master-General of the Ordnance; transport and supply were, of course, ruled by the Treasury, except marine transport and supply oversea, which were committed to the Admiralty. Militia, yeomanry and volunteers received their commissions from the Lord Lieutenants of counties and were accordingly dominated by them, while the Lord Lieutenants themselves corresponded with the Home Office and received from the Home Office all of their orders. However that may be, upon the appointment of a new Commissary-General—a Mr Coffin—in 1806, Central Commissaries were abolished, and with them both the master-bakers and the store-keepers.

* *Home Establishment of the Commissariat in* 1805: one Commissary-General, nineteen District Commissaries, twenty-five Assistant Commissaries, twenty-three clerks, eighty-three store-keepers, five master-bakers, one Director of waggons, one Inspector of waggons, two conductors.

Strangely enough, throughout all this period the Commissary-General at home had no control over Commissaries abroad, so that any officer who went oversea, on active service or on routine duty, passed beyond his jurisdiction and lost touch with him completely. It should further be noted that the Commissariat's duties, whether at home or abroad, were still limited, as in Marlborough's time, to the provision of bread for the men, forage for the animals, and, if troops were encamped, of wood for fuel. All other supplies were furnished by the departments of the Quartermaster-General, Barrack-Master-General, and Medical Board; and the sole function of the Commissariat in respect of these articles was to stir up the right department.

With the Waggon Train, beyond the procurance of the necessary funds from Parliament, the Treasury and the War Office had no concern; nor was the slightest use of it made by the Commissariat for the training of its officers. The Commander-in-Chief, in fact, owing to the many departments which contested his authority over the Army, was occasionally obliged to improvise creations of his own. Thus, the engineers being under the control of the Ordnance, he was obliged to call into existence the Staff Corps—we may call them the Commander-in-Chief's engineers—whose officers did all the work of surveying in the Peninsula, and made, among other remarkable engineering feats, the suspension bridge over the Tagus and the bridge of boats over the Adour. The Waggon Train was just such another child of the Commander-in-Chief and had nothing to do with the Treasury. This peculiarity may account for the tendency of the Military Train of later days to reckon itself among the combatants, and to look down upon the non-combatant branch.

So things continued until 1809, when a new departure was made. A fresh Commissary-General was appointed, who took over the superintendence of the Commissariat both at home and abroad, and became the sole channel of communication between the Treasury and the subordinates of the Commissariat oversea. The officer selected for the post was Colonel Willoughby Gordon, whom we have already met as Wellington's Quartermaster-General in 1812. After the old fashion he received his appointment and £4 a day from the Treasury, his commission, £3 a day and a Major-General's field allowance from the War Office. Though in many ways the reverse of a fascinating individual, he did really good work during his two years' tenure of the post of Commissary-in-Chief. He could not abolish the practice of equipping his subordinates with two commissions from two different departments; but he contrived at least that they should receive their salaries from his own department, and he did something by statutory regulations to encourage good conduct and discipline among them. Thus, for one thing, he ordained that all Commissaries should begin their careers from the bottom and serve for a certain time in every grade before they could gain promotion to the next. And this was the more creditable to him because all powers of advancement were vested exclusively in himself. He also showed courteous attention to all of Wellington's wishes and representations concerning his department. But his reign was too short for him to leave any deeper mark on the Commissariat.

Upon Gordon's resignation a successor was found to him in Mr Herries, a civilian and a politician, who had made some reputation both as a Colonel of Volunteers and as a financier. His appointment gave peculiar satisfaction to a body of Commissioners, who had been appointed to enquire into military expenditure. The duties of this office, as they averred, were all civil and should therefore be executed by a civilian. Even if the Commissioners were ignorant, as they probably were, of the immense trouble with which Wellington had built up his transport and supply service, they had still no excuse for repeating this venerable blunder. General Don, an officer of great experience, had recently laid down certain rules which should have guided the Commissioners into the right track. All Commissariat officers, pronounced Don, should be properly trained for their work in the field. No army should enter on a campaign without a field bakery. No expedition should be sent on active service without taking with it a part of the Waggon Train, to be attached to regiments, battalions and departments. A Commissariat train also should accompany it to bring forward bread and forage; and only transport additional to this should be hired by contract. Don further recommended that bread and forage should be supplied to the troops by the Commissariat in peace as well as in war, and at home as well as abroad, in order to teach Commissaries their duty. Briefly, General Don, two generations in advance of his time, wished to place the Commissariat upon a military basis and, in fact, to form an Army Service Corps. He spoke to deaf ears, as is generally the fate of a true prophet.

For the rest, though the war lasted with very brief intermissions for twenty-four years, the reforms of the Commissariat were initiated too late to put an end to a great many of its abuses. During the operations in the West Indies between 1794 and 1797 many Commissaries had by shameless frauds made large fortunes. One had amassed as much as £87,000, probably in St Domingo, where every kind of rascality was rampant among the French planters as well as the British Commissaries, and where officers and men died so fast that it was almost impossible to trace many transactions.*

* The operations at St Domingo, or at any rate the later stages of them, are among the very few of which I could find no printed record of any kind whatever. This is exceedingly rare. Even the obscurest expeditions at far remoter times than the end of the eighteenth century generally find some chronicler. If it was successful some one who had

These evil examples infected the whole service of the Commissariat. There was much malpractice at home owing to the greed of forage contractors, and more than enough abroad, even in the Peninsula, despite of the vigilance of Wellington and of the British Minister at Lisbon. Such is almost inevitably the case when men in receipt of small emoluments are entrusted with the handling of large sums. The temptation is too great, and in Portugal from 1808 to 1814 it was the greater because Assistant Commissaries there received only 5s. a day, whereas their brethren of the same rank in England received 15s. There seems to have been little wisdom in the heads of the Treasury.

To sum up, then, it must be concluded that the service of transport and supply made little real advance in the course of this long and exhausting war. Wellington indeed showed what could be done, even with the untrained Commissaries who accompanied him to the Peninsula; but his work was allowed to fall to pieces immediately. Old prejudices and the jealousy of politicians still insisted that the work of the Commissariat in the field was a civilian's business. The Commissariat itself could not throw off the evil traditions of fraud and peculation which it had inherited from the seventeenth century. The combatant officers continued to despise the non-combatants who kept them alive, and to accuse them, whether with or without reason, of dishonesty. And the non-combatant Commissaries, who knew, as they alone could know, their own difficulties, and had endured hardship, fatigue and danger, so that the combatants might want for nothing, received the sneers of their fighting comrades in silence, but nourished bitter and implacable resentment.

shared in it wished to vaunt it; if it were unsuccessful the commander put forward his defence. A Jamaican, Mr Bryan Edwards, was actually at work on the story of St Domingo but died before he could complete it. In fact St Domingo seems to have meant death to all who touched it.

CHAPTER VI

FROM WATERLOO, 1815, TO THE CRIMEAN WAR, 1854.

THE forty years which followed upon the decisive battle of Waterloo were among the most dismal of the Army's history. The nation, as Lord Liverpool, the Prime Minister, said, was peace-mad, and the soldiers who had saved it were cursed as plagues. A General could not ride down Piccadilly in uniform with an orderly dragoon at his heels, officers could not form a club—what is now the United Service Club—as a means of social intercourse, but politicians must denounce such doings as a military conspiracy to enslave England. Englishmen are never quite so great as during the continuance of a dangerous war, never quite so silly as when it has come to an end. Yet a new Empire had been won, and an army was necessary to guard and to consolidate it; but the country would never provide money enough to pay for a sufficient force. As an inevitable consequence, the Army, and especially the infantry, was shamefully overworked. Three out of every four battalions were always abroad and sometimes four out of five. Whether at home or abroad the men were infamously housed, abominably overcrowded and senselessly fed. The mortality among them was terrible, but nothing could induce Parliament to believe that it was false economy to give recruits a bounty to enlist, and, when once they had enlisted, to kill them as rapidly as possible. In tropical garrisons vast numbers of men were done to death by a monotonous diet of salt beef, which drove them to drink. It would have been easy, and frequently not more expensive, to give the soldier fresh meat; but the Treasury always thought of the Army not in terms of living men, but of pounds, shillings and pence. A ration was a ration, and, if the soldier could not live on it, he must die, which contingency was duly provided for by regulation. If he were quartered in the remote and dreary solitude of Australia, where food was cheap, he was not allowed to profit by it. He was charged twopence to threepence above cost price for his victuals, so that his comrade in the West Indies might be fed more cheaply. When, as occasionally happened, a drought sent food in Australia up to famine price, then the remedy was simple—to reduce the soldier's daily meals from three to two and give him oatmeal instead of wheaten flour. There was no deliberate inhumanity about this, nothing more than a false idea that it signified real economy. Yet the cost of the men lost through bad feeding and bad housing must have exceeded enormously any paltry sums thereby saved. But the Treasury could not rid itself of the notion that it existed to look after money and not after men; and this was always the weak point of the Commissariat so long as it was part of the Treasury. Even Bissett, as his book plainly shows, is obviously more interested in accounts than in the mobility of the Army and the welfare of men and beasts.

It is hardly too much to say that the Army would have perished from sheer inanition but for the constant effort of the regimental officers to alleviate the soldier's hard lot; and it may be broadly stated once for all that every improvement for the health and welfare of the rank and file has been initiated by the regimental officer and tardily adopted by the State.

Where the combatant branches were so badly treated,

it is no surprise to find that the Waggon Train was a constant target for the shafts of false economists in Parliament. Officers of experience pleaded that some nucleus should at least be preserved for expansion in case of war; but the answer of the ignorant was that surely soldiers were not needed merely to drive waggons. For nearly twenty years the Waggon Train existed rather as a shadow than as a substance, until in 1833 it was finally swept away. The Commissariat dropped back into its old groove of accountancy; and when a small force of five thousand men was sent to Portugal, for political reasons, in 1826, Wellington thought it as well to draw up instructions for their transport and supply exactly as he had done when he first landed in the Mondego in 1808. The strange thing was that during the forty years which followed upon Waterloo wars of greater or less scale never ceased in some part of the Empire; and it is now necessary to glance at these distant campaigns and to examine them for any light that they may throw upon our subject.

THE NIPAL WAR OF 1814-15. The first of these is the war with the Gurkhas, which was forced upon us by their aggressive encroachments. It was the first hill campaign ever undertaken by the Indian Government, but this peculiarity, though formidable, was not the greatest difficulty of the enterprise. The Gurkha frontier was roughly seven hundred miles long. Little was known of Nipal, and it was no easy matter to decide what should be the objective. Lord Moira, the Governor-General, who was also an extremely accomplished soldier, ultimately decided to invade with four columns, one from Patna, moving upon Khatmandu, the other three at different points on the hundred and twenty miles of front from Dehra Dun westward to the Sutlej.

The novelty of a campaign over a succession of trackless wooded ridges was too much for most of the old Indian Generals, one of whom was so utterly unnerved that he deserted his army. Supply was a matter of extreme difficulty, and for transport at the front the chief dependence was upon hill porters and elephants. The only effective work done was by the most westerly column, based upon Rupar, about fifty miles east of Ludhiana. There was a General, Ochterlony, who knew his business, but he was only able to reach his enemy by employing thousands of villagers to make roads, and by moving with great deliberation. The final and decisive blow, however, was struck by this same General on the line between Patna and Khatmandu. The ground was so rugged and rain so frequent that it was extremely difficult to coax elephants up the road constructed by the pioneers. The establishment of dépôts at very short intervals was imperative, and thus the operations were very slow. Indeed the movement which finally cowed the Gurkhas was a most dangerous advance through a dry watercourse, where the troops could progress at no swifter rate than two hundred yards an hour, and thence up a dangerous ascent. The men had orders to carry three days' rations with them; but it was a full week, during which the pioneers worked unceasingly at the roads, before supplies could be brought forward to them.

There is unfortunately little record of the campaign, which remains exceedingly obscure. The Gurkhas were a brave, active and enterprising enemy, but the great difficulty was to enter their country at all. In fact, unless there had been an enormous abundance of native labour on the Sutlej to make roads, it is doubtful whether Ochterlony himself could have succeeded in that quarter. On the line between Patna and Khatmandu he took the risk of having his force annihilated with comparative ease, and came out with triumph.

THE PINDARI WAR OF 1817–19. Next came the task of pacifying Central India which was in a state of anarchy. The total force employed was about one hundred and fifteen thousand fighting men, of which forty-five thousand were assembled on the Jumna, between Allahabad and Delhi, to move south, and seventy thousand to advance northward from the Narbada, thus driving the enemy into each other's arms. Both armies were of course equipped with the means of movement by the usual arrangements with native contractors, the northern after the fashion of Bengal, the southern after the manner of Madras. As it happened there was a drought in Hindustan and an unusual prolongation of the monsoon in the Dekhan. Thousands of animals perished in the mere course of concentration on the Narbada. The operations before long resolved themselves into the harrying of the country, much of it difficult and wild, by mobile columns, which signified further destruction of draught-animals. Two years elapsed before the object of the war was accomplished. Cholera for the first time appeared in India and attacked the northern army, killing thousands of troops and followers; and, looking to the wasteful system of Indian campaigns, it is not surprising that the resources of India were taxed to the utmost. Evidently Wellesley's sound maxim that good drivers are as vitally important as good beasts, had been forgotten.

THE BURMESE WAR OF 1824-6. Next came a campaign in an entirely new country, of which very little was known to the Indian Government. The Burmese, like the Gurkhas, had persisted in aggressive encroachment on the north-eastern frontier, and it was necessary to bring them to reason by an attack upon the Irawadi. Seeing that this would be a river campaign, the Government decided that it would be best to begin operations at the beginning of the rainy season, when the Irawadi would certainly be navigable. Accordingly a fleet was prepared, including a single steamer—the first ever employed by the British in war—which sailed with some ten thousand troops for Rangoon in April, 1824.

Rangoon was taken on the 10th of May with little difficulty, but then the trouble began. The British had counted upon finding native boats, waggons, bullocks, ponies and probably a certain quantity of supplies on the spot. But the Burmese had a Napoleon among them, and the British found nothing in Rangoon nor for miles around it, not a bullock, not a waggon, not a fowl, not so much as a vegetable or an egg. Having no transport but the boats of the fleet, of which no sufficiency could be spared, they could only make petty raids upon such bodies of Burmese as lay within twenty miles, and for the most part were compelled to sit still and live on ships' provisions—rice, mouldy biscuit and doubtful salt pork. The result was that the troops, both British and native, died by thousands of scurvy, dysentery and fever.

This situation remained unchanged from May until November, when water transport began to arrive from India, as also a few private speculators with some scanty delicacies which only the richer officers could afford to buy. Then a few weeks' operations sufficed to thrust the Burmese army back some fifty miles from Rangoon. Bullocks reappeared, and a bazaar was opened. Finally at the end of 1824, seven months after the army had landed, seventeen hundred draught-cattle from India were safely disembarked.

Reinforcements having arrived, the force pushed up the river, but once again the Burmese systematically laid waste the country before it. All villages and towns were deserted, and everything that could be of service was destroyed or carried off. The Burmese further made constant attempts to destroy the British flotillas by floating down upon them fire-craft steeped in petroleum. The army had therefore with great difficulty to push the Burmese forces yet further back, so as to permit the population to reassemble in its rear. Once delivered from the terror of their own soldiers, the

Burmese became friendly at once; and the more country the British could leave pacified and re-populated behind it, the easier became the task of transport and supply. The river was of course the main source of transport, but the Burmese, fully aware of this, fortified position after position to command the navigation with artillery, so that the task of clearing the waterway was unending. Even ten months after the departure of the original expedition the transport, by land and water, was still sufficient only to permit the movement of four thousand men. The Indian Government had reckoned that the expedition would reach Ava within six weeks after landing at Rangoon. After a full year it had only reached Prome, two hundred and fifty miles below Ava.

However, water-craft, bullocks, carts and drivers were by that time procurable in abundance; and the army, after halting during the rainy season, resumed its advance in November, 1825. The tracks through the jungle were execrable and occasional heavy rain made them impassable. The way then became choked with dead and exhausted cattle, while biscuit and rice were damaged irretrievably by the downpour. Cholera broke out, and the column moved on, always through solitude. No living soul was seen except the dying. The dead villagers lay so thick that the track for fifty miles was marked by their corpses; but still every village had been destroyed and every bullock had been driven off. The column was still fifty miles from Ava when in February 1826 the King of Burma at last consented to accept the British terms. The campaign had then lasted for twenty-two months.

Simultaneously with the advance up the Irawadi in 1825 another force of about eleven thousand men was sent to Chittagong to invade Arakan, with some vague idea that it might cross the mountains which divide Arakan from the valley of the Irawadi and join hands with the column on the river. A flotilla accompanied this force, but the collection of land transport took an immense time and it was not until April that the force mastered the city of Arakan. A small column of a thousand men was then sent over the mountains, but after five days returned. Many men had fallen sick, many cattle had perished, and the survivors, men and beasts alike, were enfeebled to the last degree. With pack-mules the column might possibly have gone farther, but could never have reached the valley of the Irawadi. Few white men survived the campaign in Arakan; and indeed of the British troops engaged in this Burmese war only one man in seven returned. Very much of this loss might have been avoided had the least forethought been shown in considering the problems of transport and supply.

THE ASHANTI WAR OF 1826. The next little war took a fragment of the Army to one of the deadliest climates in the Empire, the west coast of Africa. Here, as in Nipal and in Burma, a powerful tribe, the Ashantis, had erected themselves into a formidable military power and, having subdued their neighbours, were threatening to overwhelm the British settlements.

The Governor, Sir Charles Macarthy, at Cape Coast Castle, was an old soldier who had been trained in Sir John Moore's light brigade at Shorncliffe, and he was quite ready and even eager to take command in the field. His force was of a very miscellaneous character, and the only form of transport was native carriers, for horses, mules, asses and kine cannot exist in that climate. But carriers were difficult to obtain, for they asked exorbitant wages which Macarthy declined to pay. He therefore impressed a certain number of them, who threw down their loads one after another as they threaded the forest, and disappeared. One of Macarthy's parties at the end of two days' march had not a single carrier left. However, by one shift and another, Macarthy brought his men within reach of the Ashantis and engaged them in a pitched battle; but the carriers of the reserve ammunition had flung down their loads and vanished, and the result was that the British force was utterly destroyed. The British were driven into Cape Coast Castle, which had not been properly victualled, had no proper water supply and was very scantily stored with ammunition. Even the officers could get neither flour nor meat, and only very little rice. But for the arrival of a shipload of provisions from Sierra Leone in the nick of time, every soul would have perished. The war dragged on for two years with the British always on the defensive until in August 1826 they were strong enough to sally out twenty-four miles from Accra and engage the Ashantis in a decisive action which cost the enemy five thousand casualties, and induced them to accept the British terms. The whole story is curious as an example of the neglect of the foreign garrisons at this period; it being apparently no one's business to see that there were reserves of victuals in the strong places.

THE KAFFIR WAR OF 1834. We are now suddenly shifted to another part of Africa, the Cape of Good Hope, where there had been constant trouble with the native races from our earliest occupation of the Colony. In December, 1834, some fifteen thousand Kaffirs poured over the eastern marches on the line of the Fish River, their entire front extending for about one hundred miles from the Winterberg to the sea. There were only about eight hundred soldiers to meet them, and these were scattered in various posts; and the Kaffirs had laid waste practically the entire country between Somerset and the sea as far westward as Uitenhage before any resistance could be organised. Colonel Harry Smith then took command at Grahamstown, scraped together a force of regulars, Boers, Hottentots and "loose vagabonds" and, though the enemy was far in his rear, took the offensive to carry off the Kaffirs' only treasure, their cattle. The Boers' ideas of carrying on a campaign seem to have resembled those of an Indian army in the plains. One detachment of sixty-two fighting men brought with it fifty non-combatants and twenty-eight waggons; another of one hundred and eighteen fighting men, eighty non-combatants and thirty-six waggons. Such encumbrances were not calculated to suit Smith's policy of rapid forays into the enemy's country; but he understood how to handle the burghers and make them accept his arrangements. The advanced base of operations was Grahamstown, and the nearest seaport to it being Port Elizabeth, at least one hundred and fifty miles distant, practically all supplies were carried overland. The forward bases, if the term may be used, were Fort Willshire about thirty miles north and east of Grahamstown, and Fort Beaufort, about twenty miles north and east of Fort Willshire. About two thousand men, regulars and burghers, were left in posts to guard the line from the Winterberg to the sea; and there was a second line of defence about Uitenhage to keep communications open. The striking force numbered three thousand men, half of them burghers and two-thirds of them mounted. The transport consisted, as was inevitable, of the ox-waggons of the country, at which Harry Smith at first looked askance. He says:

Our train of commissariat waggons each with twenty oxen [?sixteen] in it was immense. With the headquarters column alone we had one hundred and seventy, occupying about two miles. From the length of these teams I expected great difficulty with them, and certainly took every pains to regulate and divide them into divisions, departments, etc., appointing a captain over the whole. To my astonishment, so excellent were the bullocks that I never had the slightest trouble, and they could march over any country whatever with the troops.

It is thus clear that the hiring and loading of the transport was left to the Commissaries, but that, with the striking force at any rate, its organisation and control was entirely in military hands.

Harry Smith's flying columns moved so fast and travelled as far that the waggons could not keep up with them; and the men frequently settled down for the night with nothing to eat but the freshly slaughtered beef of the captured cattle. But the raids rarely lasted as long as even three days, and Harry Smith treated them in such a sporting spirit that the men, in spite of all hardships and danger, seem to have positively enjoyed them. Smith himself took all chances with them, faring as roughly, though he had thirty years' service behind him, and going as hungry as any of them. Nevertheless, owing to the military organisation of the transport the waggons were never far distant; and thus by sheer mobility he was able to reduce the Kaffirs to submission in seven months. It must be added that, in the face of an enemy which never overlooked a mistake, no mishap ever befell the troops under his immediate command nor any of his detachments except in one or two cases where his instructions were neglected.

THE AFGHAN WAR OF 1839–42. Our story now leads us back to India and to the most insane enterprise undertaken even by an Indian Government. This was the invasion of Afghanistan in 1839 for the purpose of placing on the throne at Kabul a prince, Shah Shuja, whom the Afghans had already rejected as their ruler but who was acceptable to the British; the idea being to turn the country into what is called a "buffer-state" to stave off possible Russian aggression. The entire plan of campaign was extravagant. Two contingents were to be employed, the one from Bengal about ten thousand strong, based on Ferozepore, the other from Bombay, about five thousand strong, to be based on what was then a paltry village at Karachi. The Bengal column was to march five hundred miles south-westward to Rohri, cross the Indus and the desert of Sind to the Bolan Pass, penetrate it to Kandahar and so march on to Kabul. In advance of it were to move by the same route some six thousand native hirelings in the pay of Shah Shuja. The Bombay column was to march three hundred miles from its port of disembarkation at Karachi and join the Bengal column at some point on the way. It is to be noted that Afghanistan was then far from the British frontier, and that the invading armies would leave in their flanks and rear the Sikhs under Ranjit Sing to north and the Amirs of Sind to south, neither of them trustworthy friends, if not actually unfriendly. However, it was expected that the march to Kabul would be a bloodless affair; and there was no difficulty in finding contractors for transport and supply after the usual fashion. The formation of dépôts of provisions along the route from Ferozepore to Sukkur was entrusted, not to skilled Commissaries who knew their business, but to the "political" officers in the various Native States upon the route. These political officers were generally, wherever stationed, extremely self-confident—not to say arrogant—and never doubted their ability to achieve anything, hardly excluding miracles.

The preparations began in August, 1838. Sir Henry Fane, the Commander-in-Chief in India, went to Ferozepore in person, for though he did not intend to command the army, he was to accompany it by water for some distance on his way to Bombay and to England. Knowing that supply would be a great difficulty, he attached special importance to the formation of magazines on the route, and was by no means satisfied with the reports of the political agents, whom he set aside as "inexperienced persons". Knowing also that it was of extreme importance for the army to traverse the Bolan Pass before the hot weather began, he had fixed the day for its march from Ferozepore on the 3rd of December. To his consternation he was informed on the 1st that the start must be delayed for a week, so as to enable food and forage to be cut for the passage of the force through Bahawalpur. Fane was furious. "This staggers my confidence in the Commissariat," he wrote, "even an hour's delay is serious...and it is a great evil to the army to be delayed by want of common foresight."

However, on the 10th of December the Bengal army began its march in five separate columns, which followed each other at one day's interval. Headquarters with the cavalry brigade led the way, followed in succession by the infantry, the artillery, the supplies and the stores. The victuals included thirty days' allowance of grain, besides slaughter-cattle "on the hoof" for two and a half months. For the supplies alone fourteen thousand camels were needed, besides a very large number for the ordnance stores. There was the Sutlej at hand to convey this heavy *matériel*, but it had been found impossible to collect water-craft enough to carry great part of it. Then came the baggage. Fane, contrary to the Indian custom, ordained that the infantry should carry their packs instead of loading them upon animals hired by themselves. He also cautioned the officers against bringing into the field large tents, large establishments and much baggage. But something more than advice was needed. There should have been strict rules laying down certain limitations, and a stern transport officer to enforce them without mercy. As things were, officers, true to the evil traditions of campaigns in the plains, loaded themselves with extravagant quantities of baggage and endless retinues of servants. It was said that one brigadier had no fewer than sixty camels to carry the articles which he deemed necessary to his own comfort. In this way the camels, public and private, attached to the Bengal army alone numbered from twenty-five to thirty thousand— enough to line the road from Hyde Park Corner to Reading if drawn up in single file, nose to croup. As if that were not enough, the followers of the army numbered forty thousand. It is true that they were supposed to be starting not on a campaign but on a military promenade; yet even so it was to be a promenade of a thousand miles, including the passage of a great river, the crossing of one hundred and fifty miles of desert and the traversing of sixty miles of mountain pass.

Trouble with transport and supply began immediately. At every stage the dépôts of grain by the way were found deficient. The Commissariat complained bitterly of the order of march, which condemned the supplies and stores to the rearmost place, and so to dearth of forage almost from the day of leaving Ferozepore. The trains left their camping-ground at daylight and were often halted for hours while the preceding columns defiled through some strait; and, when at last they reached their halting-place early in the afternoon, the camels were inevitably driven far afield to find fodder and were driven back at nightfall after only two hours' of grazing and little food. Thus, though the weather was cool, the air was fresh, the country was open and the roads were good, the unfortunate beasts were overworked and underfed; and matters were not improved by the fact that all the way from Ferozepore to Sukkur the water was brackish and slightly saline.

At Bahawalpur, two hundred miles from Ferozepore, the column halted and closed up, from the 29th to the 31st of December. The order of march was then changed, the Commissariat moving off several hours before the troops. But this only gave facilities for another evil. From the very first there had been much desertion of camel drivers; and the losses of camp equipment and of private baggage from this cause had been sufficiently serious during the first six marches alone. But matters were not likely to be improved by allowing the transport to take the lead of the army. The Sikh drivers resented subjection to so menial a service, and such a feeling is not softened by continuance. The Hindustanis nourished a superstitious dread of the unknown land beyond the Indus, and the nearer they drew to the crossing-place the more they were tempted to remove themselves and their camels to safety. The progress of the march was slow, for the camels, being ill-fed, were weak, and were dying in great numbers. A fresh supply of them, provided by the political agent, was picked up at Khanpur, about eighty miles beyond Bahawalpur, on the 8th of January, 1840; but on the 19th the startling discovery was made that the mortality of the grain-carrying camels was exceeding the consumption of their loads. Such consumption should have sufficed to relieve at any rate a certain number of camels of their burdens, if only for a few days, which might have meant the saving of their lives. But it should seem that, in the general confusion, no unloaded camel could travel far without having a burden of some kind, public or private, heaped upon its back; and thus hundreds if not thousands of beasts were sacrificed to sheer mismanagement. However, in spite of all mishaps, on the 24th of January the head of the Bengal column trailed into Rohri; and halted for the preparation of a bridge over the Indus.

We must now glance at the fortunes of the Bombay column. The first transports arrived on the 27th of November and made not for Karachi, as had been advised, but for another creek in the delta of the Indus some seventy miles to south of it. The rest came dropping in on the succeeding days, but many troops were detained on board ship for a week because the transport agent had not arrived. The Commander-in-Chief, Sir John Keane, had been given to suppose that he would land among a friendly population, but it was not so. When Keane disembarked, he found that no grain, or boats or camels had been collected, and that the Amirs of Sind were doing their best by intimidation to deter owners of boats and of camels from taking service with the British. Unable to move, Keane was fain to sit still at a short distance inland, sending one of his staff to Kach by sea to procure camels. This officer, James Outram, showed the greatest energy, but even so was unable to procure more than twenty-four hundred camels. With these Keane moved slowly forward to Larkhana in a fertile district about two hundred miles north of Karachi. Here he halted from the 3rd to the 11th of March, being extremely anxious about the matter of supplies.

Meanwhile the conveyance of the stores of the Bengal column in barges across the Indus had begun on the 9th of February, and a bridge of boats had been constructed over the river. It may be mentioned as evidence of the neglect in the general preparations that the engineers had been sent away without pontoons, without anchors, without even ropes, and that they had to collect native craft and improvise every fitting for the bridge. The Bengal column, now under the command of General Cotton, then crossed the river, and assembled between the 17th and the 20th at Shikarpur. Here the Commissary-General was anxious to halt for three weeks in order to amass supplies; and he actually sent four thousand camels to the rear to collect them. But the political officer, Sir William Macnaghten, who was to all intent in command of the expedition, pressed for an immediate advance. He had already demanded a thousand camels of Cotton for Shah Shuja's troops, while Keane, having too few animals for the Bombay force, was likewise calling upon the Bengal Commissariat to fulfil his wants. Cotton, therefore, would have done well to halt, but in obedience to Macnaghten he moved off on the 21st. The march across the desert, of which twenty-six miles was absolutely waterless, was accomplished in seventeen days, but at considerable loss. The horses suffered severely, first, from want of forage and water, and, next, on reaching fertile land again, from a surfeit (which no officer should have permitted) of green growing corn. The camels, underfed and overladen, dropped down by hundreds, and many of them and of the bullocks were carried off by predatory Baluchis, whom the "politicals" forbade the soldiers to fire at lest they should provoke a blood feud.

At Dadhar, by the mouth of the Bolan Pass, Cotton again halted in the greatest perplexity about supplies. Despite of all previous losses of animals, he had still, when he left Shikarpur, transport for six weeks' provisions. Kandahar was thirty-two marches distant, making no allowance for halts; and there was therefore little if any margin. Cotton's Commissary counted upon finding ten days' victuals at Dadhar and twenty days' more at Quetta. Dadhar, however, when it came to the point, could produce only one day's provisions; and on the 8th of March it was necessary to place the followers on half rations. A week later, on the 15th, Cotton entered the Bolan Pass. The track was so stony as to be very trying to the feet of horses or camels, while the hoofs of bullocks were soon worn to the quick. Water was plentiful but there was dearth both of fuel and forage; and the destruction of animals was very great. At every ten yards lay a dead camel, a dead bullock or a broken-down cart. One brigade lost two hundred and fifty camels in four days, and many living animals were swept away by predatory mountaineers. There was, fortunately, no serious resistance to the march, and on the 26th Cotton entered the wretched mud-built village of Quetta.

There, as has been told, he had expected to find twenty days' provisions. He found practically none. Moreover on the 28th his Commissary reported that one-third of his camels had perished and that the rest were in such wretched condition that they could carry no more than half loads. Only ten days' victuals remained for the cavalry brigade and the first brigade of infantry, and only two days' grain for the horses of the cavalry and infantry. Keane, very angry that Cotton should have moved from Shikarpur without his orders, had commanded him peremptorily to halt at Quetta; but in any case it was difficult for him to move in any direction. Kandahar was one hundred and fifty miles ahead, with the Khojak Pass, a most difficult obstacle, on the way. Shikarpur was two hundred miles in rear and not to be reached except by retraversing the whole length of the Bolan Pass. Cotton therefore placed the troops upon half rations and the followers upon quarter rations and sat still. He tried to obtain supplies from Kalat, but the harvest there had been poor, and the attempt failed. The starving followers stole food and forage from the mountain tribesmen, and the tribesmen retorted by constant thefts of camels, once carrying off as many as two hundred in a body. The whole army, from the General to the drummer, was discussing the certain prospect of starvation.

Meanwhile Keane had been slowly following in Cotton's rear, and had arranged to establish a magazine of supplies at Dadhar. Enquiring as to the transport to be furnished by the Bengal Commissariat to Shah Shuja and himself, he found that only five hundred instead of a thousand camels had been left for Shah Shuja, and that of two thousand, which Cotton had promised to leave for him at Shikarpur, two-thirds were still on the eastern bank of the Indus. The truth, of course, was that the Bengal Commissariat was furious at being called upon to furnish transport for any troops but its own. There was already jealousy enough between the armies of the various presidencies, and naturally this made matters worse. When Keane at last rode into Quetta on the 6th of April he found the Bengal column not merely croaking but sunk into the lowest depths of despondency.

There was only one thing to be done—to place the Commissariats of both presidencies under a single head and to advance at once. He moved on, therefore, on the 7th, on which morning sixty cavalry horses were shot, being unable to drag themselves farther. Bad news came from the rear. A convoy of provisions had been opposed by the tribesmen in the Bolan, and what with this trouble, bad food and lack of forage, eight hundred camels with their loads had been lost between the Indus and midway through the pass. The cavalry horses continued to die. Bad management in the Khojak Pass kept a seething mass of men and beasts heaped up along a length of four miles for thirty-six hours without food or water. Vast quantities of baggage, tents and stores were abandoned and hundreds of camels were lost. On emerging from the pass the column was more than once in difficulties for water; and, the heat being very great by day, yet more animals perished. The Sixteenth Lancers marched afoot on one day for twelve miles, goading their horses forward with their lances, both men and animals nearly dead of thirst. The Bengal troops finally reached Kandahar on the 26th of April with just two days' half rations in hand. They had marched a thousand miles in one hundred and thirty-seven days. The men had been on half rations for the past twenty-eight days, and the horses had had nothing but green forage, always scanty and often bad, for twenty-six days. The cavalry brigade was, in fact, to all intent dismounted; and it was extremely fortunate that no resistance was offered to the entry of the troops into Kandahar.

Meanwhile the Bombay column had entered the Bolan Pass on the 6th of April, to find both air and water poisoned by the rotting carcases of dead animals. They were not seriously opposed, but at every stage they lost camels by theft; and when finally they reached Kandahar on the 4th of May they reported one-fifth of their horses to be dead, a vast number of camels worn out or stolen and some hundreds of camp followers murdered.

At Kandahar matters were little better than before. There were large crops of corn, but these were not yet ripe. There was plenty of fruit and vegetables, the more welcome since many soldiers were sick of scurvy; but fruit in large quantities is not the best diet for half-starved men. There was also plenty of green forage, but the horses needed barley and grain, which were difficult to find. Again, there was none too much grain to feed both the inhabitants and the army, and the price naturally rose. The transport of provisions from the base was also unsatisfactory. On the 7th of May a convoy, nominally of two thousand camels, came in from Shikarpur, purporting to carry three hundred tons of grain; but, owing to mismanagement and the rascality of native agents, little more than sixty tons reached Kandahar. Lastly, camel-stealing soon began at Kandahar, and, when the thieves were caught and sentenced to be hanged, Macnaghten intervened to protect them, lest any severity should render Shah Shuja unpopular.

However, Keane was bound to make the best of things as they were, for he had express orders from the Governor-General that Kandahar must not be left without six months' provisions for troops and followers, and that no movement from thence must be made with less than six weeks' full rations at starting. Meanwhile his vast line of communication was weakly guarded, for want of sufficient troops, and was at best extremely insecure west of the Indus. The predatory tribes were never idle, and, owing to the incessant calls for transport at the front, none of the standing-posts had camels enough to enable detachments to sally out and destroy nests of robbers. In Sind the heat alone almost paralysed all movement. One convoy starting from Shikarpur lost six out of fourteen officers, one hundred sepoys, and over three hundred camp followers dead of heat before it reached Quetta.

However, a large convoy of four thousand camels had passed through Dadhar on the 24th of May, and after its arrival Keane hoped to be able to move. On the

23rd of June three thousand camels toiled safely into Kandahar, loaded with about one month's supplies for the army on half rations. The advent of these animals was welcome, for Keane had not at Kandahar transport enough to carry more than five weeks' full rations for the Europeans and the same allowance for native troops and followers. But the merchants, who had brought the convoy, refused either to proceed farther or to sell their camels; and the drivers, without whom the camels were useless, declined to accompany them beyond Kandahar, whether purchased or not. So Keane, who had for days been chafing at the delay, was fain to store the newly arrived grain at Kandahar and to march off without it.

He started for Kabul on the 27th of June with the sepoys still on half rations and the followers on quarter rations. On the 17th of July, a little to south of Ahmed Khel, he found grain enough to serve out full rations all round for one day. On the 21st of July he was stopped by the fortress of Ghazni. He had left his siege artillery behind, and the place could neither be mined nor escaladed. It was pretty certain that, if he could beat the Afghan field army, which so far had retired before him, Ghazni would open its gates. But that field army was reported to be at least four marches north of Ghazni; and he had only three days' supplies in hand. He must, therefore, capture Ghazni at once by some means, or perish. He did capture it with no great difficulty on the 23rd, found it to be fully provisioned for a siege, and was at last able to give his troops permanently full rations. On the 30th he marched for Kabul which he entered unopposed on the 7th of August, and then, food being abundant and cheap, his troubles for the time came to an end. Garrisons were left at Kabul and Kandahar, and in September the Bombay troops returned to India by way of Kalat and the Bolan Pass, while Keane, with three Bengal battalions and a brigade of cavalry, took the route of the Khyber Pass and Peshawar.

It would be tedious and unprofitable further to pursue the story of this war in detail. After the departure of Keane the troops were virtually placed under the command of Macnaghten; and the general commanding could never guess where he stood. These political gentlemen loved above all things to make what they called "demonstrations" of military force all over the country, and would send off little columns in all directions without thought of the wear and tear of men and animals. The General might have detached the greater part of his transport animals to revictual an important post. It mattered not. He was obliged to recall them to fulfil the wishes of the political chief; and the unlucky animals, having travelled two days' journey forth had to retrace their steps and do four days' work for no object whatever. Moreover, since the political officers never knew the strength of the tribe which they desired to overawe nor anything about the country, the military officers, desiring to take no risks, often sent a stronger force, which signified a greater body of transport, than was necessary. If the General wished to establish a line of magazines along part of the route from Kabul to Jalalabad, where Shah Shuja spent the winter, Macnaghten rejected the proposal as seeming to imply distrust of the inhabitants. Lastly, it was found, moreover, that Indian camels were useless in Afghanistan. They would not face steep ascents and they had not learned to avoid poisonous herbs. In fact, as General Elphinstone wrote, they were purchased only to be buried. Yet the Commissaries of the Bengal army, hidebound by tradition, would not resort to the use of mules, native ponies and asses. In fact, long before the final disaster at Kabul, Elphinstone was in despair about his transport.

And the state of things in Afghanistan itself was repeated along the whole length of the line of communication. Every political officer regarded himself as an independent Commander-in-Chief within his district. They likewise were perpetually calling upon the troops within their borders to make demonstrations here and demonstrations there. They would establish a military post in isolation seven days' march away from the nearest dépôt, in the heart of most difficult country, without a thought for the feeding of the garrison. The transport animals, therefore, which should have been forwarding provisions and stores to the garrisons in Afghanistan, were wasted and worn out in these petty, wholly unnecessary and often perilous enterprises. The revictualling of these isolated posts became a serious and hazardous operation, sometimes causing losses of scores of soldiers and of hundreds of camels. Difficulties were increased, moreover, by the bad spirit of the officers of the Bombay army towards the Commissariat. They were ready enough to undertake light staff duties in time of peace, but shrank from the drudgery on the lines of communication in a burning climate during time of war. Extravagant contracts were made, and regiments were sent up to Sind and Baluchistan without any record of the rate of hire agreed upon for their transport. The Bombay Government was also obstructive, refusing to confirm appointments made by the General on the spot, substituting inefficient men of their own choice and even negativing orders for so vital a matter as limitation of the number of followers. The Supreme Government at Calcutta was quite as casual in its ways. The officer in command at Quetta asked in May what force was to be kept at Quetta during the winter, since it was imperative that the troops should be protected from the cold. The Governor-General answered, after six weeks' delay, that he could not at present say, but would inform the Bombay Government as soon as he had made up his mind. So great was the confusion that Keane, before leaving Afghanistan, predicted the inevitable coming of a great catastrophe.

135

As is well known, there was a general rising of the
Afghans in November, 1841. Many garrisons were isolated or overwhelmed, and that of Kabul, withdrawing
upon the faith of a capitulation, was annihilated during
its retreat. It became necessary to restore the situation
by pushing a column under General Pollock upon
Kabul by way of the Khyber Pass. Owing to the waste
of animals during the previous operations there was the
utmost difficulty in collecting transport of any kind, and
the terror inspired by the fate of the Kabul garrison
multiplied desertion among the camel drivers. As an
example to his officers, Pollock allowed himself as baggage animals no more than one camel and two mules.
His first objective was Jalalabad, where an incompetent
officer had allowed himself to be beleaguered. Pollock
forced his way thither in April, 1842, with little difficulty
or loss; but the contracts for his carriage cattle extended
only to their march to Jalalabad, upon arrival at which
place the Commissary was pledged to return them to
Peshawar. Whether such a contract were concluded by
sheer necessity or by want of foresight, it is difficult to
say; but its results were most serious. Pollock's remaining animals were too few to enable him to move
freely about the country, and depend upon it for supplies
and forage. Moreover, for several marches between
Jalalabad and Kabul, forage was unobtainable. The
establishment of magazines along the line of route
would require so many garrisons that no fighting force
would be left to him. Even if transport animals were
more abundant, the conveyance of forage for them would
so swell their numbers that the protection of convoys
would be impossible. As the political agent—a military
officer—for the Khyber district put it, no force could
conveniently protect more than fifteen days' supplies, besides its treasure, ammunition and baggage, through the
passes. Yet General Nott lay isolated at Kandahar and
it was imperative to withdraw his force by some means.

The Indian Government in May, 1842, increased Pollock's force to fifteen thousand men and, after many changes of mind, at last made a great effort to provide him with transport. It was reckoned that he would require fifty elephants, over five thousand camels and over four thousand bullocks; and by August something approaching to that number had reached him. He then advanced and reached Kabul with little difficulty on the 15th of September. A column had meanwhile made its way to Nott by way of the Bolan Pass, bringing him money which enabled him to equip himself with transport; and early in August he sent part of his artillery and stores under escort of about one-third of his force to Quetta, and marched with the rest almost unresisted to Kabul. The whole then evacuated Afghanistan in November by way of the Khyber Pass.

THE SIND CAMPAIGN OF 1843. The war in Afghanistan found its aftermath in Sind, where a newly appointed commander, Sir Charles Napier, embroiled himself with the Amirs. His force was about eight thousand men, many of them much enfeebled by long work on the line of communication, and his transport consisted of a few hundred camels, passed over to him from those which had been used in Afghanistan, one and all weak and in bad condition. His main line of communication was the Indus, where he had a small steamer. He may be said to have had two bases, one at Karachi and the other at Sukkur, the latter, of course, being what may be called an advanced base, dependent upon Ferozepore. Curiously enough, reinforcements from up and down the river actually reached him at the same place on the same day. His camels being few, he could take the field at first only with three thousand and later with five thousand men. But he made his transport go as far as possible, first by cutting down baggage to the lowest point. Here, like Pollock, he set the example, allowing himself only five camels for his personal needs and for the conveyance of the papers and records of headquarters. Next, he emulated Wellington by sparing no pains to ensure that his beasts should be properly cared for by their drivers. How he, or Wellington for that matter, contrived to secure this most important object, we are not told; but it can hardly have been otherwise than by constant personal vigilance. Napier's diary of the campaign testifies to his constant anxiety for his transport and his satisfaction at the small mortality among his camels. It is certain that within his own command he banished instantly the wastefulness which had for so long been a tradition in the Indian Commissariat and indeed in every one of the three presidential armies.

THE CHINA CAMPAIGN OF 1841-3. We must now turn our eyes yet further east to China, where the arrogance of the Celestial Empire had forced us into a quarrel. It is not worth while to do more than mention that the operations were in the fullest significance of the word amphibious, the troops—about nine thousand in all—being employed mainly to capture shore defences which hindered the passage of the fleet up sundry rivers. They were never on shore for more than a few days together nor moved far from their ships. There was, therefore, little occasion for much land transport, which seems to have been supplied, when needed, by impressing native bearers and, on some occasions, native ponies.

OPERATIONS IN NEW ZEALAND, 1845. We now approach the wars against the Sikhs, the most formidable native enemies that we met in India; but, as a matter of curiosity, it may be worth while to glance at some very tiny operations in New Zealand, the prelude to the more serious contest which was to come a few years later. The scene was the sub-tropical country north of Auckland. The force was four hundred British soldiers; their base was a man-of-war anchored in a little bay; and the objective was a Maori fort, some ten miles away over a wilderness of swamp and forest. The Commander loaded his men with five days' biscuit, two days' cooked meat and thirty rounds of ammunition, transport of any description being absolutely unprocurable. He made a start, but was stopped by forty-eight hours of continuous rain, which ruined both biscuit and ammunition. A second attempt brought him before the fortress, when the Maoris attacked him, and he was compelled to fall back, carrying forty unfortunate wounded men with him. Once again heavy rain had upset his arrangements, impeding his progress and destroying his biscuit. In fact, he had only succeeded in reaching his objective by feeding the men on potatoes (which he found on the ground) and half rations of meat for seven days; and they returned to the ship dead beat. It was ultimately necessary to send to Australia for drays and teams. Many men would sneer at the thought that four hundred men could not march ten miles without carriage. But a mere march is one thing; a march with the prospect of a fight at the end is another.

THE SIKH WARS, 1845-6, 1848-9. With this short interruption we return to India, and for the first time we are carried to the Punjab, where, since the death of Ranjit Sing in 1839, there had been anarchy and confusion. Actual power lay with the Khalsa, or trained army, which in time of peace was ruled by regimental committees; and it was only a question of time before it should seize the reins of government. The Governor-General, Sir Henry Hardinge, was on every account most anxious to remain on good terms with the Sikh rulers, real or nominal, at Lahore; but the situation toward the end of November, 1845, was so menacing that in common prudence he was obliged to make some preparations for assembling a defensive force. Yet he was so extremely reluctant to give even a semblance of offence that when the storm broke and the Sikhs crossed the Sutlej on the 11th of December, 1845, his troops were still widely dispersed. There were seven thousand men at Ferozepore, the most advanced post; sixty miles in rear of it was the principal grain dépôt of the army at Bassian, whither five thousand men were in march from Ludhiana; the nearest force to Bassian was ten thousand men at Ambala, eighty miles further eastward; and another ten thousand lay at Mirat, one hundred and twenty miles from Ambala. The transport of all was as yet scanty and unorganised, through no fault of the Commander-in-Chief, Sir Hugh Gough, but through the intervention of Hardinge, exerted for purely political reasons. The concentration required therefrom to be hurried on with very imperfect means; and a political officer was required by Hardinge to establish at short notice supply dépôts for ten thousand men at intervals of twenty miles along the whole route from Mirat to Ferozepore. He accomplished the task by boundless energy and most high-handed methods in five days; and the whole of the rearward detachments were united on the 17th of December at Badhni, thirteen miles west of Bassian, but still forty-five miles distant from the isolated seven thousand at Ferozepore.

On the following day the army advanced over twenty miles westward to Mudki, and fought an action there; and on the 21st another action was fought at Ferozeshah, ten miles north-west of Mudki, where the army halted until the 24th. It then made two short marches north-westward to the Sutlej, where it remained stationary until the 18th of February, 1846. On this day was fought the action of Sobraon, after which the Sikhs agreed to terms, and the war came to an immediate end. The army, it will be observed, had moved neither far nor fast, when once its concentration had been accomplished.

Military men had little faith in the endurance of peace with the Sikhs, but civilians were more sanguine. A succession of wars had depleted the Indian treasury, and the need for economy was pressing. The whole of the transport of the native troops on the north-west frontier (as it then was) was therefore discharged. In the summer of 1848 signs were multiplied that a rising of the Sikhs was imminent and Gough begged that preparations might be made; but not until September did the Governor-General, Lord Dalhousie, allow them even to be begun. All through October troops were assembling in Ferozepore, but the arrangements of the Commissariat were in a very backward state owing to Dalhousie's delay. The most enterprising of the native contractors, one Lalla Joti Pershad, had already been concerned with the Afghan and the first Sikh campaigns. He was now pressed to provide for the immediate supply of sixty thousand bullocks to carry grain; and at first he declined, upon the ground that the Indian Government already owed him £570,000. Later, however, he relented, and by all accounts performed his part admirably; but this little detail gives some idea of the fashion in which the Bengal Government carried on its wars.

There was an advanced force of cavalry at Lahore, which was pushed on forty miles across the Ravi on the 2nd of November. Gough on the 8th wished to strengthen this cavalry with a strong brigade of infantry from Lahore; and requisition was made for ten days' supplies, with transport to carry them. The Commissariat answered that it could furnish neither the one nor the other. After forty-eight hours of strenuous work food and carriage for two native battalions were somehow provided, and these accordingly joined the cavalry.

Gough himself with the main army could not move until the 16th, when he marched and joined the advanced column at Ramnagar; his force then amounting to seven regiments of cavalry, fifteen battalions of infantry and eleven batteries, light and heavy. Then followed desultory operations for forcing the passage of the Chenab, but nothing decisive. Gough was unable to move his army entire because the Commissariat was unable to feed it. The enemy fell back to the Jhelum, and Gough halted by the Governor-General's order near Wazirabad, until the 10th of January, 1849, when he advanced against the Sikh position at Chilianwala. There he fought a severe action on the 12th, and remained stationary until the 15th of February, when, having been strongly reinforced, he moved eastward by short marches against the Sikhs at Gujrat. There he fought a decisive action on the 21st. His cavalry pressed the pursuit with such energy that they traversed over fifty miles in seventy-two hours, when they halted for three days, having evidently outmarched their supplies and found little food or forage in a country already exhausted by the Sikh. By the 14th of March the pursuing column received the final surrender of the remains of the Sikh army at Rawal Pindi.

It will be remarked that, until the Sikh army had been utterly shattered, no great distances were traversed, and no very rapid marches were made, while two prolonged halts facilitated the task of the Commissariat. With a proper service trained to the management of transport and supply the campaign could certainly have been much shortened.

THE BURMESE CAMPAIGN OF 1852. The next trouble came in Burma, where the Court of Ava had already forgotten the lesson taught in 1824-6. This time the Indian Government, learning from experience, sent out its expedition, about six thousand strong, at the beginning of April, and provided it with plenty of steamships. Rangoon was easily taken, and the inhabitants speedily returned to it to run up shelter for the British, while the bazaar was well supplied with fresh fish, poultry and vegetables. Nothing much was done until October, when the strength of the force was doubled, but even then it found itself powerless without land transport.

Dalhousie, for the sake of economy, had hoped to depend wholly upon water transport; but the Burmese soon discovered that they had only to move three days' march from the river to be perfectly free from molestation, and that they could choose their own time for returning. They could also attack the British outlying posts by the river whenever it pleased them, while the garrisons, having no transport, were unable to sally out and disperse them. Moreover, even the smaller watercraft were liable to be entrapped and overpowered. One chief, in an almost inaccessible stronghold, made a practice of devastating the districts friendly to the British and was always on the watch to pounce upon any unwary boat. In fact, communication by water was insecure without clearing the banks; and this without land transport was impossible. Eventually Dalhousie was obliged to provide land transport, chiefly in the form of elephants; and, in fact, three hundred elephants walked from Arakan into the valley of the Irawadi.

A revolution at Ava shortened the task of the British, but a remarkable march was made by a column of two thousand men, six hundred of whom were white soldiers, the remainder Indian. They started on the 14th of January, 1853, into a tract of unexplored forest, carrying one month's supplies, four heavy howitzers, four light mortars and rocket tubes. Their transport consisted of one hundred and twenty elephants, three hundred bullock carts with teams, and some hundreds of spare bullocks. On the 14th of February they picked up some fresh supplies which had been forwarded by water to a convenient point. There eleven hundred men were left; ten days' supplies for nine hundred men were placed in boats; ten days' more supplies were loaded on the land transport; and on the 23rd of February the nine hundred men reached their objective without the firing of a shot. The whole distance traversed was two hundred and forty miles.

This expedition showed the fallacy of attempting to conduct a river campaign without land transport.

THE KAFFIR WAR OF 1850–2. Meanwhile, ever since the close of the Kaffir War in 1835 there had been constant trouble at the Cape; and in the spring of 1850 (it must be remembered that south of the line October corresponds to April in the northern hemisphere) the unrest among the Kaffirs was stimulated by a terrible drought, which burned up all forage and forbade the sowing of corn. Then swarms of locusts ate up anything green which had survived the drought, and both settlers and Kaffirs were in despair. At the end of December the Kaffirs broke across the frontier; and, worse still, there was a mutiny of Kaffir police and a rebellion of Hottentots on the British side of the marches. In fact there was great danger of a general rising of blacks against whites.

Sir Harry Smith, who had been Governor since 1847, resolved to stand firm on the frontier, despite of the danger in his rear. His advanced base was King William's Town, depending chiefly upon a marine base at East London, from which a chain of posts ran for some sixty miles westward through King William's Town, Fort White and Fort Cox; the lower reaches of the Buffalo River, from King William's Town to the sea, being guarded by a friendly Kaffir chief. But communication with the next important station in rear, Grahamstown, being insecure, Smith was obliged to act upon a double line of operations and establish a second marine base at Port Elizabeth, with a chain of posts running thence north-eastward to Grahamstown. The chain was from that point bifurcated northward to Fort Beaufort, and eastward to Fort Hare, the latter being an intermediate post between Forts Beaufort and Cox. These multitudinous posts very seriously diminished the force at disposal for offensive movement. Smith's British troops did not exceed three battalions, with a few sappers and artillery, to which were added a variety of levies disciplined and undisciplined. Of a total of about nine thousand of all ranks, little more than five thousand five hundred could be counted as a field force.

Transport was an enormous difficulty, oxen being scarce and weak owing to the drought. Much of the country, moreover, was so rugged that pack-animals were substituted for all carriage except the rolling magazines of the mobile troops; the forest, in which most of the operations were conducted, being impassable by wheeled vehicles. The whole problem of supply was baffling in the extreme, for the victualling of the various posts even for a few weeks compelled the use of large unwieldy convoys, every one of which demanded a strong escort. Again, the accumulation of any great bulk of victuals in any one of these posts—say, sufficient to furnish a week's rations for a mobile column—almost inevitably signified an increase of the garrison. In fact it was impossible to collect any great store of provisions without collecting also more mouths to consume them. The men suffered greatly from hardship and fatigue. Mobile columns escorted so many days' supplies from some post to the scene of action (the hardest of the work was done in the Amatola mountains), fought there until those supplies were exhausted, and then escorted the transport back to the dépôt to be refilled. Tents, except little dog-kennels which a man could carry under his arm, were unknown. One brigade was in the field for seven weeks with only one blanket to each man. The soldiers had to move with musket, bayonet, water-canteen and three days' rations through thorny forest, which tore the clothes off their backs, against a wary, dangerous and invisible enemy, returning wearied out to bivouac in a sea of mud. Sometimes a bitter blast from the mountains would chill them to the bone. Then the wind would change and they sought shade from the overpowering heat of the sun. The natural result was much sickness, which put a fresh strain upon the transport. But though it was physically impossible to give the men adequate clothing and shelter, Harry Smith recorded with pride that they had never gone without food; and this, in the peculiar circumstances, was something to boast of.

This was Harry Smith's last campaign. He had fought in South America, in the Peninsula from beginning to end, at New Orleans, at Waterloo, in South Africa, in India and again in South Africa. He had served also in time of peace in Nova Scotia and Jamaica. He was, perhaps, Wellington's most brilliant pupil, and, like his great master, he understood the vital importance of transport and supply.

CHAPTER VII

THE CRIMEAN WAR; THE LAND TRANS-
PORT CORPS AND THE MILITARY
TRAIN. 1854–1867.

The Crimean War of 1854–6. In 1854 England drifted into war with Russia in a fashion which is still not very easy to explain. If there were any sound reason for hostilities, it lay in the advance of Russia eastward towards India, and in the expediency of maintaining Turkey as a standing menace upon her southern flank. However that may be, the bare facts are that Russia invaded Moldavia and Wallachia in October, 1853, that Turkey declared war upon her immediately thereafter, and that France and England thereupon severed diplomatic relations with Russia. An open rupture might still have been avoided, but England and France in the spring of 1854 peremptorily required the Tsar, on pain of war, to withdraw his troops from Moldavia and Wallachia. The Tsar returned no answer, and on the 28th of March hostilities were finally proclaimed.

Ever since Waterloo the British Army had been maintained at a strength quite inadequate to the many duties thrust upon it, and had, it must be repeated, been worked almost to death. But for the peculiar system which regulated the tenure of commissions in the cavalry and infantry, and the traditions of regimental pride which had been cherished for generations, the Army might well have perished altogether. But it

147

survived as a collection of regiments, and the House of Commons took good care that it should be no more. All the auxiliary services so carefully built up by Wellington in the Peninsula were gradually pared down until at last there was little of them left to abolish. The Quartermaster-General's Staff Corps, which had done such wonderful work for Wellington, was thoughtlessly swept away. The last remnant of the Waggon Train had been destroyed in 1834. There was no Commissariat Establishment in England. That in Ireland, despite of the entreaties of the Treasury for its maintenance as a nucleus that might be expanded in case of emergency, had been done away with. Sir Charles Trevelyan, the Secretary of the Treasury, had in 1850 protested very earnestly against the fatal policy of keeping no reserve of trained Commissariat officers. "An army", he had written, "is quite as helpless without a properly trained Commissariat as without ammunition." His warning was unheeded. British Cabinet Ministers had still to learn, in spite of two centuries of teaching, that a soldier must eat before he can shoot.

The British troops were in the first instance sent to Malta, whence they were gradually transferred by the end of May either to Gallipoli or to Scutari. They numbered about twenty-six thousand, and their commander, Lord Raglan, contemplated the transfer of them to Varna in Bulgaria, where, with the help of the French, who were about thirty thousand strong, they would support the Turks in resisting a Russian advance upon Constantinople. But the Commissariat department was so weak in officers that the Commissary-General, Mr Filder, a veteran of the Peninsula, doubted his ability to feed the army in Bulgaria. Upon this luckless department fell the entire burden of providing money, of making all contracts for supplies and stores, and of furnishing provisions, forage, fuel and light, besides transport, whether by land or sea. Filder himself toiled indefatigably from morning to night, but he could not do everything himself, and his few subordinates had most of them no knowledge whatever of their business. From the very first disembarkation at Gallipoli all and sundry had cursed the Commissariat for its inefficiency. "We are all disposed to throw a stone at it", wrote Raglan. It was a repetition of the story of the Peninsular army in 1809. Raglan did not join in the cry, but in June wrote to the Secretary for War, asking him to form and send out to him a land transport corps.

Meanwhile the troops were gradually landed at Varna, and by the end of June were all, except some of the cavalry, upon the spot. Filder's misgivings were for the time banished, for on the 22nd of June the Russians, repeatedly worsted by the Turks, had fallen back from the Danube to the Pruth, their retreat being secured by Austria, who occupied Moldavia and Wallachia, under an agreement with Turkey, with her own troops. The Allies, therefore, remained stationary, suffering much from the climate, and Filder was able to collect a sufficiency of pack-animals from Turkey, Syria and Tunis. There were many deaths from dysentery, typhus and cholera, and even the sound men were weak, pallid and depressed. This went on until August, when the Allied commanders received orders from their Governments to attack and destroy Sevastopol, Russia's most important arsenal and naval station in the Black Sea. This enterprise had long been discussed at home and clamoured for by the press; but a veteran general warned the Secretary for War that it was sheer madness. Sevastopol was invulnerable on the side of the sea, and it would be difficult to force the line of defence on the side of the land, because any besieging force would be exposed to attack in rear by all the forces in the south of Russia. Raglan knew and appreciated the folly of the plan as well as anyone. The naval Commander-in-Chief, Admiral Dundas, expressed grave misgivings as to his ability, not to land the army, but to supply it when landed and to re-embark it in case of mishap. It was, however, certain that if these officers refused to undertake the operation, the Government would send other commanders, who were more complaisant; so Raglan and Dundas prepared to obey.

The embarkation of the troops was accordingly begun at Varna on the 24th of August. Filder dared not embark his pack-animals, from uncertainty of obtaining forage for them; but on approaching the Crimean coast on the 13th of September he sent home a requisition for two thousand tons of hay. On the 14th of September the infantry of the allied armies landed unopposed on an open beach thirty miles to north of Sevastopol. At noon the wind rose and the surf was so high as to forbid the landing of the cavalry until the afternoon of the 15th. So there the Allies were, some sixty thousand strong, including a small force of Turks, with no base but the floating base of the fleet, with which bad weather might at any moment sever communication. Men were still dropping down with cholera, but the British had left their ambulance waggons behind, either from lack of horses or insufficiency of tonnage. The British had no land transport of any kind and the men were one and all too weak to carry their packs. The Quartermaster-General, before many of the battalions had been landed, swooped upon a small Russian convoy, of which he had caught sight, drove away the escort and so secured seventy or eighty bullock carts loaded with flour and wood. These he carried off, hoping to use them for the transport of camp equipage. They were, however, promptly claimed by the Commissary and were yielded up as of right to him, though he returned a few for the carriage of hospital tents, hospital comforts and entrenching tools. About three hundred carts in all were collected, with their teams and drivers, during the following days, and thus on the 19th the army was able to advance. On the 20th it won the battle of the Alma, which cleared the way to Sevastopol; but, owing to the hesitation of the French Commander-in-Chief, it did not again move until the 23rd. Making a flank march, it rounded the defences of Sevastopol and came up before the south side of the fortress on the 26th. Riding ahead, Raglan caught sight of the harbour of Balaclava and saw a British man-of-war steam into it. The French Commander-in-Chief handsomely offered him his choice of that or of two other inlets, Kamiesch Bay and Katcha Bay, a few miles further to the north, only stipulating that, if Raglan should select Balaclava, the British should take the right of the line, which had hitherto been occupied by the French. The right of the line signified the section over against the south-eastern front of Sevastopol, some eight miles from Balaclava; the left of the line meant the south-western front, no more than three or four miles from the bays of Kamiesch and Katcha. On the advice of Admiral Lyons, the second in command of the fleet, Raglan decided to take Balaclava as the British marine base. It was perfectly safe, but it measured only six furlongs in length by one in breadth.

However, it was something to have regained safe communication with the fleet, even through the medium of so tiny a haven as Balaclava, though the situation even so was anxious. For the Russians on the night of the 22nd had barred the entrance to Sevastopol harbour by sinking twelve ships across its mouth, so that, even if the fortress were speedily taken, it might be long before the allies could use the harbour as a base. Moreover, it was impossible for the allies to invest the place completely, for their numbers were too weak; wherefore the Russians could, and did, pour reinforcements continually into it from the north side. The position of the allies was on a scarped plateau overlooking the fortress, with a general front to the north; and the southern border of this plateau was so steeply scarped by nature as to make their rear impregnable. The French marine bases, being more or less within this impregnable line, were safe; but Balaclava lay two miles outside it, so that it was always possible for the Russians to threaten the British communications. Lastly, the only metalled road to the British position on the plateau—the Woronzoff Road—ran not from Balaclava, but east and west across the open plain two miles to north of it, so that the Russians might impede operations greatly by the mere seizure of this road even if they failed to capture Balaclava itself. A line of redoubts was, therefore, thrown up on some low heights for the protection of this road, and was committed to the guardianship of the Turks.

Regular investment being out of the question, it was decided to bombard Savastopol heavily and then to storm it out of hand. Fatigue duties, in the dearth of animals, fell very heavily upon the troops; and even so the preparations went forward slowly. The first bombardment was opened on the 17th of October, but there was no assault. On the 25th a Russian field-force established itself at Tchorgun, within six miles of Balaclava and advanced against the British marine base. It was beaten back but retained control of the Woronzoff Road. On the 26th part of the garrison made a reconnaissance in some force of the extreme right of the British position, about Inkerman; and on the 5th of November they delivered a combined attack by the garrison of Sevastopol and the field-force at Tchorgun against the same point. They were again defeated; but the British, already much weakened by fatigue and hardship, suffered severely. After the action Raglan realised that the army must winter upon the plateau and that, though nominally the besiegers, they were really besieged. On the 7th he took measures for the metalling of the direct road from Balaclava to the British position by parties of Turks; but on the 10th the work was stopped by heavy and constant rains, which reduced both trenches and roads to seas of sticky mud. The work of bringing up provisions now became very difficult; but the hay applied for in September had not yet arrived, though part of it was nearing Balaclava, and consequently Filder still dared not bring over his pack-animals. The want of land transport had made itself felt in other ways also. Camp kettles, in the ratio of one to every five men, had been issued to the troops on landing; but the men not having the strength to carry even their packs, these kettles soon disappeared. The soldiers were therefore reduced to cooking in their mess tins, which would not hold enough water to extract the brine from their ration of salt pork. The result was that they frequently ate it raw; and this, added to cold and exposure in the trenches, induced diarrhoea and dysentery. Every name added to the sick list of course meant more work for those who remained in health; and thus was established a vicious circle which threatened slowly but surely to exterminate the army.

The crisis was hastened by a catastrophe of nature. A violent circular storm burst over the camp on the night of the 14th, laying every tent flat, overturning waggons, and drenching the plateau first with rain and later with sleet and snow. One party of one hundred and fifty men returning to camp from the trenches in the teeth of the gale took four hours to march five miles, and left seven of their number prostrate behind them. At sea the captains of all the craft off Balaclava raced for the harbour, where there was not nearly room for them, and many vessels were badly damaged. But a formidable number were lost outright, one in particular filled with warm clothing, and another with about fifty tons of forage, the first meagre instalment of the two thousand tons asked for two months earlier. French and Turkish shipping did not escape lightly, and nature taught a grim lesson as to the danger of insecure marine bases.

After this terrible visitation the task of bringing food

and forage, to say nothing of clothing, material for huts and stores of war, became desperate. The track from Balaclava to the camp became a sea of mud knee-deep, littered with the corpses of exhausted beasts. Men and horses died like flies of starvation and exposure. In spite of much confusion in the stowage of ships, there was abundance of everything at Balaclava. The wharves erected by the overworked engineers had, it is true, a frontage of less than thirty yards, but by sheer resolution and hard work huge cargoes had been discharged. The Commissariat, it is also true, being short-handed and in want of proper buildings, could not keep their goods in order. Yet, if soldiers had strength to reach Balaclava they never returned empty-handed. It was three thousand miles, roughly speaking, from England to Balaclava; three thousand miles and eight from England to the camp; and it was the odd eight miles that made the difference. Cavalry horses and artillery horses were pressed into the transport service; but there was no forage for them. All efforts of the Commissaries to procure forage locally had failed. The horses ate each other's tails and the spokes of the gun wheels in their hunger and died.

There was great indignation in England when the facts became known, and violent outcry against the General and his staff. But the whole fault lay with the Government. It was they who, in the first instance, had dictated an insane plan of campaign. Ever since June, 1854, Raglan had been asking for a land transport corps. There was no attempt to form one till March, 1855. Ever since August Raglan had been enquiring where the army should winter and what preparations he should make and where he should make them. The Government's only reply had been that he must land in the Crimean peninsula. The Commissary-General had asked for two thousand tons of hay on the 13th of September, 1854. Up to the end of November only two hundred tons had been received, and the whole quantity did not reach the Crimea until June, 1855. In November, 1854, Raglan asked for three thousand tents and for a floating steam bakery. The tents took from five to seven months to reach the Crimea, and the bakery made its appearance in May, 1855. Such were the fashion in which the British Government dealt with the requirements of war. It was, of course, nothing new. There had been quite as serious lapses in Flanders in 1794. The nearest parallel to the disastrous winter of 1854-5 in the Crimea was that in Flanders and Holland in 1794-5. Yet a vast deal of experience had been accumulated between 1795 and 1815. Abercromby had laid it down strongly in 1799 that an army cannot move without horses and waggons. But all experience was thrown away upon Ministers, or rather upon the House of Commons which appointed them.

Under the stress of public indignation the Government which had drifted into war was turned out of office, and a new administration began to set things right in the usual way by wild squandering of money. Steps were taken to convert Balaclava into a better base, though no money could increase its area. A corps of labourers was sent out to build a railway from Balaclava to the camp. The Commissariat was suddenly and violently transferred from the Treasury to the War Office, and the Land Transport Corps began to take shape under the command of Colonel McMurdo.

This corps, the first germ of the present Army Service Corps, was not at the first a success. Hastily improvised organisations very rarely are so. Money was not grudged; and the terms offered to the Land Transport Corps were, at the time, liberal. The men were enlisted for ten or twelve years, terminable with option of discharge after five years or at the end of the war. The first two thousand recruits received a bounty and 1s. 8d. a day; and those subsequently levied received no bounty and 2s. 6d. a day. (The pay of a private of the line at this time was 1s. 1d. a day, of which 8½d. was deducted for rations, groceries and vegetables, while out of the remaining 3½d. he had to pay for barrack damages, washing and the renewal of forage cap, shell jacket, three shirts, razor, brushes, mits, soap, sponge and haversack.) Some of the officers were deserving non-commissioned officers selected from other regiments of the regular army, and a good many were officers transferred from the Indian Army. But, in spite of the high wages offered, many of the recruits were mere boys, without any knowledge of horses or of driving; and the demoralisation bred by good pay was not at first corrected by discipline. Again, most of the officers from India had accepted commissions in the hope that they had found an easy place, for which habits of laziness and luxury in India thoroughly fitted them. Thus, though Sevastopol had fallen and operations were practically suspended before the winter of 1855, though the army was stationary and the difficulties to be encountered were trifling as compared with the winter of 1854, yet in November, 1855, the Land Transport Corps was on the point of breaking down. Thereupon Colonel Wetherall, of the Quartermaster-General's department, took the corps in hand, made a clean sweep of bad and useless officers and by vigorous and ruthless measures created order and efficiency. By 1856, when the British Army was really fully equipped and in fine fettle, our French allies were sick of the war. At first they had outdone us in every point of organisation, for they had been wise enough not to neglect their auxiliary departments. Nevertheless after eighteen months in the field, they began to fall behind us. In all sanitary matters they were backward, and after the fall of Sevastopol they lost thousands of men from typhoid fever. But it is surprising to learn that they found the greatest difficulty in feeding a detachment of outlying troops, though at no greater distance than forty miles from Kamiesch Bay. Evidently their transport and supply service was failing for one reason or another. The British Land Transport Corps, on the other hand, organised in battalions and companies, had by this time risen to nine thousand men, of whom seven thousand were actually in the Crimea, with twenty-four thousand horses. This would have been more satisfactory if it had not come just two years too late.

It must, however, be noted that the Land Transport Corps existed for transport only. The Commissariat was still in charge of supply; and even so the calls upon it were so heavy that the Empire was ransacked to find Commissaries who had some knowledge of their business. Old retired officers were hurried out to the Crimea, but they sufficed not to satisfy the continual demand for capable men. Volunteers were, therefore, sought for in all quarters and accepted without much enquiry. Most of them proved to be useless and expensive encumbrances. But, even if the Commissariat had been never so efficient, it was still hampered by the old prejudice that restricted it to supply only. Though it had been transferred from the Treasury to the War Office it still preserved its civil status and had no control whatever over the Land Transport Corps. Thus there was one authority in charge of the waggon and another in charge of the load, which was unsound in principle; and, worse than that, the setting of supply upon a civil and transport upon a military basis, tended to make the transport service give itself the airs of a combatant corps, thus widening the breach between two services which should have been from the first united into one.

THE MILITARY TRAIN, 1856. When the Crimean War ended in 1856 the Land Transport Corps was at once reduced to twelve hundred men and rechristened the Military Train. Sir William Codrington, who had fought all through the Crimean War, and risen to be Commander-in-Chief after the fall of Sevastopol, protested very strongly in the House of Commons against this false economy. So small a train, as he justly said, would only suffice for a division*; and he urged not only that every expedition sent over sea should take its own transport corps with it, but that the corps should be trained to its duties for active service (which included ambulance work) at home. Of course so sensible a suggestion received no notice from the House of Commons. In 1858 the Military Train was further reduced to eleven hundred men, and Codrington again remonstrated in words that are rather significant. "The Military Train", he said, "should not be kept as a matter of economy to do a variety of dirty things"; it should (I condense his speech) be put to its right purpose to enable troops to move with their *impedimenta*. And once again he advocated that all arms should be trained to these duties, and that pack-horses should be kept at Aldershot.

Meanwhile the reduction itself provided some trouble. More than one hundred of the officers of the Land Transport Corps had been promoted non-commissioned officers; and it was cruel to turn them adrift without any retiring allowance. The grievance was brought forward in the House of Commons; but the Government dared not remedy it lest other officers of other branches, who lacked private means, should claim the same indulgence. The truth is that the Land Transport Corps—or Military Train—had been improvised without the slightest care or forethought. It was the original design to exclude it from the system of purchase of commissions like the artillery and engineers. But purchase crept in by stealth, for by entering the Military Train officers could avoid service in the colonies. For some years the

* An infantry division at this time counted from eight to ten battalions.

Secretary for War evaded the awkward question, pretty frequently repeated: "Was the Military Train a purchase corps or was it not?" After about ten years of existence it was finally decided, not by authority but by sheer force of custom, that it was a purchase corps. And this was a misfortune, for it tended to make it a refuge for slack officers who wished to shirk peace service with their regiments abroad.

Circumstances, which shall very shortly be narrated, gave a very curious twist to the career of the Military Train; but before following them it will be best to say a word about the work of both Commissariat and Military Train at home. In 1853, as an astounding novelty, a camp of exercise had been formed at Chobham. Such a thing had never been known before in time of peace. Dublin had been for generations the only quarter in the British Isles where it was possible to hold a brigade field day. In the same year Aldershot was purchased as an exercising-ground; and, since there was some doubt whether it should be a training-ground or a permanent station, the question was compromised by covering it with wooden huts instead of barracks. A large force of militia was quartered there during the Crimean War. At the outset it was very far from an attractive place, but the mere concentration of a considerable body of men in a single station made a vast difference to the soldier. Provisions could be bought in greater bulk and so retailed more cheaply to the rank and file. The Commissariat also established its own bakeries, and issued at Aldershot bread far superior to that produced in London. It also purchased slaughter-cattle, set up its own butcheries and issued not only the bread and meat rations but also (in return for a stoppage) tea and other groceries. In fact, as Mr Sidney Herbert said in the House of Commons in 1859, all the business of victualling was conducted as it would be in war. From Aldershot these improvements spread to foreign stations; and by 1861 the stoppages had so far been adjusted to local conditions that, for the first time in the history of the Army, the net pay of the soldier was the same all over the Empire.

With this glance at the progress of affairs at home let us now pass on to the wars which followed quickly upon the Crimean campaign.

THE INDIAN MUTINY, 1857–8. In May, 1857, there began a mutiny at Mirat which spread rapidly to the entire native army in Bengal. The disposition of the European troops was at that time so fatuous that the mischief was not easily to be arrested. There were at the moment five regiments of European cavalry and twenty-nine battalions of European infantry, of the Queen's and the East India Company's services, very widely scattered between the Indus and the Irawadi. Of the twenty-nine battalions three were just concluding a petty war in Persia, one had a wing at Aden, three were in Burma and twelve in the recently conquered Punjab, leaving only ten and a half battalions to look to the rest of India. On the immense line of communication between Calcutta and Peshawar there was one battalion at Dinapore, two hundred miles from Calcutta, and then no more until the Jumna was reached at Cawnpore, where there was a dépôt of infantry and a weak reserve company of artillery. Further up the Jumna, there was one weak battalion at Agra, and not so much as a company at Delhi. Turning north-eastward from Allahabad towards Oudh, there was only a single weak battalion at Lucknow, and not a semblance of a force of all three arms until at Mirat, forty miles north of Delhi, there were to be found one regiment of cavalry, one battalion and two batteries.

The mutineers made Delhi their chief centre; and the Commander-in-Chief at once began to concentrate a small force at Ambala to move upon Delhi. But his difficulties were great. The Indian Government, true to the British traditions, had, from motives of economy, abolished such permanent transport service as there was. The bazaars were disorganised by the prevailing unrest; provisions were difficult to collect; and contractors for supply and transport were not easily to be found. However, thirty-five hundred men arrived before Delhi on the 7th of June, the original outbreak at Mirat having taken place on the 10th of May. Though Delhi did not fall until the 21st of September, it does not seem that the force, which was gradually increased to nine thousand men, was ever in any difficulty about supplies.

On the line of communication, Cawnpore was early in peril. A little column of two thousand men under General Havelock, which was pushed up to relieve it, arrived too late, the garrison having surrendered and been massacred on the 27th of June, whereas Havelock did not reach Cawnpore until the 16th of July. The fall of this place reacted upon the safety of Lucknow where from the 1st of July the Residency was closely besieged. The Commissioner, however, Sir Henry Lawrence, had providently laid in vast supplies of grain, which were the salvation of British rule in that part of India.

Havelock's original column being too weak to force its way to Lucknow, he was compelled to halt at Cawnpore for a month to await reinforcements. It does not appear that he found any difficulty in feeding his troops there nor on his subsequent march to Lucknow, where he entered the Residency on the 27th of September. Now was revealed an extraordinary miscalculation on the part of Sir James Outram (who really commanded Havelock's column, but had allowed Havelock to lead it to Lucknow) and of the commandant of the Lucknow garrison. Both of the Commissaries in Lucknow had been disabled; no one else seemed to know or to be capable of ascertaining what supplies were actually in store; and the commandant, growing anxious, had put his garrison upon half rations. Outram, having learned of this, had hastened his march, storing his baggage at the Alam Bagh, a large building on the outskirts of Lucknow and three miles from the Residency. His idea had been to retire from the Residency immediately, taking the beleaguered garrison with him; and on reaching it he begged the Financial Commissioner to negotiate with the people at Lucknow in order to obtain for him the necessary transport. Amazing as it may seem, he had not realised that the garrison had been for four months cut off from the world and that not a cart nor a bullock could be procured. He was, therefore, obliged to stay where he was; and, since he had brought with him no bakers, no wine, spirits, tea, coffee, sugar, nor medical comforts, few medicines and no chloroform, he really made the garrison more secure indeed, but by no means more comfortable nor more healthy. Fortunately it was discovered that there was grain enough for everyone till the end of the year; otherwise it is hard to say what might have happened. Even as things were, the mortality among the garrison from want of the simplest comforts was very serious; and the whole story shows incredible want of forethought and imagination.

Outram was in turn relieved by Sir Colin Campbell in November. Sir Colin found the military authorities at Calcutta utterly helpless and incapable, but in all his operations he seems to have encountered no difficulty in collecting supplies and transport. Latterly, if not throughout, his army trailed about the country with the huge mass of *impedimenta* which was the traditional encumbrance of an army in India. An enterprising enemy could have given him endless trouble, but the mutineers, speaking generally, were not a formidable foe. All rules of strategy and tactics might be and were safely neglected against them.

More interesting is the march of Sir Hugh Rose across Central India from Mhow to the Jumna at Kalpi—a thousand miles. His force was small, not above six thousand men, and, since he wished to move rapidly, he took immense pains over his transport, depending chiefly upon camels, and ordered his officers to leave their heavy baggage behind. His movement did not begin until January, 1858, so that there was time for some of the Military Train to join him. He did not report favourably of it. It was, he said, inefficient for war. The waggons were bad whether for conveyance of freight or of sick. The officers were too much suited to the combatant branches of the Army.

Here Sir Hugh hit the real blot upon the Military Train. Being military, it looked down upon the Commissariat, which was civil, and being mounted, it gave itself the airs and graces of cavalry. The cavalry, of course, has always been the senior service in the British Army, that seniority deriving from the days when a trooper brought his own horse to the muster, thereby approving himself a man of some substance and social rank. But even within my own memory the cavalry affected to look down upon the infantry from a great height of exaltation; and they made the most of close-fitting jackets and overalls and of ringing spurs. As a matter of fact they were recruited, generally speaking, from a better class and, having their horses to look after as well as themselves, had less time to get into mischief and were consequently better conducted. The Military Train aped this superiority of the cavalry, which was well enough in its way, but forgot that it was not their business to be cavalry. During the Indian Mutiny white men were so valuable that the Military Train were readily turned into dragoons, and as such charged batteries and took guns creditably enough. But for their own legitimate business they were useless not only in India, but, as shall presently be seen, in other campaigns also. It was a very great pity that they failed Sir Hugh Rose. His greatest difficulty, as he himself said, was unorganised and inefficient transport all the way from Bombay to the Jumna. He was certainly the most brilliant commander in India during the Mutiny, and did marvels by sheer resolution and force of will. But in spite of amazing energy he could not look to everything himself, and his transport and encumbrances seem to have increased steadily with every stage of his march. Such is always the tendency unless the chief transport officer be ruthless and inexorable. The Military Train missed their chance of a tribute from a really fine officer; and two or three charges as cavalry were a poor exchange for it, since every mounted man, military or civil, was ready enough to gallop into the middle of the mutineers.

THE CHINA WAR OF 1860. The same failing was repeated in the China War which followed immediately upon the suppression of the Mutiny, and was in fact conducted by troops taken straight from India under Sir Hope Grant, one of the most successful commanders. The rendezvous was at Hong Kong; and thither came from England a battalion of the Military Train, which was promptly broken up into three divisions, denominated the Horse Transport Train. One of these divisions was sent off to Japan to buy horses and cattle. The remainder should by right have made all the arrangements for the transport, but this they were neither willing nor competent to do. Since there was no forage except such as was imported, it was desirable to employ as few animals as possible. A large corps of Chinese coolie bearers was, therefore, formed and organised by an Indian officer; and apart from them the transport was composed of horses, asses, pack-mules, bullocks and every conceivable beast that could be found, with drivers from Manila, China, Bombay and Madras—a polyglot assembly, very trying to the patience. In the middle of May the British, about fourteen thousand strong, and their French allies, seven thousand strong, embarked and sailed to the Gulf of Pechili, where the former landed at Talienwan and the latter at Chifu, to form their dépôts for the coming campaign.

There was now some delay, for the French were rather helpless, having little experience of such expeditions; but on the 20th of July the armament sailed to the appointed anchorage off the Pei-tang-ho, landed on the 30th and 31st and on the 1st of August, unopposed, and seized Pei-tang. For ten days the British were busily employed in making wharves, landing supplies and stores and repairing roads; during which interval it was noticed that the French soldiers, owing to the defects of their Commissariat, spent much of their time in hunting for food. The first objective was the Taku Forts, about ten miles distant. By the 13th the allies had advanced over eight of these ten miles, when they halted to accumulate ten days' supplies. On the 21st the forts were taken with little difficulty or loss and on the 25th the troops marched to Tientsin, which they reached on the 5th of September. There the Chinese government gulled the British diplomatists attached to the army for a week with specious negotiations, and contrived in that time that most of the drivers and beasts, which had been laboriously collected, should all vanish on the night of the 9th. Means of conveyance being thus curtailed, only one division was able to advance, and that by small detachments, upon Pekin. The second division did not come up until the 2nd of October. Pekin was surrendered on the 13th, and so the operations came to an end.

This little campaign brought out vividly the difficulties which attend the separation of transport and supply under different heads. There was constant friction between the Commissariat, which was responsible for supply, and the Navy and the Military Train, which were responsible for transport afloat and ashore. Both declined to take any orders from the Commissariat. One of the Divisional Commanders, Sir John Michel,

Commissary-General Power, and Deputy Assistant Commissary Bailey, all wrote down their opinions upon the question and they were not favourable to the Military Train.

Michel declared roundly that the officers were drawn from the wrong class, being men rejected from the Army and other professions, whereas they should be yeomen. The Military Train, in his opinion, should be a civil corps, the men being enlisted for five years and drilled only to the use of firearms. All grades should be open to the men, and promotion should be governed as far as possible by merit. "No task in war is more arduous, no drudgery more severe, no post more thankless than that of Transport Officer. He should not in war be debarred from honours." Finally, if the corps must be military, officers should receive special commissions in the transport service only.

Bailey reported that he began by putting the horse and bullock transport (fifteen hundred Orientals and forty-five hundred animals) under the Military Train. He found that the Military Train knew nothing about the work, thought it a grievance to be under the Commissariat, and wanted to be light cavalry. He complained that the officers did not understand transport work and that there was much insubordination and drunkenness among the men; and he concluded that the Transport Corps ought not to be a purchase corps, nor a combatant corps; advocating that the men should be lightly equipped with hunting saddles and unarmed except with a revolver for self-defence.

A combatant officer of the Quartermaster-General's department, Lieutenant-Colonel Garnet Wolseley, in his narrative of the campaign was even more severe upon the Military Train:

On the long narrow causeway which runs between Peh-tang and Sin-ho, where from daylight to dark strings of baggage animals and waggons were passing and repassing, you might see these semi-dragoons lolling half asleep over their holster-pipes, although perhaps some accident had occurred which they appeared to have consigned to Providence or to the unassisted exertions of the pony to remedy. As to dismounting for the purpose of assisting a Manila driver or coolie, the idea did not seem to occur to them as either desirable or necessary. After the day's work was ended, the animals were tied up by their native drivers, upon whose humanity it depended very much whether they were fed or watered.

As to the actual material, Bailey had much fault to find. The Maltese carts sent out from England were defective; the four-wheeled waggons (originally made for the Crimea) were of faulty construction; the wood had perished; and the harness, being of bad material and workmanship, had rotted with long storage.

But the hottest of the battle raged over the control of the transport. All officers of the Commissariat claimed that it should be in their hands without any restriction whatever. Commissary-General Power complained that, in China, the Navy refused to load the ships or to anchor them conveniently, as desired by the Commissariat. Naval officers would even transfer loads to other ships or unload vessels without the Commissary's knowledge; and he did not hesitate to say that, if the campaign had lasted much longer, very serious difficulties would have arisen. As to land transport, both Sir John Michel and the Commissaries agreed that the Commissariat must have absolute and unfettered command of every scrap of it; and Bailey was careful to point out that separate transport for regimental purposes—ammunition, camp equipage and baggage—must not be exempt, since often it had no work for weeks together. But the final word was spoken by Colonel Clark Kennedy, Commandant of the Military Train, in a letter of the 18th of December, 1860:

I cannot too strongly express my opinion that any system based upon the provision of the food for the Army by the Commissariat and its independent conveyance by the Military Train would result in failure in the field—in short the two branches are so indissolubly united in the field that they must work together; and any attempt to work them independently and without accord would result in loss and injury to the service.

Thus was strongly affirmed the principle that the man responsible for the waggon must also be responsible for the load. That it must ultimately prevail was certain; but whether the man responsible were to be a civilian or a military man was not so easily to be decided. The experience of the next little war was still to leave the question open.

THE NEW ZEALAND WAR OF 1861-5. Fresh trouble broke out with the Maoris in New Zealand in 1861, the scene of action being the tract, roughly speaking, between Auckland and New Plymouth in the North Island. The Maoris were a fine and chivalrous enemy whose military code favoured a pre-arranged fight at a given time and place where the best man should win. But their favourite tactic was to build strong fortifications, or *pas*, in some place from whence retreat was easy, in the hope that their adversary would butt his head against them. In this case they reckoned, most frequently with justice, that he would lose more men than they, which to them signified victory. Their main strength was that they occupied a central position, the British settlements, all weak and small, being scattered on the coast all round them. Thus, being rapid in movement, they could strike in any direction, compelling the British commander to divide his force for the protection of all points.

The British base was Auckland, which has a good port to east, and another Onehunga, with a bad bar, to west. As the chief scene of action was the west coast, Onehunga was practically the port of the base. All the ports on the west coast of New Zealand are poor, and the sea about New Zealand is proverbially tempestuous, so that the marine difficulties were formidable. Thus

168

the first petty operations were begun from New Plymouth. Now no sailing ship would ever linger off New Plymouth for a moment longer than she could help, while even steamers were constantly obliged to put to sea and remain at sea for days together. Later the scene was shifted to the Waikato River, the mouth of which is much nearer to Auckland than New Plymouth; but there was not always shipping enough to convey the stores and supplies; and then, as shall be seen, the route became a strange alternation of land and water.

The first Commissariat Transport Corps was formed by the General in command in 1861, and consisted of two companies, each of one hundred men, with three hundred and twenty-five animals, pack and draught. In 1863, when the more serious operations began, the corps rose to thirteen companies; the land companies each of three officers, one hundred and thirty-five other ranks and two hundred animals; and the water companies of three officers, one hundred other ranks and boats. The total strength was forty-one officers, fourteen hundred and sixty-six other ranks, fifteen hundred and sixteen horses and seven hundred and twenty-eight draught-bullocks. The combatant force, at its strongest, numbered ten thousand men.

The difficulties which the Transport Corps had to overcome were enormous. There was only one road running from Auckland for about forty miles south; and this the Commissariat Transport Corps had helped to make. The operations, however, extended to a distance of one hundred and eighty-two miles from the base, with ten changes from water to land carriage. Thus the first six miles from Auckland to Onehunga were traversed with carts; then came thirty-five miles, covered partly by boats, partly by a Commissariat steamer; the next fifteen miles was in charge of the Commissariat boats; over the next five miles the boats were partly from the Royal Navy, partly from the Commissariat; the next fifteen miles were traversed by boats, if the water permitted, if not by pack-animals; the next five miles were water, and the following five once more water, both of which were entrusted first to the Navy and were taken over by the Commissariat; and the last fifteen miles of all were traversed by a Commissariat steamer. The reason for all these changes was that the route wandered from creeks into rivers and from rivers back to creeks; and the rivers were no ordinary rivers, for volcanic action is still alive in the North Island of New Zealand. That the streams should be shallow, subject to rapid changes and treacherous was nothing very peculiar, but that they should run in places over submerged forest was not very usual. At first the Commissariat trusted very much to the Navy for boats, but the bluejackets plundered the supplies freely at every transhipment, making special havoc of consignments of rum. Indeed the naval authorities declined to give receipts or to take any responsibility for supplies which were committed to their boats' crews. The Commissariat therefore designed their own boats—forty-two feet long and ten feet in beam—and, as has been told, trained their own crews. In 1864 a detachment of the Military Train came out, whereupon the Commissariat represented that, unless left to themselves, they could not undertake to feed the troops. The General, Sir Duncan Cameron, wisely declined to upset existing arrangements, and sent the Military Train to work in and about Auckland. In one action only do we find them in the field, and then acting as cavalry.

The whole campaign was peculiar inasmuch as the country itself could produce nothing except fuel. The Colony was still in rather a primitive state, and almost all supplies, except now and then a few slaughter-cattle, were perforce fetched from a distance, Australia being, of course, the nearest point. It fell, therefore, to the Commissariat to provide everything, not only bread, meat and spirits but vegetables and groceries also; and they did so with astonishing success. They had an amazingly difficult country to deal with, an untamed land of forest and scrub, steep gradients and deep hollows; but they overcame all obstacles and recorded with some pride that they frequently delivered freshly baked bread from field ovens. Altogether these New Zealand campaigns redounded greatly to the credit of the Commissariat, when, as must be emphasised, it was in control of transport as well as of supply.

THE AMBELA CAMPAIGN OF 1863. The course of our history now leads us back to India, and to the most serious campaign on the north-western frontier since the Afghan War of 1839-42. The trouble was caused by some Hindustani fanatics who had settled down in 1824 in the Mahaban mountain, some fifty miles above Attock on the right bank of the Indus, and devoted themselves to thieving and murder. They had already brought one small punitive expedition upon themselves in 1858, and in 1863 they had reached such a height of mischief that the Lieutenant-Governor of the Punjab in September asked permission to send a force of five thousand men to root them out. The mountain-mass called the Mahaban forms a rough triangle with its apex to north-east, the Indus forming one side, the valley of Chamla a second, and the Yusafzai the base. It was proposed to enter the Chamla Valley, get into their rear and drive them towards the plains. It was estimated that the entire operation would take three weeks.

The Viceroy approved the expedition. Sir Hugh Rose, the Commander-in-Chief, pointed out that the interval before the coming of winter was too short to allow of the proper equipment even of five thousand men as regards transport, supply and ammunition; and urged that the operations should be deferred until the spring. His advice was ignored, and the preparations began. The troops were hastily drawn from the northern stations which were dangerously weakened; and the transport was hurriedly collected of bad animals and worse drivers. On the 18th of October the leading parties were set in motion and on the 20th the main body under Sir Neville Chamberlain closed up to them at the entrance to the Ambela Pass, which is the gate of the Chamla valley. The way lay up the bed of a stream obstructed by huge boulders and overhung by low trees and scrub; and not a single baggage animal got in that night. On the 21st the baggage began to struggle through the pass. Mules and ponies broke down in all directions and the drivers were helpless and intractable. Loads were knocked off the backs of the beasts by overhanging branches, and the pass became choked. A great effort to push forward stores for the European troops only increased the confusion, and the whole line came to a stop. Very little baggage reached the troops that night; and the rearguard of course remained far in rear.

On the 22nd the tribes turned out to resist the column, and Sir Neville Chamberlain, finding it impossible to advance, sent back his sick and wounded with every scrap of baggage that he could spare, and asked for reinforcements. By the end of the month he had changed his line of communication, making a road over the hills to avoid the difficulties and dangers of the pass; but he was still powerless to move and was attacked almost every day. The Lieutenant-Governor of the Punjab, taking alarm, gave orders for the collection of six thousand camels and mules at Naoshera; but meanwhile the onslaughts of the tribesmen became more and more serious, and the Lieutenant-Governor, losing his head, gave orders in November for Chamberlain to withdraw to the plains. These orders were overruled; Chamberlain's force was increased to almost double of its original numbers; the tribesmen were beaten into submission and just before Christmas the nest of the

Hindustani fanatics was destroyed. The expedition, which was to have been a military promenade of three weeks, had lasted three months and cost eight hundred casualties.

It is worth mentioning, chiefly because it furnishes an instructive parallel on a smaller scale, to the Afghan War of 1839. It was planned by civilians; it was supposed to be only a peaceful demonstration; and the arrangements for transport and supply were left very much to chance. The difficulties of the track leading to the pass must have caused trouble in any case, but they were nearly fatal to the entire enterprise because the transport drivers were untrained and undisciplined. The Indian Government was very slow to learn the lesson so carefully inculcated by Arthur Wellesley and Charles Napier, that, in matters of transport, drivers are as important as beasts.

THE ABYSSINIAN EXPEDITION OF 1867. The next campaign undertaken from India, at the request of the Imperial Government, was perhaps the most difficult ever carried to a successful issue by British troops. A young Abyssinian noble had overcome all rivals in his own country and in 1855 had assumed the title of Theodore, King of Ethiopia. Friendly at first to Europeans, he became demoralised by power and not only turned against all strangers but drove his own subjects to rebellion. No remonstrances from London could prevail with him to release certain Europeans whom he held imprisoned; and in July, 1867, the Imperial Government telegraphed to the Governor of Bombay to prepare to resort to force.

The situation was extraordinarily embarrassing. The nearest point of the lofty plateau of Abyssinia is divided from the Red Sea by twelve miles of salt and waterless plain. The first thing, therefore, to be provided at the base and for twelve miles beyond it, was water; the natural supply being wholly insufficient. Then came the ascent of the plateau through some fifty miles of passes to a height of seven thousand feet; and then followed an advance of three hundred and fifty miles over rugged mountain and valley to the fortress of Magdala, ten thousand feet above the sea. The troops must take with them artillery, for Magdala was a formidable stronghold; they must keep open their communications along a line of four hundred miles; and they must furnish a fighting force strong enough to strike a blow at the end. They would be subjected to the heat of a tropical sun on the salt plain and, by day, even on the plateau; but at an altitude of seven thousand feet the nights would be cold and they would require warm clothing. Sir Robert Napier, who was in command at Bombay, named twelve thousand men as the strength of the force—evidently not seeing his way to feed more—and pronounced that it would require at least twelve thousand animals for its transport.

Annesley Bay or Zula Bay was selected as the marine base on the Red Sea, and it was evident that the building of it up would be a very delicate matter. In the first place the sea shoaled abruptly two hundred yards from the shore, forbidding the nearer approach of laden boats. Obviously, therefore, a pier of that length was one of the first requisites, and its construction might be difficult since neither stone nor timber were obtainable at a less distance than twelve miles. Another complication was that there was little water and no forage on the spot, so that, until some means of producing water artificially were established, it would be impossible to keep any great number of men and animals alive. The foundation and gradual development of the base thus became a very nice problem, involving very careful calculation. The only redeeming feature was that there was a native tribe, the Shohos, on the plain, who could provide a certain amount of unskilled labour.

Next came the question of transport and supply. For this Sir Robert Napier declared the Indian system "which goes on somehow, one hardly knows how" to be for such an enterprise wholly inadequate. There were, however, at that time what were called "contingents" attached to certain districts of India for protective purposes; and the Punjab contingent, being liable to active service on the north-west frontier at any moment, had both at Lahore and Rawal Pindi mule trains under military control, the muleteers being armed and disciplined men. Here was a model which might be followed. Agents were already dispersed in all directions to purchase animals, and on the spot at Bombay was an officer, Major Warden, who had served in the Land Transport Corps in the Crimea. He urged that native non-commissioned officers and men should be selected to take charge of the smaller units of transport. The Bombay Government objected. Napier pointed out that a mob of transport animals with Egyptian, Arab, Persian and Hindustani drivers, unless most carefully organised and disciplined, would produce nothing but confusion. The Bombay Government still objected, and the formation of the transport proceeded on the old chaotic lines. Napier inspected it, pronounced that it would utterly fail of its purpose, and pressed for the adoption of Warden's recommendation. After ten days' waiting the Bombay Government finally gave way; but meanwhile seven precious weeks had been lost, and at the end of October the transport corps was still in the making.

However, work upon the base had already begun. In September a small reconnoitring party had landed to choose a base and had left behind them at Zula one hundred and forty mules with trained and disciplined drivers as a nucleus of the transport corps at the front. From three hundred to five hundred Shohos were hired to land supplies and stores (wading through two hundred yards of sea) and on the 5th of October a Commissariat dépôt was opened about twelve hundred yards from the shore. The water supply at Zula, thanks to the sinking of wells, was for the moment sufficient, but it soon began to fail, and the small escort which had accompanied the reconnoitring party was pushed across the desert to the Hadas River at the edge of the plateau. Here wells had been sunk, though the supply of water was limited. On the 13th of October a first shipload of camels arrived with their drivers and a hundred coolies; and a few days later came in a company of sappers and miners from Aden and, most important of all, a steamer for condensing water. The building up of the base seemed to be in steady progress.

Then on the 21st by some extraordinary blunder arrived an advanced brigade, including some fourteen hundred combatants (Indian troops), fourteen hundred followers, nearly five hundred horses and nearly as many mules. They were supposed to guard the dépôts on shore, but had been despatched too soon. It appears that the officer commanding the reconnoitring party had recommended that this brigade should move up at once to the Hadas and beyond it to Kumayli; but how they were to be fed and watered until they had travelled thither across the desert, he had omitted to consider. There had been no time to make arrangements for landing troops and stores. The construction both of a pier and of a tramway to the camp had been begun, but such work could not be completed in a day. Major Mignon of the Commissariat, who commanded at Zula, said plainly that he had neither food nor water for the advanced brigade and that, if they disembarked, they must land food and water for themselves daily from the transports.

So some three thousand men and one thousand animals remained mewed up in the stifling ships under the sun of the Red Sea, until thirty-two tanks had been landed high up on the beach, and smaller casks of water had been rolled or carried up by manual labour to fill them. The daily drinking ration for the advanced brigade was eight thousand gallons; and the effort to keep abreast of it was very severe. However the advanced brigade was gradually passed across the desert to the Hadas and Kumayli, after which the infantry worked at the clearing of the dry bed of a mountain torrent which formed the only pass on to the Abyssinian plateau.

Meanwhile two men-of-war had arrived on the 22nd and 28th of October to give help in the general work of disembarkation; but on the 29th the first batches of mules began to come in from Suez. Owing to the obstruction of the Bombay Government the transport corps was still in course of formation. Major Warden had not had time to collect his officers and non-commissioned officers; and there was practically no staff on the spot at Zula to receive the animals and organise them into suitable units. The Persian and Egyptian muleteers gave much trouble. The Persians refused to work for less than double the pay which they had agreed to accept and, though enlisted to take charge of five mules apiece, would only look after three. The Egyptians, if any animal lagged or broke down, simply threw off the load and left it to be plundered by the Shohos. Both Egyptians and Persians insisted upon riding every third mule, and, if prevented, would cast off a load and ride as soon as they were out of sight. As many mules as possible were sent forward to Hadas; but the difficulty was that though there was water at Hadas, there was no forage, and that though there was forage at Zula there was only condensed water. The water tanks at Zula were increased from thirty-two to sixty, but it was impossible to keep more than half of them full, and the scenes around them were appalling. As many as a thousand mules might be seen in one dense mass, fighting for a place at the drinking troughs, and the followers scrambling to share the water with them. Later, when the arrangements had been somewhat improved, the followers were still fighting for water. When one of them reached a tank he perched himself on the top of it and doled out water to all and sundry, heedless of all rules as to water rations. Then others climbed up, spilling the water over their dirty feet, and so fouling it with mud and sand that it became undrinkable. There was no order nor discipline; only waste and destruction.

While things were in this state there arrived on the 4th of December another brigade, comprising about fifteen hundred combatants (including one British battalion), a thousand followers and about as many animals. On the 6th there landed one of the divisional commanders who found utter chaos. He struggled against it for a full month before he could make any improvement, for he was practically the first responsible commandant at the base. Bad blunders revealed themselves everywhere. Instead of tethering-chains only ropes had been provided, which the mules quickly gnawed asunder. Having thus broken loose they wandered away for miles; and hundreds were thus lost, either stolen by the Shohos or dead of hunger and thirst. Again, thousands of mules had been disembarked before a single saddle had arrived to place upon their backs. With no transport officers to look after them and no means of setting their mules to work, the drivers had some excuse for negligence. A kind of spurious glanders, epidemic in the belt of desert between the plateau and the sea, attacked both horses and mules, and played havoc among them. To crown all, there was no sanitary system at Zula. Latrines were neglected; offal was not cleared away; and the air was poisoned by the unburied corpses of mules, horses and camels. Evidently the main problem of the expedition—the marine base—had not been properly thought out. The Bombay Government had certainly done untold mischief by delaying the formation of the transport corps; but the military authorities were also greatly to blame.

Meanwhile the native battalion at Kumayli had been slowly making the road practicable for pack mules through the passes—first to Upper Suru, twenty-six hundred feet, then to Undwal Wells, four thousand feet, then to Rahagedi, six thousand feet, and finally to their temporary goal at Senafe, seven thousand eight hundred feet—a total distance of twenty-eight miles. By the 7th of December an advanced brigade of all three arms was concentrated at Senafe, but only with the greatest difficulty was it fed, though the inhabitants were friendly and brought in such provisions as they could spare. It was an effort to take a convoy of mules even from Zula to the Hadas and back—a total distance of sixteen miles. Leaving Zula as soon as they had been watered at daybreak, they did not reach the Hadas until evening. Then they had to be fed and watered and, since from ten to twelve hours were needed to water the whole of them, drivers and beasts often did not return to Zula until dawn of the following day. Thus both men and beasts were overworked. The weaklier broke down, and a greater strain was thrown upon the stronger, which likewise gradually succumbed. It is a vicious circle well known to military men.

However, by the end of the year progress had been made at the base. The troops and animals were still living from hand to mouth; but one pier had been completed; a tramway had been laid down from the camp to its head; a railway was projected from Zula to Kumayli, and a locomotive engine had already arrived. Two water-condensing stations had been established so that, with the help of the ships in harbour, there was ample supply of water for all. The epidemic among the animals had died out and the troops were healthy. The road as far as Suru had been made fit for wheeled traffic. On the 2nd of January, 1868, Sir Robert Napier arrived, and shortly after him the organised mule trains from Lahore and Rawal Pindi, which gave a model of efficiency for the rest. By the end of January, the railway had been carried half-way to Kumayli, and a telegraphic line laid from Zula to Suru. Fresh animals, including elephants, came pouring in to make good casualties. On the 25th Napier, knowing that it was vital for him to reach Magdala before the breaking of the rains, decided to begin his advance.

By the 31st the entire length of the road from Kumayli to Senafe had been opened to wheeled traffic and the business of converting Senafe into an advanced base was commenced. It promised to be a work of time, for the troops and followers on the upland were consuming ten thousand rations daily, and not more than twenty thousand could be daily delivered at Senafe. Meanwhile detachments crept forward from it to Adigrat, about thirty miles to south, forming a new post there, and thence to Antalo, yet forty miles further southward. They found some forage on the way, but few supplies. Napier then decided to reorganise his transport in two divisions. The highland division was to do the work from Adigrat southward. It was modelled upon the Punjab trains, and with armed and disciplined muleteers and eight thousand mules it soon became very efficient. The lowland train was confined to the space between Zula and Senafe.

Leaving Adigrat on the 18th of February, Napier reached Antalo over most difficult and dangerous tracks on the 2nd of March, with two thousand men and a battery of Armstrong guns. Here he halted ten days while the road to the next stage was explored. Local transport, brought in by the country people, had eased the strain upon his own animals, and he now extended the range of the lowland train from Senafe to Adigrat. Meanwhile the railway remained stationary, the Bombay Government having characteristically sent out rails which were not uniform and could not easily be fitted together. On the 12th of March Napier resumed his advance. On the 18th his foremost detachment reached Ashangi, forty-five miles from Antalo, and on the 22nd entered Lat, fifteen miles further on. By that time half of the troops had become an armed working party and the other half an armed transport corps, for it had been found a great economy in time and labour to place every mule in charge of a fighting man. Napier had already cut down baggage and camp equipment very low; and now he forbade private baggage altogether and allowed no one under the rank of divisional commander to have a tent to himself. Then followed a series of terrible marches over very trying ground, which was sometimes made worse by terrific storms. The force crept on in small detachments from stage to stage, suffering much hardship, until on the 10th of April Napier engaged the Abyssinians with a total force of about fifty-three hundred men and on the 13th mastered the fortress of Magdala, all at a cost of under forty casualties. On the 19th he blew up the fortifications and began his retirement.

This was the worst part of the whole operation. At Magdala the transport animals had to travel eight miles to find water, which tried them severely after the exertions of the advance. The men too, overworked and deprived of all stimulants for five weeks past, began in the reaction after great strain to break down. The Abyssinians, who had not resisted the advance, constantly harassed the retreat in hope of plunder. Frequent storms of rain were added to other trials. It was impossible to empty many of the dépôts, and the supplies and stores therein were abandoned. On the 24th of May, the rear of the column reached Senafe. Five days earlier a sudden flood in the Suru pass had swept away seven followers and some cattle, so that the plain was reached only just in time. Had not the discipline and spirit of the entire force been perfect, the march to and from Magdala could never have been accomplished.

From first to last, twelve thousand men were landed in Zula Bay, and the deaths from disease did not exceed forty-six among the thirty-eight hundred British troops nor two hundred and eighty-four among the eight thousand Indian troops. The animals received into the transport train numbered in round figures forty-one thousand, namely forty-four elephants, eighteen thousand mules, fifteen hundred ponies, twelve thousand camels, eleven hundred draught-bullocks, seven thousand pack-bullocks and eighteen hundred asses. The casualties were seven thousand, of which about twelve hundred and fifty belonged to the highland train. The greatest losses, in fact, were at the base and must have been very largely due to mismanagement. For that mismanagement the Bombay Government must bear the main load of responsibility.

It should be added that excellent hospital ships were sent out from England, with officers of the Commissariat in charge of the supplies on board. One of these officers, Sir John Young, is still alive and gave me interesting particulars of his charge. He and his colleagues gave freely any stores that they could spare for the general use of the force, and were thus often able to make good small defects and to ease the strain of minor difficulties. In fact there were an absence of jealousy and a readiness to take responsibility which contrasted agreeably with former experience in the Crimea.

CHAPTER VIII

THE SYSTEM OF CONTROL AND ITS SUCCESSORS. 1867–1888.

THE STRATHNAIRN COMMITTEE OF 1867. It is now time to report on the general administration of transport and supply. As has been told, the whole of the military business formerly entrusted to the Treasury and the Home Office had been in 1855 suddenly thrown upon the War Office, and the natural result had been great confusion. The struggles to reduce this confusion to order were almost ludicrously pitiful. Within twelve years, seventeen Royal Commissions, eighteen Select Committees of the House of Commons, nineteen committees of officers within the War Office and thirty-five committees of military officers had met and considered sundry points of policy; yet the machinery groaned and creaked as heavily as ever, and nothing seemed to remove the friction. At last, however, one of these committees really did bear fruit. It was appointed in 1866, to consider the question of transport and supply, under the presidency of Lord Strathnairn, whom we have already met as Sir Hugh Rose; and the other members were Sir Hope Grant and Sir Duncan Cameron, both with recent experience of work in the field, the former in China, the latter in New Zealand, Commissary-General Sir William Power, Colonels Shadwell, Gambier and Clark Kennedy.

The evidence of all Commissions agreed, as was inevitable, that, if the control of transport were separated

183

from that of supply, supply could not be carried on at all. It was pointed out that the Commissariat superintended the manufacture of vehicles at Gibraltar and the Cape of Good Hope, so that they were evidently expected to know something about transport, and that this principle might very well be extended to the British Isles. More than one of them insisted on the importance of having the same system at home, abroad and in the field. One of them, Deputy-Commissary-General Fonblanque gave rather a curious account of his position:

I am in charge of the Commissariat of Great Britain, but I don't know what is going on in my department. I cannot give the order to my commissariat officer, who acts as military accountant, to pay sixpence. I do not know what the disbursements are. Contractors are paid at the War Office, and no intervention of the Commissariat is allowed. Abroad, though the commissariat officer acts as Comptroller he has no control over the transport. The absence of control over the transport is attended with the greatest inconvenience even in England.

And he gave an instance of a batch of bread being spoiled because a serjeant of the Military Train dared not, without his commanding officer's orders, horse two water-carts to carry the requisite water a distance of two hundred yards.

A vast number of documents were put in concerning recent experience of transport and supply in the field; but the substance of these has already been given in the narratives of those campaigns. A point strongly insisted upon was the weak strength of the staff of Commissariat officers. In 1844 they numbered one hundred and ninety-seven; during the Crimean War they rose to two hundred and thirty-seven; by 1864 they had sunk down again to one hundred and ninety-eight; and Commissary-General Power pointed out that, if England should be engaged in another European war, she would not have nearly enough trained commissariat officers. Even in the petty operations in New Zealand it had been necessary to supplement the twenty-one Commissariat officers by twelve regimental officers borrowed from the infantry. These facts spoke for themselves but were not very likely to appeal to the House of Commons. There was also much discussion as to whether there should be a central transport corps, and whether certain units, such as the Royal Engineers, should have their own transport as well. Commissary-General Power at the outset had laid down that there were three kinds of transport in modern armies: (1) for conveyance of munitions of war, entrenching tools, engineers' appliances, etc., (2) for collection of food and forage, (3) for conveyance of sick, wounded and hospital equipment; and at least one officer, Fonblanque, of the Commissariat was strongly against giving the Royal Engineers any transport of their own.

Another hotly contested point was whether the Military Train should retain its military status or become civil, or whether, on the other hand, the Commissariat should cast off its civil status and become military. It is perhaps worth remarking that Sir Henry Storks, a very able officer of great influence at the time, favoured the retention of military status by the transport, while, however, subjecting it to the same controlling head as the Commissariat. Thus there was plenty of room for wrangling with the possibility of not arriving at any decisive result.

As a matter of fact, however, the Strathnairn Commission seems to have been appointed in order that it might assimilate the organisation of certain administrative departments, including transport and supply, in the British Army to that of the French *Intendance*. Lord Strathnairn having been commissioner—what is now called liaison officer—at the French headquarters in the Crimea, had there learned the working of the French system and could speak with authority. Sir Charles Trevelyan, the very capable Secretary to the

185

Treasury, also favoured the organisation of the *Intendance*; and the combination of these two opinions was decisive. In 1868 a new department called the Department of Control was set up, with jurisdiction over stores (other than munitions), barracks, the business of the purveyors (roughly speaking, hospital stores other than drugs and surgical instruments), transport and supply. Thus transport and supply were at least placed under a single head; and as a solution of the much-debated question whether their status should be civil or military or mixed, it was decided that the amalgamated Commissariat and Transport Corps should be civil. No doubt this was due to the assumption of combatant airs by the Military Train; but some misgivings were expressed in Parliament. The Duke of Cambridge, then Commander-in-Chief, in the Lords hinted at the danger that the Controller might be able to override the authority of the Commanding General in the field; and, as a detail, he strongly objected to handing the control of military transport to a civilian. Curiously enough, Sir Henry Storks, in his evidence before the Strathnairn Commission, had expressed much the same apprehensions as the Duke of Cambridge. He had observed in the Crimea that the heads of the French *Intendance* exerted excessive domination over general officers. They looked upon themselves, in fact, as delegates of the Minister for War.* To avert any such peril, Storks himself was appointed first Controller-in-Chief.† However, for better or worse the system of Control was instituted, and by 1869 had already been extended to Aldershot, Ireland, Gibraltar, the Cape, the Straits Settlements, Nova Scotia, Newfoundland, Bermuda,

---

* Evidence before Strathnairn Commission, 2540.
† Hansard's *Debates*, Sir J. Pakington's speech on introducing Army estimates, March 23rd, 1868. Sir John Young (whose memory I would not lightly distrust) told me that the first Controller was Commissary-General Sir William Power, so I give my authority for my statement.

Barbados, Grenada and Australia, with the prospect very shortly of embracing every military station.*

We shall return to the fortunes of the Control System presently. Meanwhile we must follow those of the transport and supply services of the Army. By Royal Warrant of the 12th of November, 1869, a special corps to perform these duties was created with the title of the Army Service Corps. It was commanded by commissariat officers of the Control Department and composed in the first instance of volunteers, both non-commissioned officers and men, from the Military Train, the Commissariat Staff Corps, Military Store Staff Corps, and the Purveyor's branch of the Hospital Corps. The non-commissioned officers and men of the Military Train at Woolwich were formed (Feb. 15th, 1870) into Companies Nos. 1 (Dépôt), 2 and 3. A week later three more companies, numbered 4, 5, and 6, were formed at Aldershot, and four more, numbered respectively No. 7 at Shorncliffe, No. 8 at Portsmouth, No. 9 at Dublin, and No. 10 at the Curragh. The Supply and Store companies were composed on the 1st of April, 1870; the three Store companies "A", "B", "C", being stationed at Woolwich, while of the Supply companies three, "D", "E", "F", were at Aldershot, and three more distributed singly, "G" at Dublin, "H" at the Curragh, "I" at Chatham. In August, 1870, the Franco-German War broke out and, orders being issued for the augmentation of the Army Service Corps, recruits were then for the first time enlisted directly into it. While the Army Service Corps was at this stage it furnished a detachment of the Supply branch for the bloodless Red River expedition, dependent entirely upon water carriage, through which a petty rebellion in Canada was suppressed by Colonel Garnet Wolseley in 1869.

On the 1st of June, 1871, two additional Transport

* Hansard's *Debates*, Mr Cardwell's speech of March 11th, 1869.

companies, Nos. 11 and 12, and one additional Supply company, "K", were formed, the last-named being stationed in London and providing detachments for small stations. A year later, on the 5th of July, 1872, the Transport and Supply branches were separated. The Transport companies, twelve in all, comprised sixteen hundred and twenty-three non-commissioned officers and men and a thousand and eighty-seven horses. The Supply companies were fixed at seven and the Store companies at four, with a total strength of thirteen hundred and seventy-three non-commissioned officers and men.

So matters remained until 1875. The Control System, as it was called, was developed and expanded until it embraced all stations both at home and abroad; but as early as in 1872 Sir Percy Herbert, a general officer who had served with great distinction in the Crimea, began to pass harsh criticisms in the House of Commons. He pointed out that, under the existing regulations, the Controller's position differed from that of all other officers in the Army. Those regulations laid down that the Controller was to receive his orders personally from the General and from no other officer. Whatever his rank or branch of the service he could go to the General and claim to consult with him personally and to receive no orders except from him personally. The idea was to relieve the General from responsibility, but this was false. The General alone must be responsible for everything, otherwise he ceased to be in actual command.

Such a system obviously could not endure. It was almost a reversion to that of William III's time when the Commissary could wreck a General's plans by withholding money and stores. Some said that if the Controller's name had been spelled Comptroller, limiting his authority to accompts, this difficulty might not have arisen; but the truth seems to be that the traditions of the days when the Treasury governed the Commissariat were still alive. In 1875 a general officer in the House of Commons deplored the abolition of the Control Department. The Secretary for War at once jumped to his feet and answered that the department had not been abolished, but that its name only, which "had led to an infinity of confusion and jealousy," had been swept away.

The immediate result was that the united Commissariat and Transport were erected into a separate Corps which languished under discouraging conditions until 1880. Its name was then changed to the Commissariat and Transport Staff, with the provision that its officers should be taken from the regiments of the line and should have served in that branch for at least five years. The change of name evidently signified apprehension lest the Commissariat and Transport, if they assumed the more or less regimental status of a corps (like the Royal Artillery) should develop the combatant tendencies of the extinct Military Train. The old prejudice against placing transport and supply upon a genuinely military footing evidently died very hard.

Meanwhile, as was characteristic of the nineteenth century, little wars broke out in every quarter of the globe, and the problems of transport and supply which they presented were not always ready of solution. We must now see how, in succession, the Commissariat and Transport Corps and the Commissariat and Transport Staff endeavoured to wrestle with them.

THE ASHANTI WAR OF 1874. On the west coast of Africa the Ashantis, forgetting the lesson of 1826, had again become troublesome in 1873; and it was necessary to send a little force of three battalions under Sir Garnet Wolseley to repel them. A detachment of about forty non-commissioned officers and men of the Army Service Corps was sent out to take part in what Sir Garnet Wolseley termed "a horrible little campaign". The climate was, of course, the main difficulty, being equally deadly in all quarters of the scene of action. The only means of transport was native bearers, and these had already been organised before Sir Garnet's arrival by Commissary-General O'Connor. "He was a man among many," wrote Sir Garnet, "and to me he was worth any thousand other men I could have found." All details seem to be undiscoverable except that the carriers wore zinc labels, which points to the distinction of the different companies into which they were organised. The expedition duly fought its way to Kumassi, and we may guess at its experiences by following those of Sir James Wilcocks which are related on a later page.

THE THREATENED WAR WITH RUSSIA IN 1878. In January, 1878, when the Russians after nine months of hard fighting against the Turks were directly threatening Constantinople, England interposed and seemed likely to take up arms on the Turkish side. In April, the First Class Army Reserve was mobilised; Indian troops were brought over to Malta and officers of the Commissariat were sent over to form a dépôt at Cyprus, which had been tacitly lent to England by the Turks for the purpose. There were no wharves nor landing stages, and the business of unloading the stores was undertaken by officers and seamen of the Mediterranean squadron, who, as in China in 1860, were not very considerate in their proceedings. The supply officers were permitted to have no voice as to the time and manner of landing the supplies and stores, which were simply piled up in huge impenetrable miscellaneous pyramids, without a thought as to their sorting, their storage or their issue for immediate requirements. In a very short time the supply officers began to break down from overwork. One died; and the chief and his secretary were soon invalided. The incident was probably wholly unknown to the public; but the chief's secretary, now Colonel Sir John Young, took careful note of it with results that were to be seen within a year.

THE KAFFIR AND ZULU WARS OF 1877–9. Towards the end of 1877 there was a renewal of unrest among the Kaffirs which compelled the advance of a small body of troops for its repression. A detachment of one officer and six other ranks of the Army Service Corps was accordingly ordered out to the Cape in December, 1877. The trouble with the Kaffirs was not very serious and was soon ended; but in July, 1878, there showed itself a far more formidable menace on the frontier of Natal where the attitude of the Zulus had become aggressive. They were the most powerful of the native tribes from a military point of view, in South Africa, having been trained to war first by a man of genius who had encountered the British in very early days and had taken note of their discipline. By December war was seen to be inevitable, and Lord Chelmsford, who commanded in South Africa, preferred to invade Zululand.

The general base of operations was Durban, from which a railway ran as far as Pietermaritzburg. Lord Chelmsford arranged to advance in four columns, the first, or most easterly, being posted near the mouth of the Tugela, with its advanced base at Stanger, forty miles north-east of Durban. The second lay at Krantzkop, about sixty miles north and east of Pietermaritzburg, which it was designed to protect, standing on the defensive until the other columns should have made good their footing in Zululand. The third column had its advanced base at Helpmakaar, about forty miles north-west of Krantzkop, and the fourth column at Utrecht, about sixty miles north of Helpmakaar. The whole numbered close upon eighteen thousand men, of whom about forty-three hundred were white troops, regular and irregular, and the remainder natives, including the conductors, drivers and forelopers of the transport. The animals employed in the transport counted eight hundred horses, four hundred mules and ten thousand oxen, while the vehicles numbered nearly a thousand waggons and fifty-six carts.

The advance began on the 12th of January, 1879, but the second column was unable to make any serious movement until the 19th. On the 20th the greater part of it was cut to pieces, and the Zulus poured down to the invasion of Natal. They were checked, however, by a mere handful of men, who threw up hasty defences of biscuit boxes and the like at Rorke's Drift on the Tugela, and driven back with heavy loss. This fight at Rorke's Drift was a fine little feat of arms, giving much opportunity for acts of personal valour. Among those who won the Victoria Cross was Acting Assistant Commissary James Langley Dalton, of the Commissariat and Transport Corps. Though not by profession a combatant, he took a leading part in checking the first rush of the Zulus by his deadly fire with a rifle, and by the example of his calm, cool courage. In the course of the action he was severely wounded, but bore himself with the same intrepidity; and the successful defence of the little post against overwhelming numbers was due not a little to his personal energy.

The operations were perforce for some time suspended until the arrival of reinforcements from England. Among the earliest of the officers to reach Durban was Deputy Commissary-General Young, who, remembering the trouble at Cyprus in 1878, took sole charge at Durban of the landing of every man and every ounce of supplies and stores. It had been arranged by him, in perfect concert with the officers of the men-of-war on the station, that the jurisdiction of the Royal Navy should cease at the water's edge, and that everybody and everything should pass under his control from the moment of touching the shore. This, however, did not debar him from supplying labour of his own to unload ships, if desired by the officers of the Navy, with whom he worked from first to last on the most cordial terms.

With control of the short line of railway and with a disciplined body of over a thousand native labourers under his immediate orders, he did the entire work of disembarkation single-handed. The bar at Durban in those days was dangerous, and the mere mechanical problem of landing horses was sometimes formidable; but all difficulties were successfully overcome, and two regiments of cavalry, four batteries of artillery and six battalions of infantry, with all the supplies and stores for the entire force thus augmented, were disembarked without a single accident and without any loss. At the same time his vigilance put a stop to all extortion of contractors, while his tact averted all friction with the local merchants. His duties may to the ordinary reader seem prosaic enough, but officers of his corps with experience of such matters will appreciate the good service—doubly arduous in the comparatively primitive times of half a century ago—which was rendered by one who, at the time of this writing, still survives hale and hearty at the age of eighty-eight, as the father of the Royal Army Service Corps. He received unstinted commendation not only from his immediate superiors and from Commissary-General Strickland, but from Lord Chelmsford, from Sir Garnet Wolseley (who succeeded Chelmsford in chief command) and from the Governor of Natal.

By March the British were able to resume the offensive and by the first week in April to restore the situation; and the next two months were consumed in bringing up supplies for a greatly increased force. It should seem that, owing to the panic engendered by the annihilation of a British regiment, more troops than necessary were employed; while the transport was hampered by the loss of the oxen captured from the defeated column. Since ten thousand oxen were needed for Lord Chelmsford's original army, his reinforced army, which counted more than twice his former number of white soldiers, naturally required many more; and these were not readily to be found. This trouble was increased by the fact that the scene of operations offered no food for man or horse, and that even fuel had to be brought from a distance. However, at the beginning of June the advance was slowly resumed, and on the 3rd of July was fought a decisive action which broke the power of the Zulus and ended the war.

It may be added that this was practically the first campaign to test the system of short service for the Army which had been introduced in 1870. The result was not encouraging. The battalions were full of boys, who not only were less steady than the old long-service soldiers, but sickened very rapidly under the hardships of active service and thus threw an additional burden on the transport.

In 1881 there followed a short little war against the Boers of the Transvaal and Orange Free State who, their formidable enemies, the Zulus, being removed, showed their gratitude by declaring their independence. After the British had suffered three reverses, that independence was yielded to them. During the operations the work of the Commissariat (Companies Nos. 7 and 9) under Deputy-Commissary Brownrigg was most successful; and the tale of seven non-commissioned officers and men who were killed or wounded is proof that it was not without peril.

THE EGYPTIAN CAMPAIGN OF 1882. In the following year the British Army was for the first time since 1801 turned to a field of operations which was to find much work for it for some years. In the middle of May 1882 a military rebellion placed a Colonel, Arabi Pasha by name, in virtual possession of all executive power in Egypt; and it fell to Great Britain to re-establish the authority of the legitimate ruler, Khedive Tewfik. It was decided to send out twenty-four thousand men under command of Sir Garnet Wolseley. The base was

Ismailia on the Suez Canal, midway between Port Said and Suez. From thence ran a railway which struck the main line from Alexandria to Cairo at Benha, about seventy miles to west of Ismailia; and the Egyptian Army was massed at Tel-el-Kebir, about mid-way between those two points. The line followed that of a canal which branched off from the Damietta stream of the Nile to Ismailia. Upon this the force had to rely for water on its march across the desert, and to some extent also for transport.

In the course of 1881, it will be remembered, the name of the Army Service Corps had been changed to Commissariat and Transport Corps; and under this new designation eight companies were ordered for service in Egypt (Nos. 2, 7, 8, 10, 11, 12, 15, 17). The Commissary-General was Sir E. Morris, C.B. Assistant Commissary-General Reeves was in supreme command of the eight companies and Director of Transport; and Deputy Assistant Commissary-General Charles Bridge was adjutant and assistant to him.

The operations in Egypt had opened with the capture of Alexandria and with its occupation first by marines and later by troops in July. In order to deceive the enemy, every display was made of using Alexandria as a base of operations; and to Alexandria accordingly the first officers of the Commissariat repaired early in July. From thence some proceeded to Cyprus to purchase mules. On the 15th of August Sir Garnet Wolseley arrived at Alexandria, and on the 20th the whole line of the Suez Canal, together with Ismailia, was seized and occupied almost without resistance. On the 19th an advanced force of eight battalions, about six squadrons and three batteries—nine thousand men—sailed for the new base; and it was ordered that each ship should carry fourteen days' rations for the troops on board her, and that the Commissariat should carry fourteen days' rations more. This distribution proved to be quite impossible. In the first place there were not tugs enough to bring the lighters alongside the ships, and even if there had been, some ships could not receive these supplies, while the captains of others declined to take them. But the Commissariat had already loaded a store ship, the *Osprey*, which had conveyed one of its detachments to Ismailia, with victuals; and thus any ill results that might have come of this impracticable order were averted.

The accommodation at Ismailia in 1882 was very inadequate to the disembarkation of even a small force. There was only a single pier, the distance from which to the fresh water canal was a quarter of a mile. There was but one narrow bridge across this canal, and the railway station (where there were as yet no locomotive engines) lay a quarter of a mile beyond the bridge. The water in the canal itself was falling rapidly, the enemy having built a dam, to stop the flow, at Magfar about seven miles to westward. Hardly therefore had the whole of the men and horses been landed before, on the 24th, a detachment, composed chiefly of cavalry, was pushed forward to Magfar; whence, being reinforced, it advanced four miles further to Tel-el-Mahuta on the 25th and to Kassassin, where there was a lock, on the 26th. From the sheer exigency of the conditions men were disembarked in considerable numbers before any reserve of supplies had been formed. It was very evident that such a system could not be long continued. The men who advanced on the 24th carried, or were supposed to carry, two days' rations on their regimental transport; but the sandy ground proved to be too heavy for the regimental carts, and the regimental transport broke down altogether. Thus large quantities of supplies were perforce abandoned and wasted; and men and animals were short of food, with the inevitable result that sickness increased.

By the 25th it was already necessary to resort to

water-transport, to start steam pinnaces on the canal and to hasten the procurance of locomotive engines. Traffic in the canal was a matter of great difficulty. In the first place it was necessary to remove with much labour the dams constructed by the enemy at Magfar and Tel-el-Mahuta, and, in the next, no big launches nor lighters of any great draught could pass Mahuta, so that all cargoes had to be unloaded and reshipped, causing endless and hopeless confusion in way-bills. Meanwhile, the enemy threatened the advanced troops at Kassassin, and it was necessary to augment them until the strength of the force at the front by the end of August reached a total of nearly eleven thousand men and over four thousand horses. Simultaneously the water in the canal fell lower and lower, while the rolling stock upon the railway was still quite insufficient. Orders had been given to form a reserve dépôt of thirty days' supplies at Kassassin; but this would have required daily fifty-five railway-trucks, whereas there were at hand only ten, and the daily transport of forty tons by canal, whereas the number of lighters that could be passed through it was steadily reduced by the fall of the water. Between the want of landing accommodation at the base and the lack of transport along the line of communication the task of feeding the troops at the front continued to be most anxious.

On the 3rd of September, one hundred and fifty pack-mules were at last ready to relieve in some slight degree the pressure upon the railway and upon the canal; and during the two following days there was considerable improvement in the canal itself as the obstructions were removed. Meanwhile fuel presented a problem very difficult of solution. It was very badly needed at the front, if it could only have been moved thither, but meanwhile it overwhelmed the space on the Commissariat Wharf at Ismailia. Even the men on the spot forebore to consume their ration owing to the fatigue of drawing it. The railway, with its very limited rolling stock, was still used chiefly to take troops to the front; but on the 13th a decisive action at Tel-el-Kebir to all intent ended the campaign at a stroke. The capture of large quantities of supplies removed all immediate anxiety at the front. The seizure of ten engines and one hundred carriages on the railway at Zagazig at 4 p.m. enabled communication to be opened at once with Kassassin; and the surrender of Cairo on the 14th virtually restored to Egypt its normal conditions. The campaign, though brief, was most trying to the Commissariat. Sir Garnet Wolseley had deliberately landed more men than he could easily feed, on the calculation that fewer lives would be sacrificed by a single swift blow than by more methodical operations prolonged over thrice the time during the late summer of the Egyptian climate. The rapid and decisive close of the campaign vindicated his judgment; and, though the men for a short time went hungry, neither they nor anyone who understood the situation blamed the Commissariat.

THE SUAKIN EXPEDITION OF 1884. Before the rebellion of Arabi in Egypt there had been a movement of insurrection against Egyptian rule in the Sudan, and in August, 1881, a fanatic, Mohammed Ahmed, proclaimed himself the Mahdi, divinely appointed to save the Sudan. After some vicissitudes, his power steadily increased, and in 1884 General Charles Gordon was sent out as Governor to Khartoum to restore order. Meanwhile another leader, Osman Digna, had arisen to kindle revolt in the Eastern Sudan; and he cut to pieces a force of Egyptian troops, which had been sent to quell him, in February, 1884. The British Government therefore decided to undertake the defence of the port of Suakin in the Red Sea; and a force of four thousand British troops from Egypt under General Graham was concentrated on the 28th of February at Trinkitat. It was accompanied by a detachment of the Commissariat and Transport Corps then quartered in Egypt. There had been some talk of an advance from Suakin to Berber, but this project was abandoned upon the news of the steady advance of the Mahdi's power. The expedition was withdrawn on the 27th of March, after a stay of just one month, during which it made one or two raids and fought one or two actions but never strayed more than fifteen miles from its base.

THE NILE EXPEDITION OF 1884–5. Meanwhile the conquering progress of the Mahdi threatened the safety of General Gordon in Khartoum; and the British Government decided to send an expedition to his relief. Lord Wolseley, to whom the command was entrusted, decided to advance along the Nile, which signified a line of communication, roughly speaking, fourteen hundred miles long from the sea southward. Of this distance three hundred and twenty miles were covered by the railway from Alexandria to Cairo and thence on to Assiut. For the next three hundred and twenty-five miles from Assiut to Assuan, the river was open to navigation by steamer. At Assuan lies the first cataract, extending for about seven miles; from the head of which navigation is again open for about two hundred and thirty miles to the second cataract at Wadi Halfa. From Halfa to the third cataract at Hannak is two hundred and thirteen miles; from Hannak to Dongola is forty miles more; and one hundred and thirty miles beyond Dongola lies Korti, where the Nile (as the stream is ascended) makes a great bend north-eastward to Abu Hamed before it resumes its usual course north and south. In case of urgent need Lord Wolseley prepared to send a force across the desert from Korti south-eastward to Metemmeh and thence one hundred miles southward to Khartoum. Immense preparations were therefore necessary of boats for transport by water and of camels for transport by land, more particularly along those extensive tracts where navigation was obstructed, perhaps for fifteen or twenty miles at a stretch, by cataracts. It is true that both at Assuan and at Wadi Halfa there were railways, though not as yet very complete, along the length of the cataracts; but these did not get over the difficulty of shifting loads as the means of transport changed, and to the almost inevitably resulting confusion in the matter of way-bills and accounts. In fact, there was to be a repetition on a much larger scale of the experience in New Zealand, as the following table of stages will show:

From Alexandria and Cairo to Assiut	Railway
From Assiut to Assuan ...	Barge or steamer
From Assuan to Philæ ...	Railway*
From Philæ to Wadi Halfa ...	Barge or steamer
Ten miles Wadi Halfa to Sarras	Railway†
Ten miles Sarras to Semneh ...	Boat and camel
Across Semneh, portage... ...	Camel
Ten miles Semneh to Ambako ...	Boat
Across Ambako, portage ...	Camel
Fifteen miles Ambako to Dal ...	Boat
Across Dal, portage	Camel
Thirty-five miles Dal to Kajbar	Boat
Across Kajbar, portage	Camel
Kajbar to Abu Fatmeh	Boat
Across Abu Fatmeh, portage ...	Camel‡
Abu Fatmeh to Dongola and Korti	Boat.

Before leaving England Lord Wolseley declared his intention of taking the control of the transport out of the hands of the Chief Commissariat Officer; and Lieutenant-Colonel Furse, who was appointed Director of Transport, left England for Cairo in advance both of Lord Wolseley himself and of Colonel Hughes, who had been specially selected as Chief Commissariat Officer.

* 1st cataract. † 2nd cataract. ‡ 3rd cataract.

It was further ordained, as an experiment, that the Chief Commissariat Officer should be attached to the staff not of the Commander-in-Chief but of the General commanding the line of communication, Sir Evelyn Wood.

In September, 1884, two companies of the Commissariat and Transport Corps left England for Egypt, the 9th under Captain Edwards and the 11th under Captain Lea, with Major Nugent in command of both. Their establishment as transport companies was fixed before their departure.* Among the senior officers of the corps there were employed also Lieutenant-Colonel Skinner, Majors Boyd, Whitley and Rainsford and Captain Rogers. It was October before they reached Assuan and the stations to south of it, and then they found rather a curious state of affairs. The specially appointed Director of Transport had issued no instructions as to his particular business along the line of communication, and indeed, despite of his title, he had no control over any railway nor over any boats. Over animal transport he was, indeed, nominally supreme; but a great many— indeed most—of the eight thousand camels purchased for the expedition had been acquired before his arrival. No one seemed to know exactly wherein his appointment signified the separation between transport and supply. Major Rainsford, of the Commissariat, did indeed receive from Colonel Furse at Assuan in October certain instructions which purported to bring about such separation; but Major Rainsford was shifted farther south before he could discover any change. His successor, Major Boyd, anxious to avoid any misunderstanding, addressed his immediate commander, General Grenfell (later Lord Grenfell and Field-Marshal), on the subject. The General answered that, without positive instructions, he would not recognise Colonel Furse as

* Three officers, one quartermaster, four conductors, twelve sergeants and corporals, forty-eight privates, six artificers, nine interpreters, and six hundred and four camels, with one driver to every three camels.

Director of Transport, and that meanwhile Major Boyd was to carry on all transport duties as heretofore. To one of the very best officers in Egypt, therefore, the appointment of a Director of Transport evidently came as an unpleasant surprise; and it is difficult to understand exactly what Lord Wolseley intended by it.

The truth is that the Director of Transport seems to have been a superfluity. When he visited the stations up the river, he took over local control of the animal transport duties for the time being. When he left that station, the control reverted at once to the commandant of the station, under the orders of the General commanding communications, without any reference to the Director of Transport whatever. As a matter of fact the transport duties at all the important stations from Assuan southwards were, as well as the duties of supply, fulfilled by the officers of the Commissariat. The only trouble was that these officers were not sent out early enough, that there were too few of them to extend to the important station of Dongola, and that the transport animals allotted to them were insufficient. In fact a mistake seems to have been made in not tapping one of the best sources of Egypt both for numbers and quality of animals—the Delta—and keeping the supply at Dongola as a reserve. Whether this error were due to Colonel Furse or not is doubtful; indeed it is difficult to say who was responsible for anything. Both the General commanding communications and the Chief of the Staff gave frequent orders, directly, concerning both transport and supply, to the commandants at stations.* In fact, the responsibility for transport and supply was not divided, though it was shared by these two officers. Thus the principle that the person answerable for the waggon must also be answerable for the load

* The stations on the lines of communication numbered in all sixteen: Cairo, Assiut, Assuan, Korosko, Wadi Halfa, Sarras, Semneh, Ambako, Tanjur, Akashah, Sarkamatto, Amara, Absarat, Kajbar, Abu Fatmeh, Dongola.

was in practice respected, though, for some reason, the senior Commissariat officer was supposed to have nothing to do with transport. The junior Commissariat officers, however, sought the advice of Colonel Hughes upon matters of transport and accepted that advice as orders. It was lucky that they did so for, but for Colonel Hughes, there would have been no records nor accounts for the transport whatever. These little points seem to have been overlooked by the Director of Transport.

Meanwhile eight hundred specially constructed whale-boats had been brought up to the second cataract, from whence the troops all through November and December were slowly moving up, with the help of three hundred Canadian *voyageurs*, to Korti. Each boat contained twelve men and their rations for one hundred days which, however, were not to be touched until active operations should actually begin. The feeding of the soldiers on the way, therefore, fell upon the Commissariat, though on the Commissariat fell likewise the task of checking over seventy thousand packages which contained the nine hundred and sixty thousand rations. By the 18th of November, something over ten thousand men were echeloned between Assuan and Dongola, more than half of them south of Wadi Halfa. By the 25th of December rather more than two thousand troops with eleven hundred and nine riding camels and two hundred and seventeen baggage camels had arrived at Korti. News that imminent danger threatened General Gordon at Khartoum had by that time decided Lord Wolseley to send one column under Sir Herbert Stewart across the desert to Metemmeh, while a second under General Earle should pursue its course up the river. As the troops moved up the river, the divisions of the two Commissariat companies moved up after them, so as to deal with the pressure at each station in succession.

Lord Wolseley arrived at Korti on the 15th of December, and found that camels which he had expected from Dongola were not forthcoming. It was therefore impossible for him to send his desert column, with its supplies, in one body; and he decided to despatch a convoy to the wells of Jakdul, on the way to Metemmeh, and there to establish a post. The convoy numbered about eleven hundred of all ranks of British and two hundred and twenty natives, with twenty-two hundred camels of all descriptions. Two officers, twenty-seven of other ranks and six hundred camels belonged to the 9th company of the Commissariat. The convoy started on the 30th of December and reached Jakdul, ninety-eight miles, on the 2nd of January 1885, having found a very little bad water at two halting-stations on the way. About half of the force was left at Jakdul, and the remainder returned to Korti on the 5th of January. Only thirty-one camels had been lost, but the remainder had suffered greatly in condition. On the 7th of January another convoy of a thousand camels, eight hundred of them carrying supplies, set out for Jakdul, and on the 8th the main body under Sir Herbert Stewart—about sixteen hundred British and three hundred natives with twenty-two hundred camels—advanced to the same destination, which it reached on the 12th. On that day at Jakdul the entire 9th company found itself united for the first time since it had received its animals and equipment.

On the 14th Sir Herbert Stewart made his final movement towards Metemmeh with a force of about eighteen hundred combatants and twenty-nine hundred camels, of which eight hundred and sixty belonged to the Commissariat. Majors Nugent and Rainsford were the two officers with this force and there were also thirty-three of other ranks of the 9th company. On the 17th an action was fought at Abu Klea which cost the British over one hundred and sixty casualties; on the 19th there was a second action which added one hundred and twenty more casualties and on the 20th the Nile was reached at Gubat. The force, however, had arrived too late, for Khartoum had already fallen; and after lingering at Gubat until the 15th of February, the column retreated to Korti. During the retirement it was necessary to dismount all the mounted men—over twelve hundred of them—and to take their camels for general transport.

Another column, about three thousand strong, under General Earle advanced up the river from Korti on the 28th of December, being accompanied by two divisions of the 11th company of the Commissariat with three hundred and thirty camels. The bulk of the troops moved by water in boats, and the camels lived upon growing crops. A little action at Kirbekan at the head of the fourth cataract cleared the enemy away, and the column continued its advance to within fifty miles of Abu Hamed, when on the 24th of February it was recalled. It then dropped down the river to Korti in nine days whereas the ascent had taken thirty-one days.

The difficulties of the expedition were of course enormous. The mere carriage of water by the desert column was an appalling problem. But it should seem, apart from all prejudice, that the appointment of a Director of Transport who had not been trained to the duty was a very grave mistake. In the first place he did not obtain camels enough by at least two thousand,* and in the second he did not appreciate the importance of husbanding the strength of the transport animals by proper care. All branches of the Army, the Commissariat not excepted, had much to learn about the management of camels; but there were at least some of the officers of the Commissariat who had gained considerable experience, and could have trained others of their own corps. The two Commissariat companies should have been expanded, and more officers of the corps should have been sent from England, and sent at

* This is Lt.-Col. Skinner's estimate. Captain Lea of the 11th company said that the line of communication required roughly double the number of camels actually present.

the very first. It was expert officers that were needed, not privates of the Commissariat and Transport Corps, who were found to be impatient and unintelligent in their treatment of the native drivers. On the contrary the Director promoted the formation of a company of officers and men of no experience, who worked hard and did their best, but from sheer ignorance of saddling and loading wore out great quantities of camels. The animals of the Commissariat were overworked with the task of taking up the loads at the various portages and carrying them from the feet to the heads of the rapids; and they were only with great difficulty kept serviceable. But the Director of Transport allowed the mounted troops—camel corps, as they were called—to exchange any bad camels of their own for good camels of the Commissariat; which was not encouraging to the Commissariat officers. Moreover, it was false policy; for a soldier, mounted or afoot, is useless unless he can be fed.

Then, when the time came for the advance, the transport companies were swept up from the line of communication and the 9th was bidden to march across the desert, with its exhausted camels. Naturally the unfortunate beasts succumbed. It is easy to be wise after the event; and it must be admitted that the British Government so long delayed their decision to rescue General Gordon that the military authorities had hardly a fair chance. There is no more exacting task than the effort to overtake lost time. But it does not seem that Lord Wolseley approached the vital problem of transport and supply in the most helpful spirit. Though a very able man and accomplished soldier, he always conceived that the Commissariat was a civilian's service (as it had been when he joined the Army), and that, though transport might be turned into a military service, any trouble with supply might be got over by hanging a Commissary. He would not realise that a transport officer is untrained unless he understands supply and that a supply officer is untrained unless he understands transport. Hence, though he appointed an inexpert Director of Transport, which was in itself a bad thing, he reported that his experiments generally were a success. But he was not aware that his Director of Transport counted practically for nothing; and that Sir Evelyn Wood and Sir Redvers Buller, not the less truly because unostentatiously, reversed his policy of divorcing transport from supply. He mentioned the names of eleven officers and six of lower rank of the Commissariat and Transport Staff with commendation in his final despatch; but whether he realised how completely they ignored in practice the whole of his new organisation is extremely doubtful.

Meanwhile, the outstanding fact remains that the expedition failed in its object. It might not in any case have reached Khartoum in time to save Gordon; but the desert column was too weak to advance to the city after reaching the Nile at Gubat, and it was too weak because it lacked the transport to make it stronger. Whether matters would have been better managed if the whole business of transport and supply had been left in the hands of Colonel Hughes, it would be unprofitable to discuss. But at least he would have been held responsible for any failure, whereas, as things actually fell out, the miscarriage was attributed to the decrees of Providence. It was due chiefly to the fact that the British Government undertook the whole enterprise too late.

THE SUAKIN EXPEDITION OF 1885. In February, 1885, the British Government contemplated the construction of a railway from Suakin to Berber and the suppression of Osman Digna's power with a view to seconding Lord Wolseley's operations. A force of nearly eleven thousand British and some three thousand Indians was therefore sent thither under the command of Sir Gerald Graham. The preparations were upon a liberal scale, and it was wisely decided to entrust the entire business of transport and supply to the senior Commissariat officer, Lieutenant-Colonel Robertson. The Indian troops, which brought their own transport, worked likewise under his orders with perfect concert.

There was already a small British garrison at Suakin, and the three Commissariat officers with it were hard at work before the arrival of the troops. Their duties were rather difficult because they had been set ashore at Quarantine Island, from which the only access to the mainland consisted in a narrow causeway, carrying a light railway; and great exertions were needed to prevent overcrowding in the island itself. On the 5th of March the Commissariat Staff landed, consisting of companies 3, 5, 7 and 12; and from that day onward camels began to pour in from many quarters. As fast as they were disembarked, they were organised and distributed as follows:

No. 7 Company. *Base and local transport at Suakin.* Five officers, six warrant officers, ninety-two other ranks, one interpreter, three hundred and ninety-seven natives, eleven mules, nine hundred and thirty-nine camels.

No. 3 Company. *Lines of Communication and Railway Transport.* Four officers, six warrant officers, sixty-five other ranks, two interpreters, six hundred and fifty-eight natives, eleven hundred camels.

No. 5 Company. *1st Infantry Brigade.* Six officers, three warrant officers, eighty-eight other ranks, one interpreter, three hundred and ninety-five natives, thirteen mules, six hundred and eighty camels.

No. 12 Company. *2nd Infantry Brigade.* Six officers, five warrant officers, eighty other ranks, two interpreters, four hundred and thirty-two natives, fourteen mules, six hundred and sixty-six camels.

Supply Detachment. Clerks, eight warrant officers, fifty-one privates; fifty-four bakers; twenty-seven butchers.

The Indian transport included thirteen officers, four warrant officers, nineteen non-commissioned officers, seventeen hundred and eighty-eight natives, one hundred and fifty-two mules, twenty-five hundred camels. It had been organised in India, and all of its European superiors, knowing the language and customs of their men, had an advantage which was denied to the British Commissariat who had to deal with Maltese, Greeks, Egyptians and men from Aden. The Indian transport was consequently most efficient, and was accordingly entrusted with the carriage of water and with transport for expeditions.

Regimental transport was made up of pack-mules, thirty-four being allowed to a battalion. It was specially laid down that all transport, when unemployed by the units to which it was allotted, should be at disposal for general purposes.

The great complication of the campaign was that there was no water fit for any human being (except a Sudani) to drink. The same difficulty upon a minor scale had occurred in the Abyssinian expedition, but at Suakin in 1885 it dominated all other considerations. It was overcome by the presence of no fewer than nine condensing-ships, from which the water was pumped ashore and distributed into tanks. Many descriptions of vessel were tried for transporting the water to a distance —wooden, leathern and galvanised iron—of which the last only was satisfactory. The ration of water was two gallons per man in Suakin and one gallon anywhere outside Suakin. The animals fortunately did fairly well on the brackish water obtainable from wells already existing or newly sunk; and it was arranged that the Royal Engineers should look to the pumps for raising water at these wells and that the Commissariat should take over responsibility for the water when it had reached the surface.

The operations undertaken would, but for the question

of water, have seemed trifling. The first forward movement was made to Hashin, about seven miles from Suakin, which was occupied on the 20th of March. A second post was established at Tofrek about six miles from Suakin on the way to Tamai on the 22nd. This had hardly been formed before it was attacked by the enemy, who were not repulsed without difficulty. The Arabs actually broke into the camp at one point and, reaching the transport, killed twelve men of the Commissariat and destroyed seven hundred and twenty-three out of a thousand and eighty camels. On the seven succeeding days further convoys were sent to Tofrek making up the supplies and water there to seven days' allowance. One of these convoys was attacked, and one hundred and seventeen camels with their loads were lost. However, the post at Tofrek answered its purpose as a stage on the way to Tamai, to which the troops marched on the 2nd of April, returning to Suakin on the 4th. This done, Tofrek was evacuated on the 6th; and on the 7th a steady advance was made to cover the construction of the railway westward. This involved collecting six days' reserve of rations and water for eight thousand men at Handub, about seven miles to west of Suakin, with forage for six hundred horses, five hundred mules and three thousand camels. The work continued until the 30th of April, when the force was withdrawn by order of the British Government, and operations came to an end.

All had gone smoothly enough. Field ovens were rendered unnecessary by a contractor who provided good bread at Suakin; and fresh meat was brought in the shape of Russian oxen from Odessa. The two serious shortcomings were the omission to provide sufficient officers at the landing-place and a dépôt for reserves of men and animals. To make good the former deficiency officers were taken from other corps, who did their best but, from lack of experience, were not very successful.

For the reserve dépôt an additional company of the Commissariat, the 17th, was asked for and sent out, but naturally arrived rather late. Moreover, it was found that more vehicles would have been acceptable for loading and for carrying water over short distances. There were about eighty of one description or another on the spot, but these were not enough. From first to last the animals employed by the transport on this expedition numbered one hundred and twenty-three horses, one thousand and fifty-four mules, one hundred and fifty-five asses and eight thousand two hundred and twenty-seven camels. Considering that the troops never moved ten miles from their base until they had begun to lay a railway behind them, the expedition shows the limitations imposed on an armed force by dependence on a water supply carried by animal transport.

THE BECHUANALAND EXPEDITION OF 1884–5. Simultaneously with these operations in the Sudan a small expedition was sent to Bechuanaland, rather as a measure of policy than to conduct a regular campaign. Few troops of the Regular Army were employed, most of the combatants being irregulars under military officers; the whole amounting to about three thousand men with five hundred native guards and a thousand drivers and followers. Altogether there were about five thousand men and twenty-three hundred horses to be fed. The main base was at Capetown; the advanced base, five hundred and seventy miles away and connected by rail with Capetown, was Orange River Terminus; the next important posts were:

Barkly, 110 miles	Mafeking, 50 miles
Taungs, 76 miles	Kanya, 65 miles
Vryburg, 46 miles	Molopololi, 45 miles.
Sitagoli, 50 miles	

The total length of the line of communication was therefore just over a thousand miles. The Commissariat and Transport establishment employed on this expedition numbered, including No. 10 company, nine officers, eight warrant officers, and one hundred and thirteen other ranks, of which two officers, one quartermaster, two first-class staff-sergeants, six conductors of supplies and sixty-three other ranks were set apart for duties of transport.

The camp at Orange River was laid out seventeen miles north of the station, and in consequence of a long drought there was no grazing and consequently no cattle. It was therefore necessary to purchase water carts and to equip them with mule draught. At Barkly ox transport was hired at 30s. per waggon and team per day; and the regiments were provided with regimental transport to carry the usual baggage and stores, seven days' rations for men and two days' forage for animals. The rest of the transport was divided into sections under a civilian contractor or a non-commissioned officer of the Commissariat. But No. 10 company was distributed into four transport sections at four principal posts, where all vehicles were inspected by the officer and, if necessary, repaired by the artificers.

Altogether the purchased transport included forty-four mule waggons, forty-two water carts, fifteen smaller carts, fifty-one horses, six hundred and thirty-seven mules and sixty-four oxen. The hired oxen numbered eight thousand one hundred and twenty-eight, which would mean roughly five hundred waggons.

The object of the expedition was attained without bloodshed within six months; and the casualties among horses did not exceed 8 per cent., among mules 5 per cent., and among oxen 7 per cent.—figures which become interesting when compared with those of the mortality among animals during the Boer War of 1899–1902.

CHAPTER IX

THE NEW ARMY SERVICE CORPS
AND ITS WORK. 1888-1898

THE RE-CREATION OF THE ARMY SERVICE CORPS. In November, 1887, the Quartermaster-General at the Horse Guards, Sir Redvers Buller, took occasion to represent that the establishment of the Commissariat and Transport Staff provided for two hundred and forty-four officers, but that only two hundred and twenty-four existed. He pointed out further that for the mobilisation of two Army Corps two hundred and twenty-four of these officers were required, and that no more than one hundred and thirteen could be produced. The higher ranks were full, but there was a shortage of subalterns, for which he at once accounted. "I do not myself believe", he wrote, "that we shall ever get a ready flow of officers into a service which offers no permanent prospect of employment and promotion." The old system, contrived with some hope of building up a reserve, had been to take officers of the line into the Commissariat for a term of five years, with possibility of extension to ten years, at the conclusion of which period they reverted to their regiments. This had obviously broken down, and it was necessary to replace it by a new one.

It was, therefore, decided to do away with the Department called the Commissariat and Transport Staff and to replace it by a regiment, wholly military,

213

called by the old name of the Army Service Corps, which an officer would join when young, and where he could make Transport and Supply his career. Pay, promotion and pensions were fixed on the lines of those in the Royal Engineers. The principle of taking officers from the line was not wholly abandoned, for sufficient reasons. An officer who had served for a short time with a company of infantry or a squadron of cavalry would, on active service, take greater interest in the subsistence of the fighting men and, at a pinch, would not be helpless if called upon to defend a convoy. But any officer joining the reconstituted Army Service Corps was accepted only on probation until he had passed through a regular course of theoretical and practical instruction. The great point, however, was that the men entrusted with the most difficult and often perilous business of feeding soldiers in the field should take their rightful place as brother-soldiers, and not be treated as mere clerks and servants. Then they could feel a pride in their calling, which would be of benefit not only to themselves but the Army at large.

And here perhaps I may be allowed to say a word of the creator of the Corps, Sir Redvers Buller. His family and my own are neighbours in Devon, and I knew him first when I was a boy and later still better as a man. He was, as befitted the son of a country squire, happier out of doors than in a library. He had no gift for languages, but was a fair mathematician and was very early interested in the science of architecture. He was a fair fisherman, a fair shot, a good horseman, a still better whip, and a really good sportsman. In his youth he had served in Canada and always spent his leave in the wilds, becoming an expert canoe-man and axe-man and something of a trapper. He loved a horse and could shoe a horse himself, and mend harness and saddlery. Succeeding to his father's estate after the death of an elder brother, he took to practical farming and stock-

General Sir Redvers Buller. V.C. G.C.B. G.C.M.G.

breeding, and there was no finer judge of Devon cattle. In fact there was little about cultivation, stock and horses (for he had made some study of veterinary surgery) that he did not know. He could produce working drawings for the building of a house, and he knew every detail of construction and every technical term of the builder. He made a special study of carriage-building and of butchers' meat for behoof of the Army Service Corps, and he told me that he searched all Great Britain for a colour printer who could faithfully reproduce the difference in hue between old and young beef. He had served in India, China, the Red River, Ashanti, South Africa and the Sudan, which gave him acquaintance with five different descriptions of transport. Thus it will be seen that, though he had not gone through the training school for transport and supply (he had passed the Staff College), he had most of the knowledge needful for a good officer of the Army Service Corps.

The warrant for the creation of the new corps was dated the 11th of December, 1888, and the new system was launched in the following year. Naturally time was needed before the changes in the constitution of the corps could take their full effect. With the exception of a few seniors at the very top of the list, most of the officers of the Commissariat and Transport Staff were transferred to the Army Service Corps; and some, though by no means all, of them were a little slow to adapt themselves to the new conditions. Old habits and traditions do not easily perish; and, in spite of the active work done by Commissariat officers in charge of transport and of transport animals in the field since the days of Wellington, there still lingered on men of the old school who, consciously or unconsciously, regarded transport and supply as still within the domain of the Treasury and conceived that the most important part of its business was of a sedentary nature, to be transacted in an office. Constant little campaigns, however, during the last decade of the nineteenth century were continually affording opportunities for experience, practically all of them in Africa, either to south or to west or to north. It is not necessary to dwell upon these at any great length. The motto of the Royal Artillery—*Ubique*—Everywhere—is even more appropriate to the Army Service Corps; for small expeditions may take the field without cannon but cannot even be called expeditions without food. Moreover, the nature of the transport in different parts of Africa is (saving mechanical appliances) always the same—in the north chiefly camels, in the south chiefly oxen, on the west coast human carriers. A very brief notice will, therefore, suffice for most of these petty enterprises.

In July, 1893, the Matabele were in rebellion in what is now called Rhodesia. Captain H. Donovan, A.S.C., who happened to be shooting big game in the country, joined the force for suppression of the revolt as a volunteer.

In November, 1893, and February, 1894, two little expeditions on the Gold Coast, known as the Sofa Expedition and the Gambia Expedition, called for the services of Captains F. W. Steel and D. Webb, of the Army Service Corps, who were then quartered at Sierra Leone. For the Sofa Expedition Captain F. W. B. Koe was also sent out from England. In the Gambia Expedition Captain Steele more than once took command of mixed forces as a combatant officer and received the Distinguished Service Order.

THE ASHANTI EXPEDITION OF 1895. The Ashantis, a conquering race and very unwilling to acknowledge a master, had failed to carry out the terms of the treaty imposed by Lord Wolseley in 1874; and it was necessary to bring them to reason. The troops to be employed were about seventeen hundred, three-fourths of them native African troops and the remainder British. The Army Service Corps were the first of the British to arrive on the scene, having sailed from Liverpool on the

16th and 23rd of November. Lieutenant-Colonel Ward, Major Clayton, twelve more officers, sixteen warrant officers, and some twenty non-commissioned officers composed the whole body.

Seven more officers drawn from various native corps were attached to the Army Service Corps for duties of transport, and the work of enrolling carriers began immediately.

By the 21st of December over eight thousand carriers had been enrolled, and their organisation into companies had begun.

A company in the first instance consisted of one officer, one warrant officer of the Army Service Corps, one interpreter, ten superintendents, forty headmen and forty gangs of twenty each, making eight hundred carriers; and the various companies were distinguished by coloured armlets.

The transport was divided into three parts:

(1) *Local transport*, which was employed in conveying supplies and stores from the base to the advanced base at Kwisa or to any one of the intermediate stations between them, viz.: Mansu (thirty miles from Cape Coast Castle), Prahsu (seventy-one miles), Essiaman Kuma (ninety-one miles), Akusirem (one hundred and nine miles), Kwisa (one hundred and twenty-four miles).

This work was done in part by the organised companies, in part by floating gangs which were engaged or discharged as required. The local transport was reckoned at seven thousand four hundred carriers.

(2) *Regimental transport.* This was allotted to each unit to carry baggage, reserve ammunition, medical stores and three days' supplies. To the more important units, four in all, an officer of the Army Service Corps was allotted, and to the rest a non-commissioned officer.

This duty absorbed nearly fifty-four hundred carriers.

217

(3) *The hammock train or sick transport.* This employed twenty-one hundred carriers more.

Altogether at its maximum the transport counted close upon fifteen thousand carriers.

The operations were bloodless. The final march into Kumasi was made on the 17th of January, 1896, and by the 7th of February the troops had begun to re-embark from the West Coast. The Army Service Corps returned to England in February and March. Lieutenant-Colonel Ward received the C.B. for his services and Major Clayton a brevet Lieutenant-Colonelcy. Fortunately the officers did not suffer greatly from sickness, for there were none too many, even including the attached officers, for the work. Fortunately also not a shot was fired, otherwise the difficulty of obtaining carriers among the tribes nearest the coast, who are abject cowards, might have delayed operations seriously.

ASHANTI EXPEDITION OF 1900. It will be convenient here to depart from strict chronological order and to pass to the next campaign on the Gold Coast. The next collision with the Ashantis, arising always from the old quarrel, was a more formidable affair. They broke out into revolt without any warning; the whole of the country north of the Prah joined them, and the Governor, Sir Frederick Hodgson, with his small garrison was besieged in Kumasi. This took place at the end of April, 1900. The whole affair was so sudden and so startling that for a time no one seems to have realised the situation. Reinforcements of native troops arrived in driblets and were pushed up country; but they remained scattered and isolated. The various posts between Prahsu and Kumasi, each holding a tiny garrison, were more or less beleaguered, and had no reserves either of food or of ammunition. Not until a new Commander-in-Chief, Sir James Willcocks, arrived on the 26th of May, was the full peril of the situation realised.

Everything was unpropitious to the new Commander. In the first place nearly every officer and man of the Regular Army and Reserve Forces was already employed in South Africa. Next, the rainy season, signifying continuous heavy rain for weeks, was just setting in. There were no stores at Cape Coast Castle. No provisions of any kind had been collected nor even ordered from England. Lastly, there was no transport, the tribes about the coast proving themselves worthy of the contempt in which the Ashantis had always held them. They refused to cross the Prah, and Prahsu was but half-way to Kumasi. Even if they had crossed it they would have thrown down their loads at the first shot and deserted into the forest—an abject race, of fine physique, but with too little heart even to carry a load in peace, much less in war. There were no white troops to be spared, though there were good native African regiments, and even native Indian troops, if it were possible to bring them to the spot in time. All really depended on about two hundred British officers and non-commissioned officers, and they had to do their work in a deadly climate at the most unhealthy season of the year within six degrees of the equator.

Among them was Lieutenant Willans of the Army Service Corps, who was serving in Northern Nigeria but was lent by the High Commissioner to Sir James Willcocks at this crisis. For the moment he could only buy up all the rice, tinned meat, biscuits and so forth that were obtainable along the coast from Sierra Leone to Lagos, and telegraph to England for the supplies, ammunition and equipment that were necessary. Simultaneously Sir James Willcocks begged for the despatch of carriers from all the British territories in East as well as West Africa, as well as for reinforcements of troops. In the first week of June, the first carriers began to arrive in batches of about five hundred at a time. These were Mendis and Timanis from Sierra Leone, men with no sense of honour or morality of any kind, who could not be kept from pilfering their loads nor from accusing each other of every imaginable crime. Their cheerfulness and good humour, however, were inexhaustible, and, though at first they were inclined to run away when they came under fire, they soon learned to set down their loads and take cover behind them. They had been organised at Sierra Leone in gangs of twenty-five under a headman and, as they could all talk some kind of barbaric English, they could be directed by any British officers. They were, therefore, set to work immediately to fill a dépôt at Prahsu, whither headquarters moved up on the 8th of June.

Meanwhile two of the posts between Prahsu and Kumasi had fallen into the enemy's hands and communications north of the Prah were absolutely severed. It was necessary to send supplies and stores to the stations north of the captured posts by a circuitous path. These convoys of course required an escort, for they had to fight their way for every yard of the advance; and the difficulties of progress through the forest, what with bogs and swamps and swollen streams and fallen trees, were appalling. The carriers often had to move for long distances almost up to their necks in mud and water. They were short of food and liable to come under fire at any moment, but they toiled on with indomitable cheerfulness and endurance, faithfully carrying their loads. Even when they had reached their destination they were often detained for many days or even weeks before an escort could be collected to take them back, which added enormously to the troubles of Major Willans.

However, by the end of June preparations were sufficiently far advanced to enable Sir James Willcocks to advance with a thousand men upon Kumasi, though his reserve of supplies was so small as to make the operation in the highest degree hazardous. The danger to Kumasi was, however, so urgent that he felt bound to take the risk; and Kumasi was duly relieved on the 15th of July. Thenceforward it became the advanced base of operations.

Meanwhile fresh carriers arrived from various quarters. First came three hundred Haussas from Northern Nigeria, who were employed exclusively in carrying guns and ammunition. Faithful and fearless, they took a pride in their loads, and in action stood behind the guns to watch the effect of their fire. Next landed seven hundred and fifty men from British Central Africa. They were unfortunate in suffering from an epidemic of pneumonia, which killed thirty-seven of them on the voyage. Apart from this sickliness they were disheartened by separation from the native soldiers whom they knew. Not until the stronger among them had been collected at Kumasi did they begin to recover, in time to do some good work at the close of the year.

Lastly came two thousand men from Mombasa and Zanzibar under two British leaders. They were very superior, self-respecting men, organised in gangs of one hundred, each under a trustworthy headman and two subordinates. They held themselves aloof from all the other carriers; they worked steadily; they went under fire without hesitation and they were scrupulously honest, never attempting to steal from their loads. In fact, they were ideal carriers.

Thus gradually the service of transport and supply—under a single head, be it observed—was built up. As far as the Prah the degenerate tribes could be utilised. Beyond the Prah only the imported carriers could be trusted; and, since Kumasi was the centre from which flying columns were pushed out for the pacification of the country, it was necessary to amass there very large reserves and a very considerable force of carriers. A regular service of convoys was instituted and the Etappen system was put into force. The stations, four in number, were from sixteen to twenty-two miles apart, and at three of them eleven hundred carriers were stationed. Convoys started on three, four or five days a week. Half of the carriers in each station moved north and half south, so that they met half-way between two stations and handed over their loads to be carried forward or returned.

Considering that the whole service was improvised under unspeakable difficulties, and that no one knew anything about transport and supply except Lieutenant Willans, the rapidity of its development was remarkable. None of the officers assigned to him had the slightest experience of such duties; and the business of returns and accounts was at first most puzzling to them, the more so since there were no printed forms nor proper stationery to help them. They each received a few minutes of hurried instruction from Lieutenant Willans, after which they did their best to accomplish their clerical work without any clerks and on any paper that they could find. A telegraphed request for stationery to be sent out from home was answered first by the despatch of a mass of forms to Sierra Leone. This was rather like sending to the Shetland Islands goods urgently required at the Land's End. At last in September the expected stationery arrived at Cape Coast Castle and was found to consist of forms for hired vehicles and boat notes. The former would have been most useful at Cape Town, and the latter had had their value on the Upper Nile; but neither were of the slightest service on the Gold Coast. However, the officers even so did their work efficiently; and, though the point may seem a small one, it must compel admiration among the understanding. It is wearisome enough, as the writer knows by experience, to draw out forms for returns and fill them up, even with every comfort and facility, in the tropics. What must it have been to men worn out with toil and shaking with fever, writing on their knees or on some rude makeshift, without any of the aids of the office table?

By the middle of December the campaign had been successfully ended, but few of the British officers or non-commissioned officers were by that time left standing. The climate and Ashanti bullets had killed not a few and laid low many more. All Europeans, whether nominally combatant or non-combatant, took the same risks, for a transport officer with a convoy was as freely exposed to fire as any of the escort. Lieutenant Willans himself was wounded in action on the 30th of September; and, on the same day and in the same combat, there was wounded one whom Sir James Willcocks describes as "a fine old veteran of the Army Service Corps who had come out at the end of his service to see a fight".—Sergeant-Major Shanley. Happily the Colonial Office, knowing that all depended on the little handful of British, did its best to keep them in health by abundance of the very best supplies. Fresh meat, in the shape of cattle and poultry, could only be gathered in by purchase from a point on the coast many hundreds of miles distant; but it was obtained, and the regular issue of it thrice a week contributed much to keep the Europeans in health. It may be noted that their weekly ration included half a pound of tea, coffee, cocoa or chocolate (any two of them that they might prefer), a bottle of whisky and half a bottle of rum; nor can there be doubt that all three were needed by men overworked, both physically and mentally, in that exhausting climate. Altogether it was "a horrible little campaign," in which the Army Service Corps bore a very honourable share. "Willans never failed me from start to finish in Ashanti", wrote Sir James Willcocks, and Lieutenant Willans was the Army Service Corps. Of course, as we have just seen, there was another member of the Corps present in the person of Serjeant-Major Shanley, but he seems to have taken on a combatant status for the occasion. However that may be, it will probably be long before the Army Service Corps can

223

again show such a record as that of Ashanti in 1900. *Present*, two officers; *casualties*, two officers wounded.

MASHONALAND, 1896. In 1896 a second revolt of the Matabele called for suppression by the local troops; and Lieutenant W. E. Barnes of the Army Service Corps was sent up to join them in June. He was killed in action on the 10th of August, but meanwhile Lieutenant-Colonel C. H. Bridge, two warrant officers and a corporal had been sent out to Mashonaland from England. At the close of the operations Colonel Bridge received the C.B. and Staff-Serjeant Field was promoted to commissioned rank as Quartermaster.

THE SUDAN CAMPAIGNS, 1896–8. In this same year 1896 the first steps were taken towards the reconquest of the Sudan. The work was begun by the Egyptian Army under British officers, and was undertaken at leisure, for there was no General Gordon at Khartoum to be rescued against time, as in 1885. The railway past the second cataract at Wadi Halfa was reconstructed, the Dervishes (as the Mahdi's followers were called) were thrust back, and the railway was carried on into the province of Dongola. Thus much was accomplished in 1896. But in 1897 a new departure was taken and a railway was built across the desert from Wadi Halfa south-eastward to Abu Hamed, cutting across a great bend of the Nile. The work was begun on the 1st of January and completed by the 1st of November, a flying column having driven the Arabs from Abu Hamed in August. But military considerations made it imperative to push on at once to Berber, and therewith the difficulties of transport were for a time greatly increased. The loading and unloading along the line of communication was still a source of much trouble.

From Cairo to the first rail-head, now extended for 100
    miles north of Assiut, was 340 miles;
  from thence to Assuan by river, 205 miles;

from thence to the head of the cataract by rail, 6 miles;
from thence to Wadi Halfa by boat, 226 miles;
from Wadi Halfa to Abu Hamed by rail, 248 miles;
and thence came in successive stages
45 miles by boat,
13 miles round a cataract by camel,
25 miles more by boat,
11 miles round another cataract by camel,
and finally 22 miles more by boat.

In March, 1898, the Egyptian force at the front was increased to fourteen thousand by the addition of a British brigade, which added to the strain on the transport; but by July the construction of the railway from Abu Hamed to the British camp at the Atbara, twenty miles south of Berber, had been completed, and thenceforward all was comparatively easy. The enemy's position on the Atbara was stormed on the 8th of April. For the final advance on Khartoum in September, 1898, there were concentrated some eight thousand British and eighteen thousand Egyptian troops; but what with the railway and with plenty of steamers on the river, they moved with no more land transport than thirty-five hundred camels, nine hundred mules and two hundred and thirty asses. The final and decisive action of Omdurman was fought on the 2nd of September, 1898.

As to the actual organisation of the transport and supply service, it is a little difficult to speak. Sir Herbert Kitchener commanded the line of communication as well as the fighting force at the front; and not an ounce of food was issued from the reserves at Assuan and Wadi Halfa without his direct sanction. The accumulation of these reserves, however, was the work of Lieutenant-Colonel Rogers of the Army Service Corps and the Egyptian Army. The supply officers under him, a captain and two lieutenants, all belonged to the Army Service Corps. But the Director of Transport was Lieutenant-Colonel Walter Kitchener, brother to Sir Herbert, and his four assistants were all drawn from the British infantry. Three additional officers of the Army Service Corps were sent out to the Sudan in 1896, and of the whole number there were mentioned in despatches Lieutenant-Colonel Rogers, Captain Drage, Lieutenant Blunt, and Lieutenant Howard, while Captain Morgan received the Distinguished Service Order. After the occupation of Abu Hamed Captain Drage was again thanked in despatches, his name, however, being linked with those of transport officers. For the final campaign of 1898 seven officers of the Army Service Corps left England in January and four more in April. After the action of the Atbara Staff-Sergeant Wyeth of the Army Service Corps was mentioned in despatches; and after the action of Omdurman the list of Army Service Corps officers distinguished in despatches is long—Lieutenant-Colonels Hope and Rogers, Majors Drage and Morgan, Captains Sargent, Blunt, Coutts and Howard, Lieutenant Pigott, Quartermaster-Sergeant Osburn, Staff-Sergeant Beville, Sergeants Parsons and Topliss, Second Corporal Pawley, Shoeing smith Peter Smith (who was wounded), and Private Darling. Lieutenant-Colonel Hope received the Companionship of the Bath, Captains Bernard and Blunt brevet majorities, and Lieutenant Frank Hunnard the Distinguished Service Order. The Distinguished Conduct Medal also was awarded to Staff-Sergeants Beville and Wyeth, Sergeants Parsons, Topliss and Titterell, Quartermaster-Sergeant Osburn, Second Corporal Pawley, Shoeing smith Peter Smith and Private Darling.

It is to be remarked that the Army Service Corps in these campaigns was debarred apparently from any share in the work of transport, and that the duties of transport and supply were absolutely separated. But the expeditions were really Egyptian rather than British, and Sir Herbert Kitchener himself probably furnished the link that bound transport and supply together. In such comparatively small affairs it was possible for one man to combine in himself a considerable number of functions, and Sir Herbert Kitchener was certainly not averse from doing so. Moreover he had Lord Wolseley's example to justify him in placing supply and transport under different heads, and probably he had no knowledge of the actual, as opposed to the ostensible, working of Lord Wolseley's system. The operations had begun on a small scale, and the arrangements for transport and supply were simply expanded to meet increasing needs, not indeed without temporary strain but without such exacting demand as might require examination of first principles.

Meanwhile in this same year the Transport Branch of the Army Service Corps was increased by forty officers and one thousand men to meet the deficiency existing in the number of transport units required for mobilisation. The organisation for the field had also taken definite shape. The Army had until very recent times been not an army at all but a collection of regiments; and regimental feeling (which alone had kept the Army together for two centuries) was still so strong that, upon working out the details for mobilisation, the regiment or battalion had been selected as the lowest unit to be self-equipped.

The first division of transport, therefore, was:

1. The *Regimental Transport*, which fell into two parts,

(a) The Fighting Transport for the conveyance of ammunition, entrenching tools and so forth.

(b) The Subsistence Transport, carrying one or two days' rations of food and forage for the unit.

An officer, a sergeant and (in an European war) drivers were furnished by the unit for this Regimental Transport.

2. The second division of transport was the *Supply*

Column or *Replenishing Transport*, also calculated to carry one or two days' supplies. The supply columns were organised for four distinct units: Cavalry Brigade, Infantry Brigade, Divisional Troops and Corps Troops. Each was under the charge of a company of the Army Service Corps—trained men under trained officers with all the necessary equipment for the preparation and issue of supplies and for keeping account of the same.

3. The third division, technically called the *Supply Park*, was the Travelling Dépôt or Rolling Magazine, organised to carry at least three days' food and forage for the men and animals of the Army. This of course was under the Army Service Corps.

4. A fourth division, in the event of there being no railway, was the *Auxiliary Transport*, for the replenishing of supply parks.

It was said, as a homely illustration, that the Regimental Transport corresponded to the store cupboards of a household, the Supply Column to the tradesman's carts which deliver supplies daily at the door, and the Supply Park to the tradesman's dépôts to which the carts return, when empty, for a fresh load. This is true enough so long as it is remembered that an army is a collection not of stationary but of moving households, with which the tradesmen's carts and dépôts must contrive to keep pace. But it is just this movement which makes the problem of transport and supply so puzzling. It is difficult enough when the movement is forward; but when it is backward—in fact a retreat with an enemy pressing hard upon the rear—it becomes a very high problem indeed. It is better, therefore, not to press illustrations too far, and to note simply that in this organisation the Supply Park represented the handling of goods in bulk, and the Supply Column the handling of the same in detail, and that it was important that their functions should not be confounded.

CHAPTER X

THE SOUTH AFRICAN WAR OF 1899–1902

W E come now to the first great test to which the newly organised Army Service Corps was to be subjected—the South African War of 1899–1902. The broad question at issue, evaded in 1881, was whether the British or the Dutch, namely the Boers of the Transvaal and the Orange Free State with their compatriots in Cape Colony, were to be masters in South Africa. The contest between the two parties had become acute since the discovery of gold in the two Dutch republics. The precious metal had attracted to the Transvaal a vast swarm of foreigners—Uitlanders as they were called—so many indeed that they considerably outnumbered the Boers. But though they were heavily taxed and provided the greater part of the revenue, the Boers steadily refused to give them any voice in the government of the country. In June, 1895, the Uitlanders attempted an insurrection in arms which, being very foolishly contrived, was easily repressed; while the incident gave the Transvaal Government an excuse for continued denial to them of civic rights, and a pretext for laying in vast stores of munitions of war. Negotiations to end this unsatisfactory state of things were initiated in May, 1899, but to no purpose; and then weak reinforcements were sent out to the British garrisons in South Africa. Shortly afterwards, on the 11th of October, the Transvaal Government declared war, and was supported in its defiance by the Orange Free State.

Nervously anxious to take no step which could be construed as aggressive, the British Cabinet had refrained from sending out troops enough for security against attack; but preparations had not been wholly neglected. In July Colonel Charles Bridge and four more officers of the Army Service Corps had arrived in Cape Colony to make enquiry as to animals, vehicles and harness. Moreover, between the 8th of July and the 30th of September forty-eight officers and two hundred and twenty-four of other ranks of the transport branch of the Corps embarked for South Africa, besides two hundred and twenty-one clerks, bakers and butchers. Hence it was, that on the day after the declaration of war a first contract was signed with Julius Weil for seven hundred ox waggons. But the fighting men on the spot were as yet so few that for several weeks the British possessions lay at the mercy of the Boers. Fortunately the latter were not very enterprising enemies, and failed in great measure to take advantage of their opportunity.

In the days before railways and steamships the conquest of the two Dutch republics would have been an impossible task owing to the vast extent of the country. Everything, therefore, turned upon the railways, of which there were three main lines. The western railway ran from Capetown by Kimberley to Mafeking and beyond it to northward. The midland railway started from Port Elizabeth in two more or less parallel lines, the western branch through Graaf Reinet, the eastern through Cradock, which, uniting at Rosmead Junction, pursued the way north by Springfontein, Bloemfontein, Kroonstad and Johannesburg to Pretoria and beyond. The eastern railway ran from East London by Queenstown, Stormberg and Bethulie, joining the midland railway at Springfontein. From east to west these three main lines were linked together within British territory by branch lines running from Stormberg on the eastern railway to Rosmead on the midland, and from Naawport on the midland to De Aar on the western railway. On the side of Natal a line ran from Durban to Ladysmith and Laing's Nek and struck the midland railway a little to south of Johannesburg. Thus from all four of the principal ports, Capetown, Port Elizabeth, East London and Durban, railways converged upon Pretoria.

On the side of Natal the British frontier was strategically very faulty. The northern part of the colony ran up into a sharp salient, having the Transvaal on the eastern and the Orange Free State on the western flank. Within this salient lay Ladysmith which, though in a hopelessly indefensible position, became, through the drift of circumstances, the principal dépôt of supplies and stores for the British in that quarter. Its garrison, which included a detachment of the Army Service Corps, numbered about twelve thousand men. The Boers began early to close round it. The British struck at them with some success on the 20th, 21st and 24th of October, but failed in a more serious effort on the 30th; and by the 2nd of November Ladysmith was closely invested. Its relief involved forcing the passage of the Tugela River and breaking through a series of nearly impregnable positions beyond it.

On the side of Cape Colony, Kimberley, about five hundred miles north-east of Capetown, with a garrison of four thousand men, was likewise beleaguered, as also was Mafeking, with a garrison of two thousand, some two hundred miles further to the north. Neither was in any urgent peril, but the investment of Kimberley cut off, while it lasted, the resources of Bechuanaland, which affected the cost of hired waggons in the contracts made in 1899. Furthermore, some thousands of Uitlanders had fled from the Transvaal to Natal and to Cape Colony, which raised the cost of all supplies very seriously. In fact, until in November vast shipments of provisions were made from England, Colonel Richardson, the Director of Supplies in Cape Colony, lived in a state of painful anxiety. He knew that some forty thousand troops would arrive shortly and was at his wits' end to accumulate any reserve of victuals for them.

Happily the Army Service Corps was sent out in advance of the fighting troops. On the 6th of October no fewer than nineteen companies embarked for South Africa, and a twentieth followed on the 21st, making, with the six companies already on the spot, a total of twenty-six in all. On the 30th of October, the Commander-in-Chief, Sir Redvers Buller, reached Cape-town, having left England on the 14th. By that time not only were Kimberley and Mafeking, on the side of Cape Colony, invested, but the enemy had occupied the road bridge at Colesberg and the railway bridges at Norval's Pont and Bethulie and were marching on Colesberg. To oppose them Buller had of regular troops no more than three and a half battalions, three batteries of artillery and three squadrons of cavalry. Of the three railways, the western was blocked at Kimberley; the midland was insecure owing to the hostility of the Dutch settlers at Graaf Reinet and Cradock; and the eastern was held by the British as far north as Queens-town. On this side Sir Redvers sent one fraction of his little force under General French to Naauwport, and another fraction under General Gatacre to Queenstown, and hoped for the best. A week later the Boers in Natal advanced southward; and the danger to that Colony became urgent.

On the 9th of November troops began to come in from England. Three brigades were sent round to Natal, and one division, under Lord Methuen, was directed to advance up the western railway to the relief of Kimberley. As each unit was disembarked it was at once provided with transport, according to the scale laid down by regulation, without a day's delay. To enable Methuen to leave the railway, if necessary, he received transport enough to carry five days' supplies. His orders were, if he reached Kimberley, to reinforce the garrison, bring away non-combatants, fall back to Orange River and there halt, until all was ready for a general advance. He was then to move eastward and seize the bridges over the Orange River. Supplies were therefore to be accumulated for him at De Aar and Orange River Stations on the western railway, as also at Port Elizabeth and East London, so that, as he moved eastward, he should open up new lines of supply. As a matter of fact, large quantities of supplies had already been pushed up to De Aar and Orange River, though at considerable risk, for there were not troops enough to protect them. Sir Redvers's last act was to divide for the time (though against all of his own principles) the control of supply and transport, thinking that the combination was too heavy a charge for one man. He therefore made Colonel Richardson Director of Supplies and Colonel Bridge Director of Transport, in full confidence that they would work well together. This done, on the 22nd of November he left Capetown for Natal.

Meanwhile Methuen had begun his advance on Kimberley. In three engagements on the 23rd, 25th and 28th of November he drove the Boers back; but in a fourth attack on the 11th of December he was repulsed. He then came to a standstill by Modder River.

On the previous day General Gatacre had attempted an offensive movement about Stormberg and had also been driven back.

On the 15th of December Buller with about twenty-one thousand men made his first effort to force his way to Ladysmith and was likewise repulsed.

The news of these mishaps caused great excitement in England. It was clear for one thing that the army sent out to South Africa was not nearly strong enough for its purpose, and for another that one man could not possibly direct operations from bases a thousand miles apart, as were Capetown and Durban.* Every regular soldier that could be spared was sent out; corps were formed of militia, yeomanry and volunteers; the Colonies contributed contingents; and altogether between October, 1899, and September, 1900, there were despatched to South Africa two hundred and fifty thousand men. Lastly Lord Roberts was appointed to the chief command in South Africa with Lord Kitchener for the Chief of his Staff.

Foremost to arrive among the reinforcements was of course the Army Service Corps, three companies having embarked at the end of November, three more in the middle of December, three more in the first days of January, 1900, one more at the beginning of February, and three more in the middle of March. But these were naturally quite insufficient for the very large force (comparatively speaking) which was pouring into South Africa. The strength of the Corps had been fixed without any idea that it would have to provide for such numbers, and the question of expansion became urgent. According to the regulations a force of one division of cavalry and three of infantry—say forty-three thousand men—would require twenty-three transport companies, including six for the lines of communication. Since there were only thirty-four transport companies in all, there remained but eleven to deal with, at a moderate computation, one hundred thousand men. Such a situation was bound to present difficulties. Probably the best method of meeting them would have been to withdraw one or two companies from each infantry division and to use them for the new brigades and divisions, at the same time expanding both them and the remaining companies to make good the pressing need. There had been no complaint against the transport so far. Everything had worked smoothly and well. The extension of

* In Europe it would be like asking the same man to direct operations at Havre and at Lisbon.

the existing organisation would probably have accomplished what was necessary with the least possible friction or confusion. Had Lord Wolseley or Sir Evelyn Wood or Sir Redvers Buller been in supreme command, they would most likely have adopted this course, for they thoroughly knew the British Army and all of its departments.

Most unfortunately neither Lord Roberts nor Lord Kitchener had the slightest knowledge of the British Army at large, nor of the course of events which had led to the reconstruction of the Army Service Corps in 1888. Nor can they be blamed, for Lord Roberts had served all his time in India, and Lord Kitchener had been tied for the greatest part of his career to Palestine and to Egypt. It is difficult to guess exactly what happened; or to say whether Lord Kitchener had resolved, even before he landed, to reorganise the transport according to his own ideas. He had certainly for some reason made up his mind on the outward voyage that it was in disorder. In any case both he and Lord Roberts seem to have imagined that, because the transport had been allotted to units on the regulated scale, it was therefore irrevocably and inseparably bound up as part and parcel of those units, and furthermore that no other transport existed. They were completely mistaken upon both points. We have the evidence of Lieutenant-Colonel Clayton before the Royal Commission that there was plenty of transport when Lord Roberts arrived; and it was very plainly laid down in Sir Redvers Buller's orders that *all* transport was under the orders and at the disposition of the senior transport officer on the spot, and that regimental transport in particular could be withdrawn for general purposes at any time. It was indeed true that transport had been delivered to units which were to remain stationary; but for that the Director of Transport could not be blamed. No one confided to him which battalions were to take the field and which to guard the lines of communication. Indeed so many orders and counter-orders were issued on the subject that little seems to have been known by anyone. In such circumstances the Director hesitated not to equip all units with transport, since he could at any time take back any part of it.

However, Lord Roberts, or Lord Kitchener for him, determined that he would change everything. It is very clear, from Lord Roberts's evidence before the Royal Commission, that he had not the slightest idea what the existing transport organisation was. He seems to have thought that there was nothing but regimental transport; and it was necessary to remind him of the existence of supply columns and supply parks. Lord Kitchener's ignorance appears to have been at least as profound, though it manifested itself in a different fashion. When Colonel Bridge spoke to him about ammunition parks and supply parks Lord Kitchener simply stared at him blankly and ejaculated, "I don't know what you mean". It should seem, however, from such evidence as can be gathered, that the distribution of transport generally, and of regimental transport in particular, was fundamentally distasteful to him. Regimental transport, it will be remembered, was of two kinds, the first line or fighting transport (ammunition, water carts, entrenching tools, etc.) and the second line or subsistence transport (one day's ration, kits, etc.). Lord Kitchener decided to leave the first line untouched, but to sweep the second line and all the rest of the transport—ammunition columns, ammunition parks, Royal Engineers' units and supply columns—into one common stock, to be at disposal for any purpose.

The companies of the Army Service Corps were then each of them split up into two; their numbers were taken from them and they were designated by letters, the lowest number becoming A and B, the next C and D and so on. In this division of the companies the

Army Service Corps officer in command remained with the right half, and the subaltern was assigned to the left half, so that he might be of assistance to the new commander, who would possess no expert knowledge. For, of course, in order to complete these new companies it would be necessary to draft into them a number of officers from every branch of the service. As an attraction, presumably, to these stranger officers, it was arranged that all of them should receive staff rates of pay and allowances, though few of them had the slightest experience of transport. The officers of the Army Service Corps, who knew their business, were left with only the much smaller allowances originally arranged for them; and thus it came about that young militia officers drew double the emoluments of the Army Service Corps officer under whom they were serving. In one instance, indeed, the senior transport officer of a division, happening to belong to the Army Service Corps, received less pay and allowances than any of his subordinates. It was, however, recognised that mere emoluments could not make good the lack of knowledge and experience; so in order to save these inexpert officers from the responsibility for financial details and for keeping accounts, it was ordained that the Army Service Corps officer, who had commanded the original company, should be answerable for the books, accounts, records and so forth of the two divisions into which it had been parted, as also for their equipment, their animals and the pay of the non-commissioned officers and men.

The new companies were then organised for mule transport and ox transport (see table, p. 238).

The general idea underlying these changes was that two mule companies should furnish the transport required for an infantry division, supplying detachments for each of its units in place of the old regimental transport. Each unit was to have transport sufficient to carry two days' rations and forage; for supply columns, it must be repeated, had been utterly abolished. The transformation of the old organisation into the new was accomplished in a very brief space of time; and both Colonel Richardson and Lieutenant-Colonel Clayton pronounced it to be—as undoubtedly it was—an amazing piece of work. The strain thrown upon the Army Service Corps was terrific, and more than one officer broke down under it. But orders were obeyed; Lord Kitchener's theory was converted, so far as possible, into practice; and it remained to be seen how the new system would work in the field.

Mule Company	*Ox Company*
1 Major or Captain	1 Captain
1 Subaltern	1 Subaltern
1 Warrant Officer	1 Warrant Officer
4 Sergeants or Corporals	1 Company Sergeant-
2 Second or Lance-Cor-	Major
porals	2 Sergeants
20 Drivers (including 2	2 Corporals
"cold shoers")	1 Trumpeter
2 Farriers	2 Farriers
1 Wheeler	1 Wheeler
1 Collar Maker	10 Drivers (batmen and
16 Horses	cooks)
520 Mules	10 Horses (public)
49 Buck waggons	*Civilian Establishment*
4 Scotch carts	28 European conductors
1 Water cart	200 Native drivers
Civilians	20 Horses
5 Conductors	1600 Oxen
124 Natives	100 Waggons
	1 Water cart

After review of the whole military situation Lord Roberts decided to concentrate near Lord Methuen's camp on the Modder River, turn the left flank of the Boer force under General Cronje, which barred Methuen's advance, and strike eastward upon Bloemfontein. In other words, he was going to march with thirty thousand men a hundred miles away from the western railway until he struck the midland line; and this signified the need of a very large supply park and of very perfect arrangements for transport and supply. The new companies were duly portioned out to the various brigades and divisions, and were then distributed among the various smaller units. It was distinctly ordered that the transport thus allotted was to be considered as attached to its unit only while actually on the move, and that, if need were, it might be withdrawn at any moment. Upon this principle transport was doled out to the ammunition columns of the artillery and to various units of the Royal Engineers, necessitating the presence not only of the officers of those arms, who were responsible for the loads, but of transport officers to keep a jealous eye on animals and vehicles. For other units the *personnel* of the Army Service Corps was subdivided to extremity in order to provide men who knew their business. Under the old system, it will be remembered, each battalion of infantry furnished a trained officer and a few trained men to look after the second line of regimental transport. Lord Kitchener preferred to dispense with these and to replace them by a detachment of amateurs, stiffened by a sergeant and one or two drivers of the Army Service Corps. Some units had actually to content themselves with a single driver. The Royal Artillery had borrowed six hundred of the Army Service Corps's drivers, so that it was lucky if even a single driver could be spared. However, the great thing was that Lord Kitchener had carried his point about throwing the whole of the transport into one common stock. He seems to have supposed, though no order was actually given, that, when the force came to a halt, all transport should be concentrated in a central camp.

Under these conditions Lord Roberts set his force in motion on the 11th of February, 1900, and on the same day a supply park of two hundred ox waggons under Major Long of the Army Service Corps crossed the Orange River into the Orange Free State. The ox is a beast whose ways, in South Africa at any rate, must be studied and respected. He cannot work during the heat of the day. He will not drink until the sun has been up for some hours, nor after sunset. His working hours are therefore from 2 or 3 a.m. until 9 a.m.; his grazing and resting hours extend, roughly, from 9 a.m. till 4 p.m.; and he will work again from 4 p.m. till 8 or 9 p.m. The officer commanding the escort of the supply park insisted on marching during the heat of the day on the 11th, with the result that one hundred and five oxen dropped out and died. Fortunately Major Long chanced next day to encounter Lord Roberts, who issued orders to forbid the practice.

On the night of the 13th, after issuing rations to the troops, the park, now reduced to one hundred and eighty loaded waggons, moved to Waterval Drift on the Riet River and spent the night of the 14th crossing the drift. In spite of Major Long's repeated requests, no adequate escort had been provided, and on the morning of the 15th the Boers opened fire upon the park from a line of hills about twelve hundred yards in advance. Thereupon Major Long sent back all the cattle to the drift, out of harm's way, and took, with his officers, measures for the defence of the waggons. There was a small party of infantry and another of mounted infantry with the convoy, and they made successful resistance until 1.30 p.m., when the Boer fire slackened. Thereupon Major Long's combatant superiors gave orders for the cattle to be brought out of the drift and for the supply park to move on. This was a mistake, if only because it abridged the oxen of two of their resting hours, and, tactically, it was a fatal blunder. No sooner did the oxen reappear than the Boers reopened fire. The oxen, being hungry and seeing good grass before them at the foot of the Boer position, rushed towards it and, notwithstanding all of Major Long's efforts, could not be stopped. Thus twenty-five hundred cattle, through sheer mismanagement not of the Army Service Corps but of other officers, ran straight into the enemy's arms. There remained the waggons, round which an entrenchment was dug as night fell; but at midnight orders came to abandon them; and abandoned they were. The whole incident was the result of bad staff work, for which no excuse could be put forward; and it bade fair to wreck Lord Roberts's operations for the moment. By a curious coincidence, at this very time Lord Roberts relieved Colonel Richardson of the control of the transport and transferred it to Sir William Nicholson, an able officer from the Royal Engineers, who, however, had no experience nor special knowledge of transport and supply.

On the same day, the 15th, General French made a forward movement with the cavalry division, which relieved Kimberley. He had refused to part with his supply column, maintaining that cavalry, owing to the greater rapidity of its movements, could not dispense with it; and indeed it is difficult to see how, without it, the cavalry division could possibly have accomplished all the hard work which it did between the 10th and the 16th. Meanwhile the whole of Lord Roberts's troops were placed on half rations; and on the 17th they came to a halt before Paardeberg, about twenty-five miles east and north of Modder River Station, where Lord Roberts had succeeded in surrounding the Boer force under General Cronje. On the evening of the 17th Major Long, who had returned to the railway, started again with another convoy of one hundred ox waggons from Jacobsdaal for Klip Drift on the Modder River, about eight miles west of Paardeberg. Arriving at 6 a.m. on the 18th, he found all the transport of the cavalry division (including of course the supply column) awaiting him, with orders to victual not the cavalry division only but the entire army at Paardeberg. In fact, by declining to part with his supply column, General French saved the troops before Paardeberg from starving certainly for twenty-four and possibly for forty-eight hours.

Having surrounded Cronje's force, Lord Roberts decided not to end matters promptly by an assault but to wait for hunger to do its work. The army was then kept stationary until Cronje surrendered on the 27th. In that period a good quantity of supplies was accumulated at Paardeberg, but the troops remained upon half rations of biscuit, while forage was so scarce that the animals were starving. The oxen suffered much from heavy rain at this time and from waiting about to load up the sick and wounded when about to return to the railway for more supplies. Among other changes, Lord Kitchener had reduced the ambulance waggons for each division from twelve to two, with the result that the sick and wounded were carried for miles in springless, uncovered ox waggons. Lord Roberts in his report contended that these ox waggons compared not unfavourably with the regulation ambulance. Captain Ford, who succeeded Major Long in command of the supply park, was not so confident. "It was", he wrote, "a pitiful sight to see some hundreds of wounded men leaving in open ox waggons for the base in pouring rain."

On the 1st of March a slight forward movement was made, but the army did not fairly get under way for Bloemfontein until the 6th. Even then large quantities of biscuit and oats were left behind, though horses were dying for want of forage. The destruction of the old system of the Army Service Corps had evidently upset all the old bases of calculation. The supply column of the cavalry division once again came to the rescue and saved the abandoned oats; but the lack of a complete service of supply columns was felt acutely. The flow of supplies caused endless worry and anxiety, for the next convoy behind the supply park were always a full day in rear; and there was no means of sending back to meet and unload it. Ultimately the army occupied Bloemfontein without resistance, and then sat down exhausted and paralysed.

Lord Roberts in his evidence before the Royal Commission declared that during the march from Modder River to Bloemfontein the total loss of mules was seven hundred and ninety-six out of eleven thousand, three hundred and sixty-two, or 7 per cent. Major Long, who became senior transport officer to the 9th Division on the 24th of February, reported that this division had entered the Orange Free State on the 13th of February with sixteen hundred and thirty-eight mules. It arrived at Bloemfontein with twelve hundred and forty-eight mules, showing an actual loss of three hundred and ninety; but of the survivors only eight hundred and ninety-six were fairly fit for duty, and three hundred and fifty-two were so completely worn out as to be useless for several months, if indeed they were ever useful again. Thus the real losses of the 9th Division amounted to seven hundred and forty-two out of sixteen hundred and thirty-eight, or not far from 50 per cent.; and the mules of the 9th Division had fared not worse but better than those of other divisions. It is, therefore, quite plain that the figures furnished to Lord Roberts by his Director of Transport were absurdly inaccurate.

The paralysis of the army at Bloemfontein from want of animal transport continued for nearly two months.

The supply park resolved itself into a supply dépôt. The mules, which were starving, were excused from all duty, and the whole of the garrison work was thrown upon the oxen. As they were neither shod nor fed and were in the yoke all day, they had little chance to recover condition. However, in the short period from the 11th of February to the 13th of March a good many lessons were taught to those who had designed the new organisation for transport and supply.

In the first place, the withdrawal of all transport to a central camp as soon as the force came to a halt proved, as might have been foreseen, to be ludicrously impracticable. The idea seems to have been grounded upon the conception of a compact force of three or four thousand men, engaged in a savage warfare, rather than of a body of thirty thousand men spread over miles of country. It was not realised by the theorists that, when such a force halted for the night, possibly only a portion of each vehicle might be unpacked; nor was it remembered that transport was required to carry food and blankets to the outposts, perhaps two to three miles distant in front and flanks. When these difficulties were pointed out, it was suggested that at all events the greater number of the mules might return to the transport lines. But those who suggested this remedy ignored the fact that the only means of securing animals for the night is to tie them to the pole of a vehicle, and the only means of feeding them is a canvas manger, arranged to be hung on either side of the pole. Transport duties were evidently not well understood by Lord Roberts's Staff.

Owing to the general confusion already reigning in the transport service, a conference was called of senior transport officers, one and one only of whom belonged to the Army Service Corps. Having met, they, being actually in the middle of a campaign, gravely debated as to what should or should not be carried by an army in the field. It never occurred to them that these matters had been thought out and that tables of carriage had been formulated long before this sudden appeal to their wisdom. Half of them did not know what a supply officer was. Not one (except of course the Army Service Corps officer) knew the weight of a soldier's blanket, nor of the scores of other articles which must be carried by military transport. Every one (always with the foregoing exception) calculated that, if the soldier received one pound of meal and one pound of biscuit, the two weighed two pounds, not understanding that this was the *net* weight, and that the *gross* weight was 50 per cent. more. One enlightened gentleman, specially chosen for knowledge of transport duties, argued gravely that such points did not concern a transport officer; deeming that his duties required him only to see that his native drivers moved forward, all together and correctly, at the word of command, and that they kept their dressing and their distance. It may be guessed that the conference arrived at no very valuable conclusions; but the Army Service Corps officer had at least his fill of marvel and of mirth. The bare fact that he was the one solitary representative of his corps on this memorable occasion throws a strong light on the capacity of the new Director of Transport.

It must, however, be said for him that Lord Kitchener's new system was breaking down in innumerable details. Thus, to give a typical instance, Lord Methuen's camp at Modder River was classed as a standing camp and was in consequence deprived of most of its transport. Lord Roberts, however, after the first action at Paardeberg, found himself obliged to summon the brigade of Guards from Modder River to Klip Drift. The Guards marched accordingly, with but one waggon to each battalion. They did not receive their half ration of food until 4.30 p.m. nor their blankets (though the nights were bitterly cold) until forty-eight hours later. There are worse methods than this of building up a high sick list. But indeed the withdrawal of the old regimental subsistence transport, and the substitution for it of a small transport unit under charge of a junior non-commissioned officer of the Army Service Corps, could hardly upon the very face of it be satisfactory. Under the old system regiments had taken an interest in their subsistence transport, for they furnished the trained men who were in charge of it, and looked upon it as a part of themselves. Now in the great majority of cases they no longer did so, which bore all the harder upon the non-commissioned officer of the Army Service Corps.

The abolition of the supply column, the connecting link between the fighting troops and the supply park, also caused great difficulties. In the first place it turned the supply parks into dépôts of issue on a small scale, even to individuals. Now the supply park, as has been told, was instituted to do what may be called wholesale business, the supply column doing the retail. For a single man to go to a supply park for his day's rations was rather as if an ordinary citizen should go to a Manchester cotton mill to buy a reel of cotton. There was no machinery for transactions on this minute scale, and it was quite impossible to keep account of them. Thus arose confusion, with every possibility of waste and embezzlement. Moreover, some link with the supply park was imperatively needed; and the only way to furnish it was to collect from units the necessary number of waggons and send them back to the supply park. Say that the unit was a battalion of infantry, in those days organised in eight companies. Each battalion received nine waggons, with orders to carry two days' food and forage. Naturally one waggon was assigned to each company, with the food and forage divided among them, while the ninth went to regimental headquarters. Whence then were the empty waggons to come for the work of replenishment? They could only be supplied by dumping the goods of some unfortunate company on the ground and thus causing much inconvenience and discomfort. Such a procedure was not calculated to endear the new system to the rank and file.

Next, the idea that transport allotted to ammunition columns should also be at disposal for general purposes was exploded at Paardeberg by a very rude shock. A divisional commander received orders to detach all the waggons and mules of his ammunition column to fetch supplies from Kimberley. The officer in command of the column thereupon asked what he was to do with his ammunition. Was he to dump it on the wet and sodden ground? He appealed to the chief artillery officer, who answered that he would assent to no such thing, nor would he be responsible for the consequences of damp ammunition. It was then ordered by some individual, whose simplicity shows a kinship with genius, that the waggons of the ammunition column must remain untouched, but that the mules might be taken. Unfortunately, for the purpose of carrying provisions across the veldt, mules without waggons were no more useful than petrol without motor vehicles.

The case was the same with the transport detailed for use with the Royal Engineers. It was found impossible to withdraw it for purposes of general transport. The sappers required it for their own objects and refused to yield it up. Many efforts were made to wrest it from them, all equally futile; and all ended alike in confusion, bad blood and victory to the engineers.

Next, when the new transport companies were allotted to brigades and divisions, it was assumed that they would be attached to them in perpetuity. But in the unceasing change of conditions which is the essence of war, brigades and divisions were constantly dropping some of their own troops, and receiving others from elsewhere. A battalion, for instance, would be hurriedly detached in some urgent need to seize and hold a distant post, which for the moment became a point on the line of communication. This battalion would of course be left behind, while the brigade or division marched on; and with the battalion would remain its transport, because it might at any moment be required to march. Changing circumstances would then render the post unimportant, and the battalion would be removed, probably to some other brigade, since its own had long since vanished into space. This dropping and picking up of detachments was continuous among the mounted troops; and by the time that the army reached Paardeberg—that is to say, within a fortnight of the inception of the new system—not one of the new transport companies could show itself complete. They could say no more than that portions of it had gone away with such and such units in some direction unknown; and in some cases the remnant that continued together exceeded not one-quarter of the original company.

As to the connection between the right-hand and left-hand companies, into which the original Army Service Corps companies had been bisected, it disappeared almost instantly and quite completely. During the long halt at Bloemfontein some Army Service Corps officers of right-hand companies tried to find their left-hand companies, with results that are typified in the following letter from one of them.

I found my left-hand company's head-quarters to consist of one waggon, one water-cart and one forge-cart, with a major of the Guards in command, some few military artificers and a few non-commissioned officers and men. The rest of the company had been distributed and had disappeared with units that had left the force. I may here perhaps finish the history of this poor left company, which was certainly left in every sense of the word. Many months afterwards, just after the Wittebergen operations I met at Bethlehem [about one hundred and fifty miles north-east of Bloemfontein] a weary looking sergeant, and a farrier-corporal who hailed me with delight. They told me that, so far as they knew, they were the last remnants of my left company, and had been looking for me for months. Where the rest were they did not know, and I have never discovered. It seems strange to realise that, so far as my being able to account for them went, some forty-nine waggons, four forge-carts, one water-cart, some six hundred horses and mules, and an enormous quantity of valuable equipment had disappeared.

And here it must be remarked that in the army of Natal, where the old system was retained under Sir Redvers Buller, everything worked with perfect smoothness. It was urged in explanation that Sir Redvers remained for long stationary and that he advanced ultimately along a line of railway. But, except for the march between Modder River and Bloemfontein, Lord Roberts likewise stuck to the railway; nor would that march have been so trying if, through the incompetence of the staff, the supply park had not been captured at Waterval Drift. But that mishap would have been less important if supply columns had been preserved; and, as we have seen, it was General French's supply column —retained in spite of Lord Kitchener—which saved the whole situation. The fact is that Sir Redvers Buller, foreseeing that a war with the Boers was inevitable, had designed the organisation of the Army Service Corps with a special eye to such a duty. He knew South Africa well, having served in the Kaffir and Zulu Wars of 1878-9, and took advantage of his experience. He had far harder fighting round Ladysmith than Lord Roberts ever encountered in the whole of his campaign, and, when at length he reached Ladysmith on the 1st of March, his army was not reduced to a state of paralysis. He remained halted by Lord Roberts's order until the 7th of May; but he was quite ready to advance in the third week of March.

The long period of inactivity at Bloemfontein came to an end at last, after there had been much sickness and great mortality among the troops. Much of the time was spent in quietly reviving under different names the system which had been so thoughtlessly swept away. Regimental transport officers and establishments were reintroduced, though the name "regimental" was carefully avoided. However, the responsibility for this transport was still vested in some transport company, so that it was a matter of indifference to the regimental officer to take note of the loss of a vehicle or the death of an animal. He had not to account for them; and thus one of the best features of the old system was abolished. Still, unit after unit retained the same transport from the beginning to the end of its service in South Africa; and it might just as well have been called regimental transport and might much better have been entrusted to the regimental officers. There was one battalion of the Black Watch which, having the good fortune to possess a transport officer, Major Ball, of peculiar excellence, restored, after two years of incessant marching, two-thirds of the animals and the whole of the vehicles which had originally been issued to it. Supply columns were also revived, though they were not called by that name; and by great efforts Lord Roberts's army was fed during its rapid advance along the railway to Pretoria. The railway being breached in many places, each breach in succession became the rail-head, and the supplies were pushed forward in waggons by relays of teams every ten miles. Pretoria was captured on the 5th of June, and then followed the clearance of the Transvaal to north and east, in the course of which the Natal Army on the 28th of August actually came alongside that of Lord Roberts. It should be added that in Lord Roberts's army the business of transport and supply, in spite of endless orders and counter-orders, was still in confusion, whereas in the Natal Army all went smoothly and well. Meeting Sir Redvers Buller at Pretoria in October, Lord Kitchener told him that there were only two columns which had proper transport, Sir Redvers's own and Lord Methuen's. Sir Redvers could not forbear to reply that these were the only two columns that had stuck to the old system.

After November, 1900, the nature of the struggle was changed, and guerrilla warfare took the place of more methodical operations. Divisions and brigades were broken up and replaced by small columns of all arms, which were known by their commanders' names. The enemy, having learned wisdom, devoted themselves chiefly to raids upon outlying posts or forces about the lines of communication, and having a manœuvring ground as large as France, with little bodies of British scattered all over it, they gave a great deal of trouble.

It will be profitable, therefore, to sketch the actual condition of things at the end of 1900, when mobile columns were at work in all directions.

The transport companies, one and all, were wandering about, complete or in fragments, with the various columns.

There were only one or two small transport dépôts, each of them very weak in *personnel* and incapable of producing more than a certain number of natives, fifteen or twenty waggons with their complement of mules, and perhaps a few trek oxen. In brief, there were no reserves of transport.

The war had already lasted a year, which was six months longer than anyone had expected. It had been conducted in a country practically roadless and bridgeless and in a climate so dry that no timber can resist shrinkage. Consequently very many of the vehicles had become very shaky and needed immediate repair. The harness—a standing trouble throughout the war—even more urgently required attention.

Under the regulations all but trivial repairs were carried out by the Army Ordnance Department, and accordingly the Ordnance had set up a few small repairing establishments, at Pretoria for the Transvaal, and at Bloemfontein for the Orange Free State. But no one of these establishments had more than a dozen workmen, numbers ludicrously inadequate for the mass of repairs that had become necessary.

The Ordnance Department, which was responsible for furnishing all stores, except food and medicines for men and beasts, was at its wits' end. Orders came crowding in upon it from column commanders for harness, vehicles and equipment. The Department had no means of judging whether these orders were legitimate, and could find no basis of calculation for possible future requirements.

The Remount Department, which was charged with the supply of animals, was equally inundated with orders which it could not check. The Director of Transport at headquarters tried to obtain returns and information which would enable him to ascertain exactly what the condition of the transport was. He tried in vain. No one could tell him, because nobody knew.

All in fact was in the utmost confusion; and there was imminent danger lest the transport service should break down altogether and bring the military operations to a stand.

The immediate cause of this state of chaos was as follows. There was no proper control of the transport service. Lord Roberts and Sir Redvers Buller had both of them gone home, and the command had been vested in Lord Kitchener, whose staff seems to have been quite unequal to the task of handling that very difficult matter. Commanders of columns and even of smaller units would telegraph directly to the Ordnance requiring certain articles—it might be, say, waggons or it might be spare parts of waggons. Now a great many mule waggons had been purchased in the Colony, since they could not be furnished with sufficient rapidity from home, and these were of many different patterns with, as was to be expected, spare parts which varied very greatly. The applicants for such articles frequently, through ignorance or carelessness, misdescribed them; and the Ordnance, dreading lest it should be made answerable for any breakdown, expended vast sums of public money in the purchase of superfluous stores. Thus, for one item, tens of thousands of muleshoes were ordered out from England, though the ground in South Africa was mostly so soft that not one mule in a hundred required shoeing.

So, again, some unit, newly come from over sea or locally raised, would arrive at some station; and the nearest transport dépôt would receive orders to fit them out with certain vehicles, animals and *personnel*. These last, it must be remarked, were now civilians, the Army Service Corps having long since been drained dry. Now, according to Lord Roberts's orders, the vehicles, animals and equipment thus issued remained in charge of the issuing company or dépôt. This was a necessary sequence of the theory that all transport belonged to a single central authority. Of course it was impossible for the issuing dépôt or company to follow the fortunes of the transport thus issued, or even to hope ever to see it again; but theory ignores such little complications. So away the unit marched with its valuable animals and equipment, having signed no receipt nor voucher for so much as a shoenail. After a time it would demand fresh animals from the Remounts and fresh vehicles from the Ordnance; and, since there was no means of checking their actual needs, these requisitions were perforce complied with.

Now, every army contains its proportion of rogues; and there were also, especially among the irregular and colonial corps, many individuals quite astute enough to take advantage of this state of things. If unlimited transport were to be had for the asking, why not get as much of it as possible? No doubt some of it changed hands, and ill-gotten gains passed into some pockets. But the general motive was less guileful. Everybody

253

was sick to death of the war and anxious to carry it on as comfortably as possible. The irregular troops seem to have set the example, and the regulars soon caught the infection. Why should they be worse off than the amateur soldier? Unfortunately, some of the Generals were the most shameless offenders. One general officer —it need hardly be said that he came from India—with a staff of four more officers and some thirty servants and orderlies, allowed himself transport enough to provide for an infantry-battalion. Another took even more; and with hardly an exception all took more than they were entitled to. The table of allowance of transport for all ranks, carefully drawn up and enforced by Sir Redvers Buller, was entirely ignored. Lord Roberts and Lord Kitchener had changed all that. The campaign might have been one of the old-fashioned sort on the plains of India, when a brigadier took sixty camels to keep himself in comfort.

Another evil, arising from the principle that a central authority was responsible for all transport, was that commanders were scandalously careless in the matter of working their mules to death. The issuing of mules to some of them, in the words of an indignant critic, was like pouring water into a sieve. Yet these same officers at home would have been furious with a servant who broke their cups and saucers. Again, mules captured by these mobile columns—sometimes to the extent of hundreds—were very rarely shown in any report; and there was no means of checking the numbers, because no voucher had been given for the animals originally issued, and there was no trustworthy return of casualties.

The state of the ox transport was, if possible, even less satisfactory than that of the mule transport. As has already been told, the waggons and teams had been hired under the impression—no less general than false— that the duration of the war would be short. The price, it may be repeated, was at first £2. 15s. 0d. per waggon per day, the sum covering the cost of the waggon itself, sixteen oxen, two natives and one European conductor and sub-conductor to every ten waggons, though both natives and conductors were entitled to free rations at the public expense. The value of a good ox waggon ranged from £60 to £70; the highest value of a good ox at the beginning of the war was £15. Taking £100 as the extreme value of the waggon, and £15 apiece as the price of each of the sixteen oxen, the total cost would amount to £340. Now £340 would be exactly the price of one hundred and thirty-six days' hire of the same waggon and team, so that, even allowing for the drivers' wages, six months' hire (one hundred and eighty-two days) would more than pay for the purchase of waggon and team outright.

In these contracts it was of course stipulated that the contractor should replace any animals that died or proved inefficient, unless such death or inefficiency could be ascribed directly or indirectly to military operations. On the other hand, it was part of the agreement that all captured waggons should be handed over to the contractors to make good these casualties— after which the British Government proceeded to pay heavily for their hire. Thus, when the Boers surrendered at Paardeberg, over two hundred waggons, mostly ox waggons, were a part of the spoil. They were solemnly delivered to the contractors and as solemnly redelivered in return for the stipulated hire. When the army was broken up into mobile columns, these frequently captured waggons complete with oxen, and as frequently requisitioned others from Boer farmers, giving receipts for the same. Such waggons were all absorbed into the general transport of the column and, beyond the wages and rations of native drivers, should have cost the country nothing. Yet an order was issued from General Headquarters that such waggons were to be made over to the contractors for ox transport, after which they were hired from them again. One column alone had accumulated some twenty to thirty captured waggons with teams. They were sold to the contractor at £200 apiece—say £6000 in all. They were then hired at the rate of at least £60 a day or £21,900 a year, giving him a profit of nearly £1. 10s. 0d. per waggon per day. It is not surprising that, in some quarters at any rate, the war was popular in South Africa.

Of course it had been presumed that the contractors would draw their ox transport from Cape Colony, Bechuanaland or some other quarter not involved in the war, and that they would take over captured stock for which they would give a receipt and in due time pay. But it is beyond question that a very large proportion of the oxen furnished by the contractors were simply seized by their agents. From the time when the British army entered the Orange River Colony until the end of 1900, the agents and other employees of the contractors were little better than cattle reivers. They ranged the country as the troops advanced, capturing or stealing oxen whenever they could, or compelling Boers and natives by intimidation to sell them oxen at £4, £3 or even £2 a head. They then charged them to the Government at the rate of four or five times that sum. The fact was early reported and was therefore well known to headquarters.

Another scandalous abuse was the contractors' practice of making use again of oxen that had fallen out on the march. This also was duly reported, with rather curious results. An order was issued that the senior transport officer of columns should be held personally responsible for all oxen that fell out, and that it was his duty to see that every such beast was branded with the Government mark or that, if it were dying, he should wait for its decease, and then cut off its tail in proof thereof. This order failed of its object. It had been overlooked that a transport officer could not always carry with him a brazier and a branding iron to mark fallen oxen. Nor could he sit, with his best bedside manner, alongside a prostrate ox, feeling its pulse and awaiting the moment of dissolution before severing its tail. He might thus be the means of delaying the rear-guard, under sniping fire of the enemy; and an ox's tail was hardly worth one or two casualties. Nor again, even if fortune were kind to him and the dying oxen showed promptitude in giving up the ghost, could he find con-venient storage for the hundreds of tails which would have accumulated even in a comparatively weak column after some weeks of marching over the veldt. In that climate a severed tail becomes putrid and stinking within twenty-four hours; and the medical officers might have raised sanitary objections. This remarkable order, therefore, was of no practical utility.

Thus in every branch of the transport there were confusion, waste, negligence, extravagance and oppor-tunities (which were not always allowed to escape) for downright rascality. And these evils had grown up under the direction not of the Army Service Corps, but of the distinguished Royal Engineer appointed by Lord Roberts. Unless this chaos were reduced to order it was only a question of time before the operations should collapse.

Now it was that the Army Service Corps came forward in the person of one of its ablest officers. To avoid excessive prolixity of detail, it will be best to describe what was done in a single large area, leaving the reader to deduce from this one example the system which was gradually extended to all.

At Bloemfontein the Assistant Adjutant-General for transport was Major Long. There lay the only transport dépôt in the Orange River Colony, known as No. 6; and in November, 1900, its reserves amounted to from twenty to thirty mule waggons, a few carts, from thirty to forty ox waggons, a few spare civilian conductors and native drivers, one small field forge and two or three artificers. At Major Long's instance the premises of the largest vehicle builder in the town were requisitioned, together with the owner and all of his workmen; and an amicable agreement was arranged with the owner that he should work (as he loyally did) for the Imperial Forces. Out of these shops as a nucleus grew up a repairing dépôt which eventually maintained over eighty trained artificers, besides some hundreds of less skilled workmen, who laboured night and day to keep the vehicles and equipment efficient. At the same time smaller dépôts of the same kind were formed, first only at Kroonstad to north and Springfontein to south, but shortly afterwards at Brandford, Winburg and Heilbron to north and north-east, and at Edenburg to south. Thus, whenever any mobile column or other force struck the railway, it would always find a transport dépôt within reasonable distance, where worn-out vehicles and equipment could be replaced and assistance could be given with repairs. At the same time measures were taken to collect all the broken and abandoned vehicles which lay littered along the whole length of the railway; and column commanders were begged to bring to the railway line every vehicle that they found, no matter how decrepit.

Other reforms not less important followed. In the first place the ox transport was purchased, and the wasteful system of hiring, with its endless abuses, came to an end. Further, it was ordered that in future no transport vehicles nor equipment should be issued directly to any unit by the Ordnance; but that all demands must be submitted to it through duly appointed transport officers from the nearest transport dépôt. All outstanding demands were sent to Major Long at Bloemfontein who went through every one of them, cancelling all items which he considered unnecessary. He then drew reserves of stores from the Ordnance, keeping that department fully informed as to the further reserves which, in his opinion, it should keep. To help the department further, he prepared tables showing exactly what would be necessary for one hundred vehicles of each description for the coming three months, giving every part in detail, from cobbler's wax or a harness needle to a wheel or a complete waggon. These tables were finally used for the whole seat of war in South Africa.

The same procedure was followed in respect of the Remounts Department. All issue of animals was forbidden except to transport dépôts according to the demands of the Assistant Adjutant-General for Transport. The dépôts then delivered animals to mobile columns or to units upon instructions from the administrative office at headquarters.

Thus was established an initial check upon all issues, and at the same time the regulations for the allowance of transport were strictly enforced. Every column or unit was bound to find its way to the railway sooner or later, and then, no matter how luxurious Generals might complain, all transport over and above their allowance was taken from them. Further, when the unit or column went on the march again, it gave a receipt for every item of its transport and was held responsible for it. Thereby not only was much scandalous waste—and worse than waste—prevented, but a reserve of transport was built up which enabled the war to be carried to a successful conclusion.

A few examples will suffice to make this clear.

Only two months after the inception of this system Christian De Wet, perhaps the most enterprising of the Boer commanders, made a swift rush upon Cape Colony. Instantly a large number of columns was entrained with all haste and sent southward by rail to head him off. So congested was the railway that their transport could not be sent with them. Thereupon the transport dépôts of the Orange River Colony produced and entrained as quickly as possible five hundred ox waggons and nearly as many mule waggons, with their full complement of animals and drivers.

Again, in April, 1901, General Elliott arrived at Glen, about twelve miles north of Bloemfontein, with no fewer than five different columns. They had been engaged in a great drive of the country from the Vaal to the Modder River, and the General telegraphed that the whole of their transport required attention. Within forty-eight hours every one of these columns was completely refitted. No fewer than ninety-six defective waggons were replaced by efficient vehicles; one hundred and twenty-four others received repairs more or less extensive; over five hundred wheels were renewed or repaired; old harness was mended or replaced by new; and finally five hundred mules were issued, three hundred of them to make good casualties and two hundred in substitution for animals that needed rest.

On another occasion a force under General Plumer, which had been hurriedly sent southward from the Transvaal by rail, arrived at Bloemfontein with its vehicles only, the rolling stock being insufficient to carry the animals. Moreover these vehicles had undergone much hard work and were many of them broken or shaky. Within twenty-four hours eighty-two of them were repaired and, when necessary, re-wheeled; and thirteen hundred fresh mules were collected and issued to the troops.

In fact, from the time when these reforms were initiated, the work of the transport was, on the whole, efficiently done. But it would have been more efficient still had the old organisation of the Army Service Corps been preserved and expanded by men who understood it. It was the hasty dislocation of the old system and the clumsy improvisation of a new model to replace it which caused all the trouble. And this trouble was the greater because this change was wrought by men who had not the slightest knowledge nor experience of the inner problems of transport and supply.

The irony of the whole situation was rather remarkable. The Army Service Corps was on its mettle, for this was its first great trial on active service. The first Commander-in-Chief, Sir Redvers Buller, was its founder and likely to see that it had fair play. He failed, however, in the field, not least because only sixty thousand men were entrusted to him to do work which required two hundred and fifty thousand. To call upon a corps, which had been framed to meet the wants of sixty thousand men, to provide for four times that number must in any case have been a high trial. If, however, Sir Redvers had remained in command, he would beyond question have stretched the old system to cover the new needs. The strain would have been great; but every member of the Army Service Corps would have known where he stood, and could have worked heartily and intelligently to make the expansion a success. They showed, even as things were, a loyal readiness which was beyond praise; but it cannot be said that they were fairly treated.

I have said enough, I think, to show that, even if Lord Kitchener's theories were not unsound in principle, at least they utterly broke down in practice. From the moment when he instituted his new organisation, there began a steady tendency towards reversion to the old system; and indeed, however the fact may be disguised by words, it was only by ignoring Lord Kitchener's reforms that the war was carried on at all. But even assuming that Lord Kitchener's theories had been sound—and they may still have their champions—was it the part of a wise and practical man to sweep away an existing organisation and substitute a new one by a stroke of the pen in the very middle of a campaign? In those days battalions (as has been told) were organised

in eight companies. They are now organised in four—
an arrangement over a century old in some continental
armies—which is admitted to be an improvement. But
if Lord Kitchener had introduced the four-company
organisation in the middle of the South African War by
a stroke of the pen it would certainly not have worked
smoothly at the outset. Yet Lord Kitchener's changes
in the organisation of the transport and supply service
were far more drastic and far-reaching than this. He
would not have dreamed of laying violent hands on
cavalry, artillery, engineers or infantry, but had no
scruple about turning the Army Service Corps upside
down.

The only excuse to be made for him lies in his
ignorance of the British Army. Whenever he was
appointed to a high command he appeared to think that
he had been called down as a *deus ex machina* to create
something which had not previously existed. Thus in
1914 he utterly ignored Lord Haldane's scheme for the
expansion of the Army and substituted for it an improvisation of his own. It was a repetition of his
treatment of the Army Service Corps in 1900. He
seems to have thought that he had been summoned to
call into being a service for transport and supply, and he
never enquired as to that which already had been carefully and with immense pains prepared. Wellington had
found his Commissariat useless in the Peninsula and
had been obliged practically to re-create the service.
Kitchener assumed that history was repeating itself,
and that he must play Wellington in South Africa.
But the trouble was that he was very remote from a
Wellington. Wellington was the very best horse master,
mule master and ox master that the British Army ever
had. Kitchener was the very worst. His ignorance of
animals was something out of the common. Soon after
the army reached Bloemfontein, with all of its beasts
starving, Kitchener learned that within twenty miles of

the place there were huge crops of green growing mealies—Indian corn. He sent for Major Long and ordered him to take his starving mules thither to graze. Major Long respectfully pointed out that, if he did so, ninety per cent. of the animals would be dead within forty-eight hours. Kitchener turned upon him furiously. "What do you mean?" "Your chief veterinary officer is here, Sir," answered Major Long, "if you do not believe me, ask him." Kitchener did so, and was told that Major Long had understated the case, and that not ninety per cent. but every one of the animals would perish. Then Kitchener revoked his order; but he had evidently never seen nor heard of sheep, oxen or horses breaking into some rich green crop, gorging themselves and presently collapsing, distended like balloons with wind, to die after a period of torture, unless relieved by surgical operation, of rupture of the diaphragm. His—to all seeming—utter ignorance of the abilities and disabilities of animals and his indifference to the mortality among them had a very bad effect upon the army at large. Vast numbers of officers, as was inevitable in an army composed chiefly of the town-bred, were quite as ignorant as he was, and fully as indifferent. To the very end commanders of columns slaughtered oxen wholesale by working them at the wrong hours. It must, of course, be admitted that the hours of oxen are inconvenient for men. It is unpleasant to move every morning at 2 or 3 a.m. But in nine cases out of ten it would have been possible for the transport to start with a small escort at 3 a.m., for the troops to follow them at 7 a.m. and pass them at their midday halt, and for the transport to come into camp late in the evening. There were, of course, times when military considerations compelled the oxen to march under the full heat of the day; and then heavy casualties among them were inevitable. Transport after all exists for armies and not armies for transport. But no amount of orders or cautions could avail to make many officers treat their oxen fairly; and the waste and the expense were consequently appalling. No one knows nor ever will know the number of oxen that perished in that campaign, nor are there trustworthy returns of the casualties even among the mules. It is perhaps as well, for the figures would not be creditable to the British Army. But I would refer the reader to an extract from a memorandum written by Wellington about oxen, which is printed on a previous page; and he may judge for himself whether the story would not have been very different if the army in South Africa had been commanded by a Wellington, who had transport and supply at his fingers' ends, instead of by a Kitchener who had not.

For the rest, this South African War, weary and costly though it was, was of inestimable benefit to the Army as training for the great struggle that was to come. Up to 1914 it represented by far the most formidable military effort made by England beyond sea.* Between July, 1900, and June, 1902, the total number of men embarked for South Africa was three hundred and fifty-nine thousand, of horses three hundred and forty-seven thousand, of mules over one hundred and four thousand, and of mule waggons two thousand. These figures, of course, do not include men, vehicles and animals found within South Africa itself. When the war ended the men receiving rations numbered three hundred and twenty-seven thousand; the horses and mules two hundred and sixty-five thousand and the oxen nineteen thousand, or, in other words, eleven hundred and twenty-five teams.†

To minister to the physical wants of this host the

* I am careful to say *beyond sea*, for quite as large a proportion of the male population was under arms from 1803 to 1814 as from 1914 to 1918.

† According to these figures the joint casualties of horses and mules (347,000 + 104,000 − 265,000) amounted to 186,000, but this calculation ignores animals which were already in the Colony. The number may safely be taken as well over 200,000.

Army Service Corps sent out two hundred and thirty-three officers and twenty-seven hundred and sixty-seven men—just three thousand of all ranks—with which effort its resources in *personnel* were exhausted. But what far outweighed the comparative smallness of their numbers was the quality of their brains. Amid the endless inevitable difficulties of war, aggravated by an unnecessary confusion forced upon them from without, they worked loyally and indefatigably, even if the strain might cost them their lives. Then, the instant that the chance was offered to them they, with astonishing rapidity, called order out of chaos, put an end to innumerable extravagances and abuses and proved that they knew their business much better than anyone could teach them. It is not too much to say that, but for them, the war would not have been brought to a successful end.

Moreover, in spite of the contentions of Lord Kitchener, and in a milder way, of Lord Roberts, the merit and value of the Army Service Corps were by the year 1902 firmly established. It was at once raised to a strength of ten thousand, and the foundations upon which Sir Redvers Buller had built it were left undisturbed. The introduction of mechanical transport, very soon after the close of the South African War, necessarily brought about some changes in organisation; but these must be described by some other pen. The present writer's province is bounded by the continuance of animal transport only. He is conscious that, even within those limitations, his work is very imperfect. But he trusts at least that he may have given some idea of the long struggle of a great auxiliary service against the jealousy of Parliament and the prejudice of combatant officers—a struggle which, after two full centuries, issued at last in recognition of the principle that the transport and supply of armies must be governed by a single head and must be constituted upon a military basis.

APPENDIX A

LIST SHOWING THE NUMBER OF COMMISSARIAT DÉPÔTS IN PORTUGAL, 1812

ABRANTES
ALBUQUERQUE
ALCAYER DE SOL
ALDEA GALLEGA
ALMEIDA
BARCA D'ALVA
BUCELLAS
CABEÇA DE MONTACHIQUE
CASTANHEIRA
CASTELLO BRANCO
CELORICO
COIMBRA
ESPINHAL
ESTREMOZ
FIGUEIRA
GALIZES
LAMEGO
LISBON
MAFRA

NIZA
OEIRAS
OPORTO
PEDROGÃO
PENICHE
PORTALEGRE
RAIVA
SABUGAL
SACAVEM
SANTAREM
SAN JOÃO DE PESQUIER
SETUVAL
SOURÉ
THOMAR
TORRES VEDRAS
VALLADA
VILLA DO PONTE
VILLA FRANCA

APPENDIX B

TABULATED HISTORY OF THE ROYAL ARMY SERVICE CORPS AND ITS PREDECESSORS

1794. Royal Waggoners formed. Five companies of 120 n.c.o.'s and men, of whom one-tenth artificers. Uniform—blue. These came to an end in 1795.

1799. 12 August. Royal Waggon Train formed. Five troops. Each of 1 captain, 2 lieutenants, 1 cornet, 1 quartermaster, 3 serjeants, 3 corporals, 1 trumpeter, 1 collar-maker, 1 wheelwright, 1 blacksmith, 2 farriers, 60 drivers.

The whole commanded by a Waggon-Master-General with rank of Lieutenant-Colonel on the continent of Europe only.

Pay of all ranks						Per day	
						s.	*d.*
Waggon-Master-General	...	...	...			18	10
	s.	*d.*					
Captain, pay	9	5 ⎫	...	...		11	5
Captain, horse-allowance	2	0 ⎭					
Lieutenant, pay	4	8 ⎫					
Lieutenant, allowance	1	0 ⎬	...	...		7	8
Lieutenant, horse-allowance	2	0 ⎭					
Cornet, pay	3	8 ⎫					
Cornet, allowance	1	0 ⎬	...	...		5	8
Cornet, horse-allowance	1	0 ⎭					
Adjutant ...	...	...	...	...	...	5	0
Surgeon ...	...	...	...	...	...	11	4
Veterinary Surgeon	...	...	...	...	8	0
Quartermaster ...	...	...	...	...	3	0
Collar-maker, wheelwright, blacksmith, farrier						3	0
Serjeant ...	...	...	...	...	...	2	2
Corporal ...	...	...	...	...	...	1	7½
Trumpeter and driver ...	...	...	...		1	3

Successive augmentations brought the total number of troops to 12 in 1810, which were reduced to 9 in 1811.

The uniform of the Royal Waggon Train seems to have been blue with red facings and silver lace. Regulations for 1803 provide that n.c.o.'s and men shall have a blue jacket and waistcoat and blue plush breeches.

1817. The Royal Waggon Train reduced to three troops.

1822. The uniform changed to scarlet with blue facings and silver lace.

1828. The Royal Waggon Train reduced to two troops, 124 of all ranks with 120 horses.

1831. The lace changed to gold.

1833. The Royal Waggon Train abolished.

1855. Land Transport Corps formed.

1856. Strength of Land Transport Corps: over 9000 men and 24,000 horses.

On conclusion of peace the corps was reduced to 1200 men and rechristened the Military Train.

Uniform—blue, facings white, lace gold.

Headdress—chaco with black plume.

1858. Oct. Commissariat Department formed on Military basis. Officers joining the department to be taken from the line, after serving not less than two years, and to serve on probation for six months, after which they may resign their military commissions and receive fresh commissions as Deputy Assistant Commissaries-General.

Grade	Pay per diem			Relative rank in the army
	£	s.	d.	
Commissary-General	3	0	0	Major-General
Deputy Commissary-General				
of 5 years standing	1	10	0	Colonel
under 5 years standing... ...	1	10	0	Lieut.-Colonel
Assistant Commissary-General ...		15	0	Major
Deputy Assistant Commissary-General		10	0	Captain
Acting Deputy Assistant Commissary-General		7	6	Lieutenant

1869. 12 Nov. Warrant for formation of the Army Service Corps, commanded by commissariat officers of the Control Department.

The non-commissioned ranks were:
Serjeant-Major.
1st class Staff-Serjeant (with army rank of Serjeant-Major).
2nd class Staff-Serjeant (with army rank of Quartermaster-Serjeant).
3rd class Staff-Serjeant (with army rank of 2nd class Staff-Serjeant).
Serjeant.
Corporal.
2nd Corporal
Trumpeter.
Bugler.
Private.

1872. 5 July. The Transport and Supply branches were separated.
  Transport: 12 companies, 1623 n.c.o.'s and men, 1087 horses.
  Supply and Store: 7 Supply, 4 Store companies, 1373 n.c.o.'s and men.

1875. March. Companies divided into half companies and each half company into two divisions.

1877. April. The Store companies were separated from the Army Service Corps.

1878. May. Five additional companies raised.
  Establishments of companies revised.
  Establishment of horses reduced to 63 per company.
  Order for recruits to be instructed in long-rein driving.

1879. Nineteen n.c.o.'s of the corps appointed to the new rank of Conductor of Supplies.

1880. March. Classes formed at Aldershot for instruction of officers, n.c.o.'s and men in the mode of judging quality of food and forage.

1881. 11 August. Designation of the corps altered to Commissariat and Transport Corps.

1883. A barrack section for the corps formed.

1885. April. Two additional companies formed.
  Sept. One further additional company formed.

1887. The 17 service companies were divided into 34 so as to furnish cadres for the companies required for two army corps.

1888. 11 Dec. Warrant for reorganising the Supply and Transport Services. The present Army Service Corps created.

1889. 1 February. New designations of n.c.o.'s and men introduced, as follows:

> Company Serjeant-Major.
> Farrier Quartermaster-Serjeant.
> Collar-maker Q.M.S.
> Wheeler Q.M.S.
> Staff Q.M.S.
> Company Q.M.S.
> Staff-Serjeant Farrier.
> Staff-Serjeant Collar-maker.
> Staff-Serjeant Wheeler.
> Staff-Serjeant.
> Serjeant.
> Corporal.
> Corporal Farrier and Carriage-smith.
> Corporal Collar-maker.
> Corporal Wheeler.
> 2nd Corporal.
> Private.
> Trumpeter.
> Driver.
> Boy (until 18 years old).

Mark VII General Service Waggon introduced.

1890. August. Designation of Commanding Officer of Corps changed from Assistant Adjutant-General to Assistant Quartermaster-General, and that of the Assistant Officer from D.A.A.G. to D.Q.M.G.

Oct. Office of the A.Q.M.G. of A.S.C. transferred to the Horse Guards, and that officer became one of the Headquarter Staff of the Army.

1891. July. Remount companies formed to look after remounts at Woolwich and Dublin.

1892. June. Title of Conductor abolished and that of First Class Staff-Serjeant-Major substituted.

Order for examination of officers in corps duties before promotion to captain or major.

Men of A.S.C. armed with carbine and trained to musketry.

1893. Corps of Military Staff Clerks abolished, and a staff clerk section added to A.S.C.

1894. Nominal establishment of A.S.C. officers fixed at

> 7 lieutenant-colonels.
> 32 majors.
> 77 captains.
> 91 lieutenants and second lieutenants.
> 40 quartermasters.
> 2 riding masters.

Rail and Water Transport transferred from the Ordnance Store Department and from all contractors to the A.S.C.

1899. April 1. Augmentation of the Transport units authorised, by 40 officers and 1000 men.

INDEX

INDEX

CAMBRIDGE: PRINTED BY W. LEWIS, M.A., AT THE UNIVERSITY PRESS

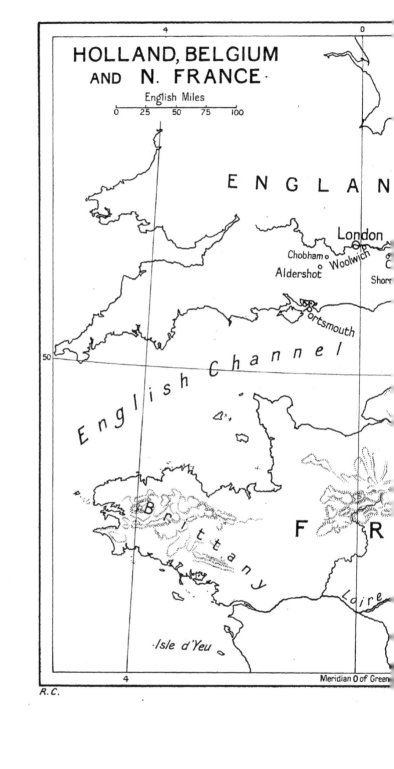

HOLLAND, BELGIUM
AND N. FRANCE·

English Miles

| 0 | 25 | 50 | 75 | 100 |

E N G L A N

London

Chobham o   Woolwich

Aldershot   Shorr

ortsmouth

C h a n n e l

E n g l i s h   C h a n n e l

B r i t t a n y

F   R

Loire

·Isle d'Yeu

4

Meridian 0 of Green

R.C.

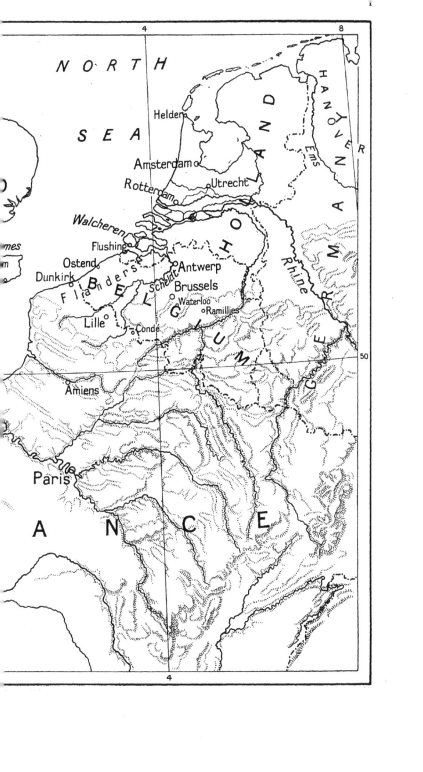

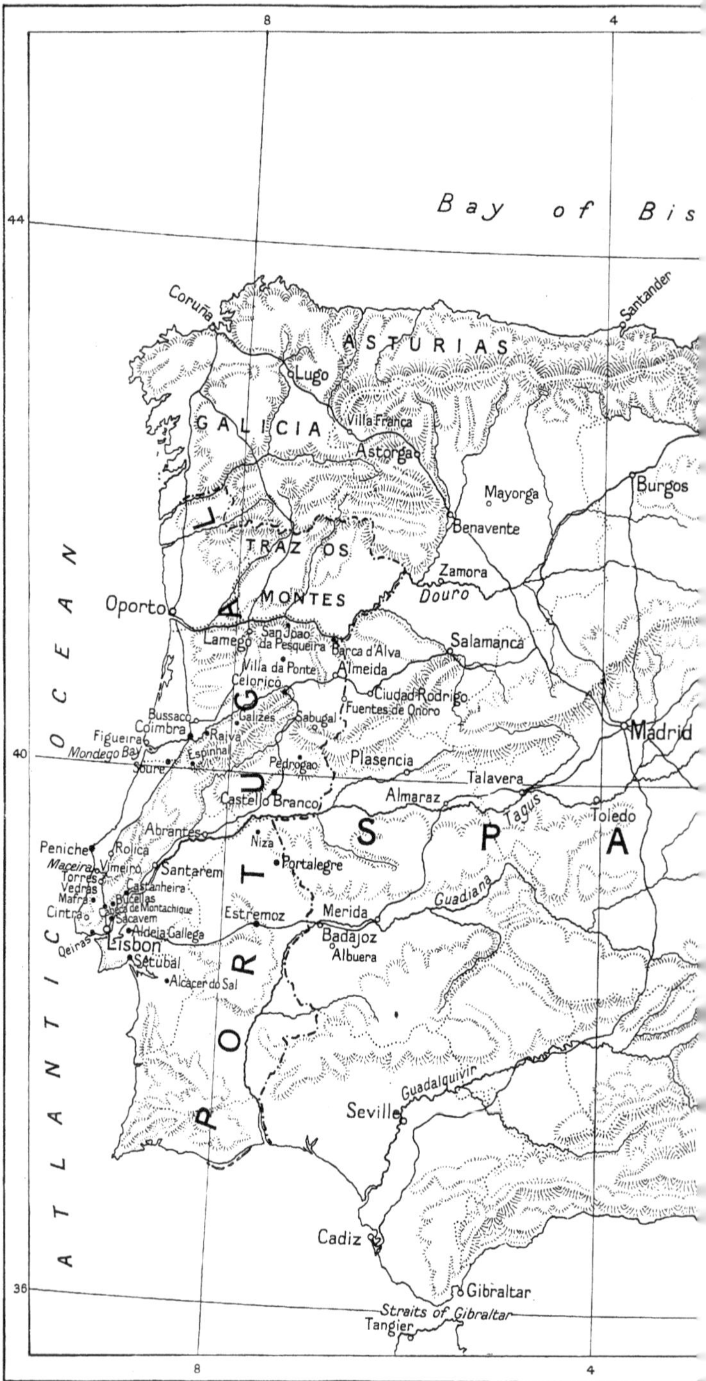
Bay of Bis
ATLANTIC OCEAN
Coruña
Santander
ASTURIAS
Lugo
GALICIA
Villa Franca
Astorga
Mayorga
Burgos
Benavente
TRAZ OS MONTES
Zamora
Douro
Oporto
San Joao da Pesqueira
Lamego
Barca d'Alva
Salamanca
Villa da Ponte
Almeida
Celorico
Ciudad Rodrigo
Fuentes de Onoro
Bussaco
Galizes
Sabugal
Coimbra
Madrid
Figueira
Raiva
Mondego Bay
Espinhal
Plasencia
Soure
Pedrogao
Talavera
Castello Branco
Almaraz
Tagus
Toledo
Abrantes
Peniche
Rolica
Niza
Maceira
Vimeiro
Santarem
Portalegre
Torres Vedras
Castanheira
Mafra
Bucellas
Cabeça de Montachique
Cintra
Sacavem
Estremoz
Merida
Guadiana
Badajoz
Albuera
Aldeia Gallega
Qeiras
Lisbon
Setubal
Alcacer do Sal
PORTUGAL
SPA
Guadalquivir
Seville
Cadiz
Gibraltar
Straits of Gibraltar
Tangier
44
40
36
8
4

R. C.

SPAIN, PORTUGAL
AND S. FRANCE

English Miles

0   25   50   75   100

—— Principal Roads
• British Depôts in Portugal

Meridian 0 of Greenwich

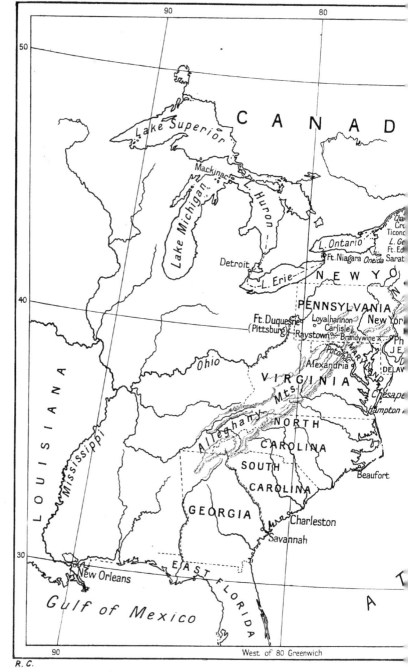

C A N A D A

Lake Superior

Mackinac

Lake Michigan

L. Huron

Detroit

L. Erie

Ontario

Ft. Niagara   Oneida

Sarat

L. Ge
Ft. Ed

Chal
Cro
Ticond

N E W Y O

PENNSYLVANIA

Ft. Duquesne   Loyalhannon
(Pittsburg)   Carlisle
Raystown   Brandywine

New Yor

Ph
J E

DELAW

Ohio

Potor

Alexandria

V I R G I N I A

Cesape

Hampton

Alleghany Mts

NORTH

CAROLINA

SOUTH

CAROLINA

Beaufort

GEORGIA

Charleston

Savannah

L O U I S I A N A

Mississippi

New Orleans

E A S T F L O R I D A

Gulf of Mexico

A

West of 80 Greenwich

R. C.

NORTH AMERICA

English Miles

0   50 100   200   300   400

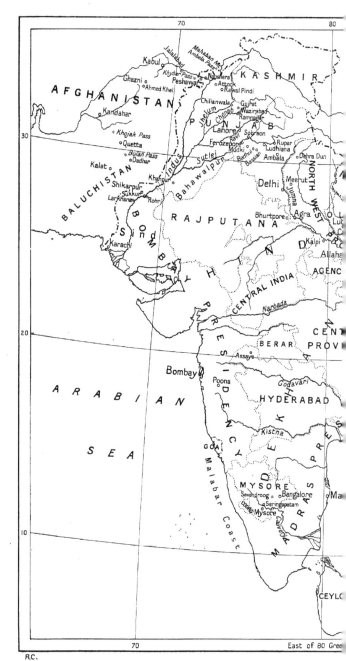

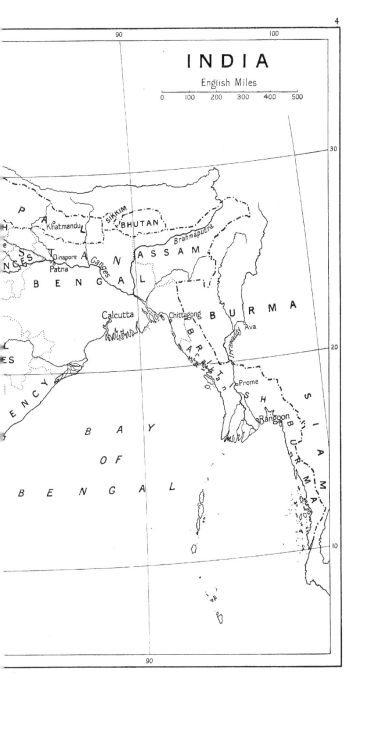

INDIA

English Miles

0   100   200   300   400   500

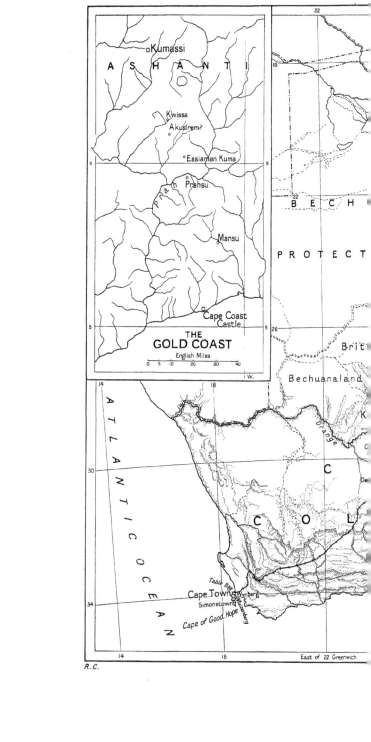

THE
GOLD COAST

English Miles

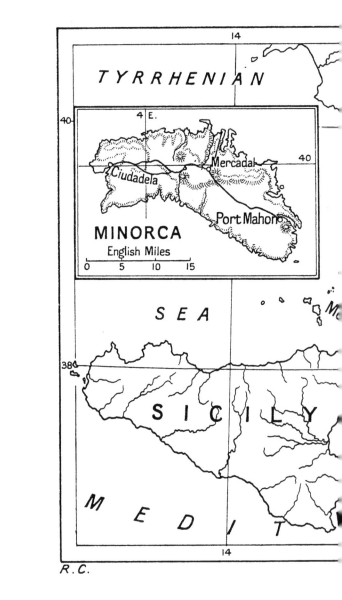

TYRRHENIAN

40

40

4 E.

Mercadal

Ciudadela

Port Mahon

MINORCA

English Miles

0   5   10   15

SEA

14

38

SICILY

MEDIT

14

R.C.

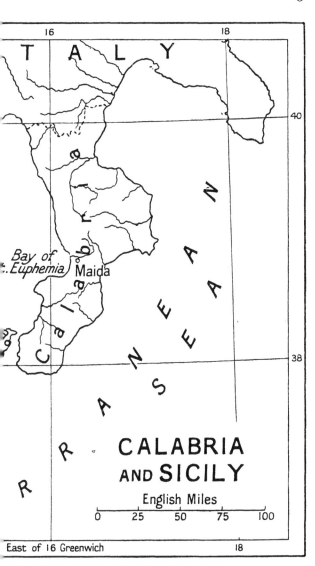

T A L Y

40

Calabria

Bay of
t. Euphemia Maida

MEDITERRANEAN

38

CALABRIA
AND SICILY
English Miles

0   25   50   75   100

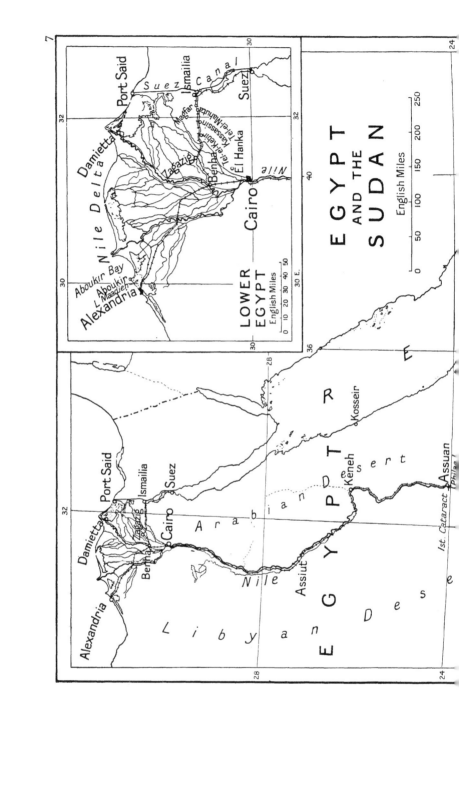

EGYPT
AND THE
SUDAN

English Miles

0   50   100   150   200   250

LOWER
EGYPT

English Miles

0 10 20 30 40 50

Port Said

Suez

Ismailia

Canal

Suez

Magfar
Mahuta
Tel-el-Kebir
Kassassin
El Hanka
Benha
Zagazig
Damietta

Nile Delta

Cairo

Nile

Aboukir Bay
Aboukir
L. Maadieh
Alexandria

Alexandria
Damietta
Port Said
Ismailia
Suez
Cairo
Zagazig
Benha

Arabian

Desert

Kosseir

Keneh

Assiut

Nile

Libyan   Desert

EGYPT

1st. Cataract Assuan
Philae

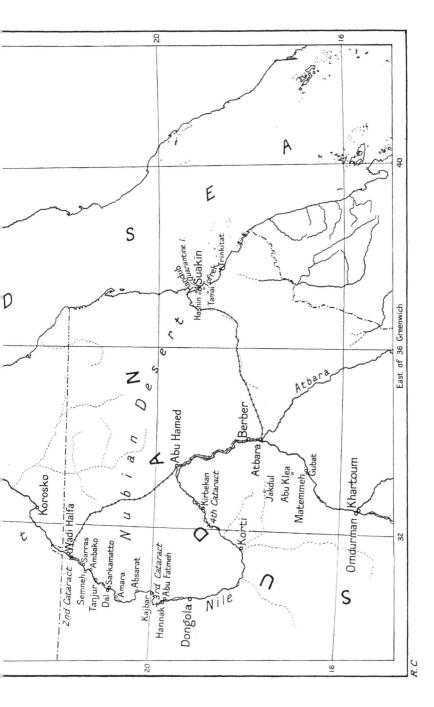

20

16

40

A

E

S

Quarantine I.
Ayub
Hashin Suakin
Tamai Tofrek
Trinkitat

D

Nubian Desert

Atbara

Abu Hamed

Berber

Atbara

Korosko

Jakdul
Abu Klea
Matemmeh
Gubat

2nd Cataract
Wadi Halfa
Semneh
Sarras
Tanjur
Ambako
Dal
Sarkamatto
Amara
Absarat
Kaibar
Hannak
3rd Cataract
Abu Fatmeh

Kirbekan
4th Cataract

Korti

Dongola

Nile

Omdurman
Khartoum

S

East of 36 Greenwich

32

16

20

R.C

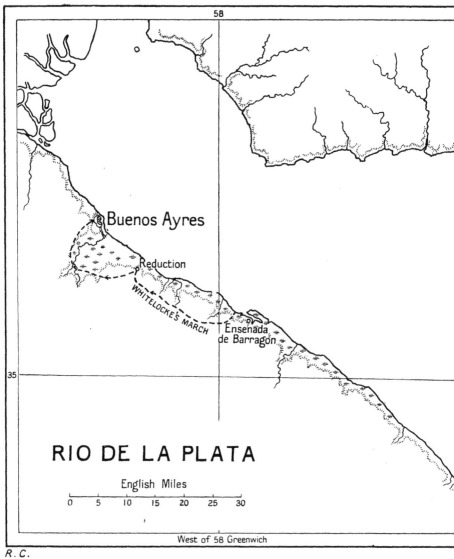

58

Buenos Ayres

Reduction

WHITELOCKE'S MARCH

Ensenada
de Barragón

35

RIO DE LA PLATA

English Miles

0   5   10   15   20   25   30

West of 58 Greenwich

R. C.

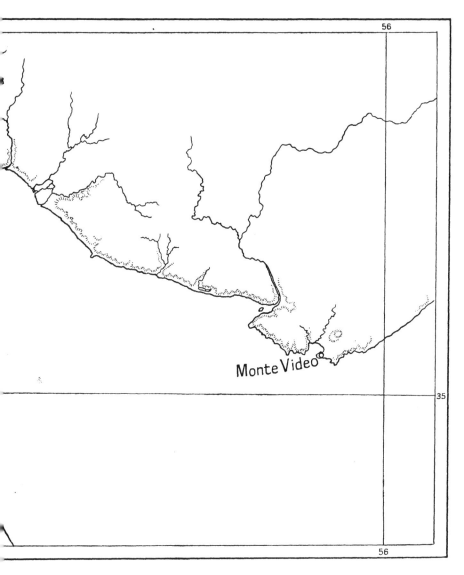

56

Monte Video

35

56

THE CRIMEA

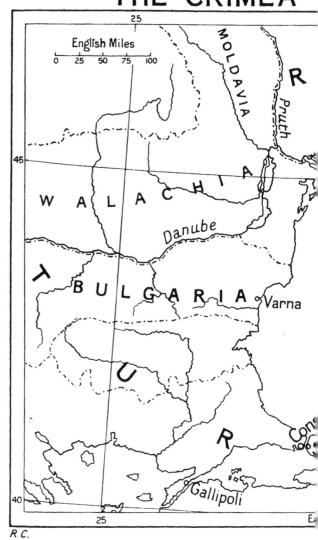

English Miles

0   25   50   75   100

MOLDAVIA

Pruth

R

W A L A C H I A

Danube

T

B U L G A R I A ∘Varna

U

R

Con
sto

Gallipoli

R.C.

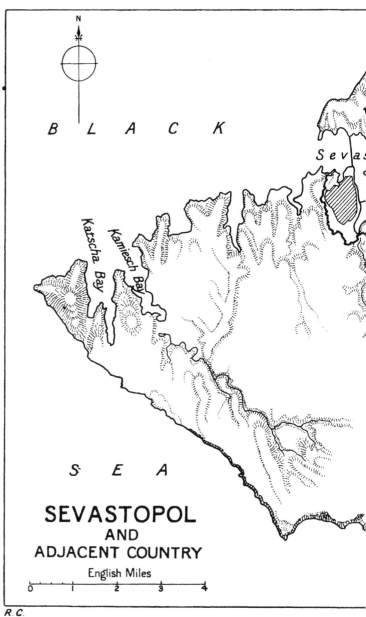

SEVASTOPOL
AND
ADJACENT COUNTRY

English Miles

R.C.

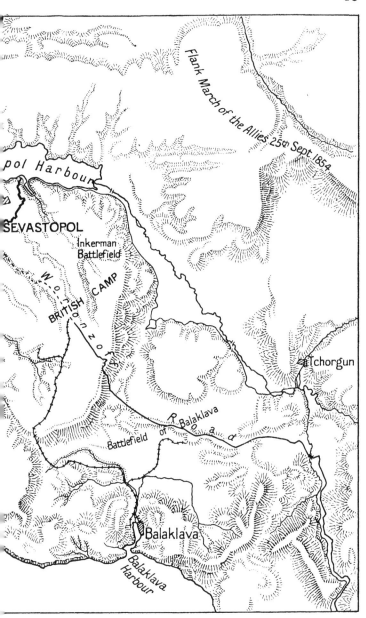

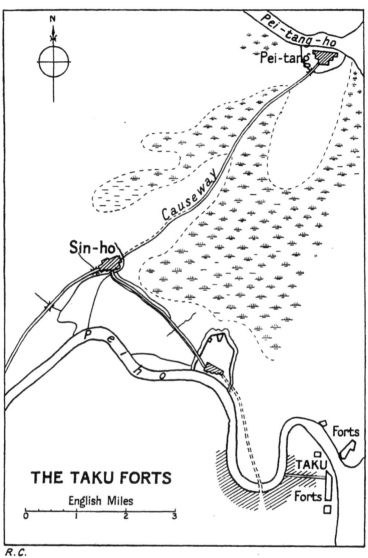

THE TAKU FORTS

English Miles

R.C.

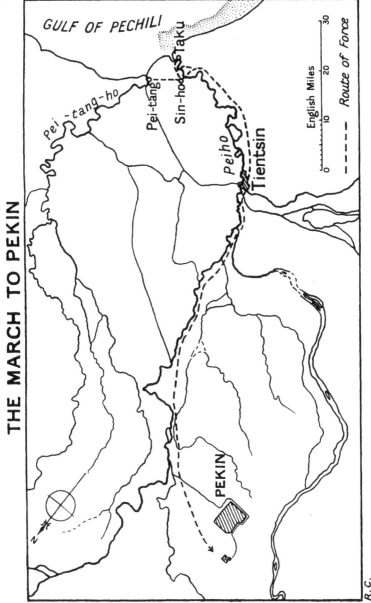

THE MARCH TO PEKIN

GULF OF PECHILI

Taku

Pei-tang-ho

Pei-tang

Sin-ho

Peiho

Tientsin

PEKIN

English Miles

0 10 20 30

- - - - Route of Force

R.C.

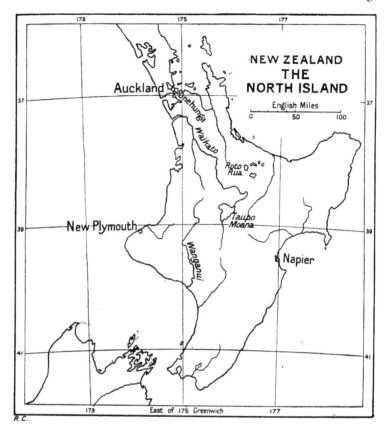

NEW ZEALAND
THE
NORTH ISLAND

English Miles

0   50   100

Auckland
Onehunga
Waikato
Roto Rua
Taupo Moana
New Plymouth
Wanganui
Napier

East of 175 Greenwich

R.C.

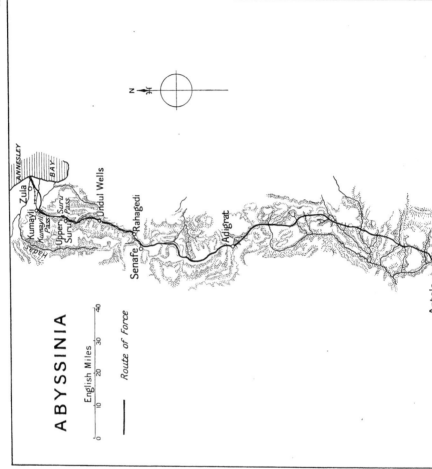

ABYSSINIA

English Miles

0   10   20   30   40

——— Route of Force

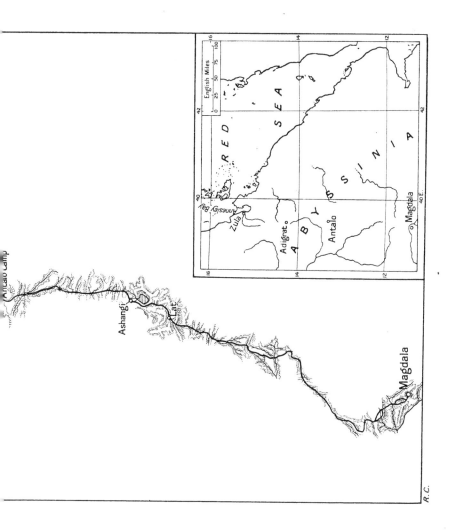